# FROM A
# WHISPER
## TO A
# RALLYING CRY

# FROM A WHISPER TO A RALLYING CRY

## THE KILLING of VINCENT CHIN and the TRIAL that GALVANIZED the ASIAN AMERICAN MOVEMENT

. . .

## PAULA YOO

**Norton Young Readers**

*An Imprint of W. W. Norton & Company*
*Independent Publishers Since 1923*

For information about permission to reproduce selections from this book, write to Permissions, W. W. Norton & Company, Inc., 500 Fifth Avenue, New York, NY 10110

For information about special discounts for bulk purchases, please contact W. W. Norton Special Sales at specialsales@wwnorton.com or 800-233-4830

Manufacturing by Versa Press
Book design by Yang Kim
Production manager: Anna Oler

Library of Congress Cataloging-in-Publication Data

Names: Yoo, Paula, author.
Title: From a whisper to a rallying cry : the killing of Vincent Chin and the trial that galvanized the Asian American movement / Paula Yoo.
Description: New York, NY : Norton Young Readers, [2021] | Includes bibliographical references and index. | Audience: Ages 13–18
Identifiers: LCCN 2020053662 | ISBN 9781324002871 (hardcover) | ISBN 9781324002888 (epub)
Subjects: LCSH: Asian Americans—Civil rights—Juvenile literature. | Chin, Vincent, –1982 | Murder victims—United States—Juvenile literature. | Chin, Vincent, –1982
Classification: LCC E184.A75 Y56 2021 | DDC 305.895/073—dc23
LC record available at https://lccn.loc.gov/2020053662

W. W. Norton & Company, Inc., 500 Fifth Avenue, New York, N.Y. 10110
www.wwnorton.com

W. W. Norton & Company Ltd., 15 Carlisle Street, London W1D 3BS

0 9 8 7 6 5 4 3 2 1

*For my dad,*
*Young Sik Yoo*
*(1938–2016)*

# CONTENTS

CONTENTS

# Slaying ends couple's dream

By BRIAN FLANIGAN
Free Press Staff Writer

Vincent Chin was to be married Monday. On Tuesday, he was buried instead.

On Wednesday, Chin's best friend talked about how much Chin — beaten to death a week ago with a baseball bat — looked forward to his wedding day.

"This ... it ended the dream," Danny Lew, 30, said haltingly.

The "dream," according to friends, began about three years ago when Vincent Chin, of Oak Park, met Vickie Wong, of Mt. Clemens, and fell in love. Late in 1980, Vincent was hired at Efficient Engineering Co., an Oak Park firm that provides mechanical engineering work for automotive and aircraft companies.

"HE HIRED IN as a computer terminal operator and a draftsman," recalled Gene Blair, Vincent's supervisor. "But he was so intelligent and industrious that we quickly realized his potential on the (drafting) board and put him on the board full-time."

Vincent received a pair of pay raises, according to Blair,

**Vincent Chin and Vickie Wong:** A tragic ending to their dream of happiness.

See **DREAM**, Page 15A

Vincent Chin's smile first caught Vikki Wong's attention when they began dating in 1978. "Vince was a happy person—positive, always on the go," Vikki told the press after his beating death made front-page headlines. They were to be married on June 28, 1982.

# "YOU DON'T KNOW ABOUT VINCENT CHIN?"

"Today's the big anniversary. Don't talk to your mom about that guy."

Jarod Lew's phone beeped. He glanced down at the screen to see a mysterious text message from his cousin.

Jarod was confused. *What guy?* he typed.

*You don't know about Vincent Chin?* his cousin texted back.

*No.*

A few moments later, his cousin simply wrote: *Look him up.*

It was June 19, 2012. Jarod sat at his desk, eating a corned beef sandwich for lunch while he worked. For the past year, the twenty-five-year-old aspiring photographer had been employed at a family-owned portrait studio just outside Detroit.

Jarod glanced around the empty office. It was near the end of his lunch break. He wasn't allowed to use the work computer for personal use, and his boss would be back soon. He quickly typed the words *Vincent Chin* into the Google search bar.

The first image that popped up onscreen was a *Detroit Free Press* front-page story from 1982. SLAYING ENDS COUPLE'S DREAM, the headline blared.

The photo to the left of the headline featured a beautiful twenty-four-year-old Chinese American woman, dressed in a trim blue button-down shirt and stylish jeans. Her wavy black hair fell past her shoulders. Her arms were wrapped snugly around a handsome young man's waist. He wore a collared white shirt, jeans, and a jade pendant necklace around his neck. They both smiled for the camera.

Jarod didn't need to read the photo caption to know the young woman in the photo was Vikki Wong. He recognized his mother instantly.

"It was a very surreal moment," Jarod remembered years later. "I definitely recognized my mom right away. I felt my heart drop a little. I looked at it, and everything became super quiet. My hands were shaking a little bit, and I'm not going to lie, my heart was racing."

Jarod immediately looked up *Vincent Chin* on Wikipedia. He skimmed the introductory paragraph in shock. On June 19, 1982, "Vincent Jen Chin (May 18, 1955—June 23, 1982) was a Chinese-American draftsman who was beaten to death by two white men, Chrysler plant supervisor Ronald Ebens and his stepson, laid-off autoworker Michael Nitz."

*June 19, 1982.* Jarod did the math—Vincent Chin was only two years older than he was now when he was killed exactly thirty years ago. So *this* was the "big anniversary" his cousin had warned him about.

Jarod clicked on more links. News headlines from the 1980s flashed across the screen:

GETTING AWAY WITH MURDER?
THE LIFE AND DEATH OF VINCENT CHIN


VINCENT CHIN CASE: JUSTICE OR MOCKERY?

A BAT, A GAVEL, A QUESTION OF JUSTICE

There were newer headlines, from 2012, as well.

RONALD EBENS, THE MAN WHO KILLED VINCENT CHIN,
APOLOGIZES 30 YEARS LATER

FIGHTING ON FOR VINCENT CHIN:
OAKLAND COUNTY MARKS 30TH ANNIVERSARY OF KILLING

There was even an official press release from the White House on the thirtieth anniversary: REMEMBERING VINCENT CHIN.

Jarod had never heard of Vincent Chin before in his life. And yet even the White House was commemorating this man's thirty-year legacy.

And then Jarod found an old newspaper photo of Vincent Chin standing with three other Chinese American men. They were all dressed in black tie, with red roses pinned to their lapels, clearly all groomsmen for a friend's wedding party.

Jarod recognized one of the young men in the photo. It was his uncle. First his cousin, then his mother, and now his uncle? How deeply intertwined was Vincent Chin with Jarod's family? "That's why my cousin was warning me not to upset my mom," he realized.

Suddenly, Jarod heard his boss's voice.

"Hey, what are you doing?" his boss asked as he entered the office. "You gotta get off Google and get to work."

Jarod couldn't bear to look at the photo of Vincent Chin on his screen anymore. He turned the computer off.

. . .

When Jarod met his mom for lunch the following Saturday, all he could see in his mind was that grainy newspaper photo from 1982 of a twenty-four-year-old Vikki hugging her fiancé, Vincent, tightly.

"I definitely had a hard time," he remembered. "I wanted to be extra nice to her, which was not the most normal thing for me because I was very confrontational with my parents."

So Jarod forced an extra cheerful smile onto his face. "Hi Mom," he said, his voice unusually upbeat. "Good to see you!"

But Vikki frowned, suspicious. Jarod *never* said things like that. What was going on with her son?

"Why are you being so nice to me?" she asked immediately. "You must want something."

Jarod's smile froze—*busted.*

"Why can't a son be nice to his mom?" he said quickly, trying to make a joke.

To his relief, Vikki smiled.

As they sat down for lunch, Jarod decided not to ask her about "that guy." Instead, he did what she had unconsciously taught him to do—bury his feelings.

"It must have been in my genes, like my mom," he said. "I just shoved it down and pushed it somewhere else. Left it hiding in a dark corner. I didn't want to deal with it."

So Jarod said nothing, even though he felt the weight of the world on his shoulders.

PART ONE

# "THE LAST TIME"

## Chapter 1

# "ONE LAST NIGHT OUT WITH THE GUYS"

When Ronald Ebens swung the Jackie Robinson "Louisville Slugger" baseball bat one last time at Vincent Chin, it was as if he were going for a home run.

Vincent wasn't supposed to be here. Not lying in a pool of his own blood in the middle of Woodward Avenue across from a McDonald's in Detroit on a warm June night. He was supposed to be out celebrating his bachelor party with his best friends Jimmy Choi, Gary Koivu, and Bob Siroskey.

Instead, Vincent was lying helpless as a drunk and enraged forty-two-year-old white man slammed a baseball bat against his head.

It was nine days before Vincent Chin's wedding to Vikki Wong was to take place. Trim and athletic, with thick, luxurious black hair, deep-set dark eyes, and a flirtatious smile, Vincent had charmed many girlfriends and had a passion for cars, football, and fishing. He was an All-American Guy.

But now, at twenty-seven, Vincent had fallen deeply in love with the brilliant and beautiful Vikki, who worked at an insurance company. He was ready to settle down and start a family with her. He had been working two jobs—as a draftsman at an engineering firm by day and as a waiter at a Chinese restaurant by night—in order to save money for their wedding and their future together. In fact, they had scheduled their wedding for a Monday because Vincent and most of his friends were waiters in Chinatown, and they made the most money in tips on the weekends.

But on Saturday night, Vincent's restaurant shift ended earlier than expected, so he impulsively decided to invite his friends for a last-minute bachelor party.

Before he left, Vincent told his mother, Lily Chin, that he would be out late for "one last night out with the guys."

Lily frowned. She didn't want her son to go out at all. "Don't stay out too late," she said.

"Mom, we're just going out to a bar," he said.

"You're getting married," Lily insisted. "You shouldn't go to these places anymore!"

Vincent smiled at his mother—he knew she couldn't help being overprotective of him. Especially after his father, David Bing Hing Chin, had passed away from kidney disease just eight months earlier. He appreciated how hard both his parents worked, from long hours in steamy basement laundries and crowded restaurants in Detroit's Chinatown, to take care of him.

"Okay Mom," Vincent said. "I promise, this will be the last time."

But Lily wasn't amused. "Don't say 'last time,'" she scolded him. "It's bad luck."

"I'll be home early," he promised.

. . .

Abandoned auto factories and smashed-up storefronts surrounded the Fancy Pants Club. Originally built in 1915 as a "movie palace," the Art Deco building later became an adult entertainment dance club for people eighteen and older, a reflection of the hard times that had hit Highland Park by the early 1980s. Since the 1967 Detroit riots (also known as the Detroit Rebellion of 1967) against racism and the economic recession of the 1970s, more than half of Detroit's white population had fled, leaving behind empty buildings.

But inside, the crowded, noisy club was far from empty. Young women danced topless, on a raised catwalk stage, to current rock and pop.

Soon after Vincent and his friends took their seats by the stage, Ronald Ebens and his stepson, Michael Nitz, entered. They had abandoned plans to attend a Detroit Tigers–Milwaukee Brewers baseball game at Tiger Stadium after hearing the Tigers were down 10 to 3. The men had been on their way home when they impulsively decided to stop by the Fancy Pants Club for last call.

Like Vincent, Ebens was an outgoing, friendly guy and a hard worker. He had climbed the ladder at the Chrysler plant from assembly line worker to supervisor. But his stepson, along with almost a quarter-million autoworkers through the industry, had been laid off recently, as competition from Japan had caused a 30 percent plunge in American auto production, not to mention the permanent closing of several plants in Michigan.

But it was a Saturday night, and Ebens just wanted to have a good time. He smiled warmly at one of the young women dancing for Vincent and his friends. She took it as her cue to leave them and dance for Ebens instead.

Vincent made a few jokes about feeling rejected by the dancer.

"Boy, you don't know a good thing when you see one," Ebens shouted at him.

Vincent's smile vanished. "I'm not a boy," he shouted back.

And that was how Vincent Chin met Ronald Ebens.

• • •

Like the other dancers at the club, Racine Colwell, twenty-four, relied on tips to make ends meet. Colwell, who was white, had worked at the Fancy Pants for the past six years. She liked Vincent's friendly smile. He was a nice customer who seemed to have an endless supply of dollar bills. This was going to be a good night for her.

Suddenly she heard shouts coming from Ebens's side of the stage. Vincent's friends Bob Siroskey and Jimmy Choi would later testify in court that they heard someone shout the racist slurs *Chink* and *Nip* in their direction, although they could not confirm that either Ebens or Nitz actually said these words.

Colwell glanced over just in time, she later said, to hear Ebens shout in Vincent's direction, "It's because of you little mother-fuckers that we're out of work!"

Colwell raced off the stage to safety as Vincent stormed toward Ebens. To this day, what happened next remains unclear. Ebens would later claim that Vincent sucker-punched him in the mouth with his fist while he was still sitting down.

But Vincent's friends remember differently. "He shoved him," Gary Koivu later testified in court. "It was in the chest. Ebens shoved back and they both started swinging and punching."

Despite these conflicting versions, one thing was clear. Vincent was angry.

The fight escalated from there. Somehow in the scuffle, a

chair slammed against Michael Nitz, ripping a bloody gash across his forehead. The whole fight lasted maybe a couple minutes at most, before the bouncers kicked everyone out of the club.

Koivu couldn't help but feel relieved that they had been kicked out. "I was hoping once the fight broke up in the bar, that was it, that we'd both go our separate ways and go home," he said later. "It didn't turn out that way."

· · ·

Out in the parking lot, Vincent, still pumped up on alcohol and adrenaline, kept taunting Ebens. At five foot ten and 149 pounds, Vincent didn't care that the six-foot-one, 190-pound Ebens was bigger than him. Nitz, an avid athlete, grabbed a baseball bat that he kept for practice out of the trunk of his car.

But as Ebens looked at his stepson clutching a wad of toilet paper against his forehead to stanch the flow of blood, his protective fatherly instinct kicked in. Ebens had married Nitz's mother, Juanita, when Nitz was twelve years old. The two had grown close over the years. They shared a love for baseball and participated in an after-work pick-up baseball game twice a week, plus batting practice at the cages whenever they had a free moment. They had started out as father and stepson, but now they were best friends. He glared at Vincent—*You did this to my boy.*

Ebens grabbed the bat from his stepson and charged toward Vincent.

Vincent ran.

· · ·

The McDonald's restaurant at 12857 Woodward Avenue in Highland Park, Michigan, where Vincent Chin was beaten. Built in 1975, it stands between an auto parts store and a mini shopping mall and has long since been abandoned.

Ebens could not keep up with Vincent, who was sixteen years younger. He returned to the parking lot, where Nitz's head was still bleeding. Ebens realized his stepson needed stitches. They got into the car and roared off.

As they drove down Woodward Avenue, they spotted Vincent sitting on the curb outside a nearby McDonald's with Jimmy Choi, who had caught up with him. They were talking and laughing while waiting for their friends Koivu and Siroskey to find them.

The more they laughed, the more irate Ebens became.

"All I could think of was that they were laughing because they really pulled one over us," he said later. "I told Mike to pull the car over."

Meanwhile, off-duty police officer Morris Cotton was working that night as a security guard at the McDonald's. He

12

was in the parking lot, helping a customer jump-start his car, when Ebens and Nitz showed up.

"It kind of shocked me," said Cotton, who is Black. "Because it's predominantly a ninety percent Black neighborhood. And to see a male white get out of the car with a baseball bat, the first thing I was thinking was maybe he was coming from the Tiger Stadium baseball game."

Inside the McDonald's, Michael Gardenhire, another off-duty police officer, was eating a cheeseburger when he noticed a commotion outside the window. He raced outside to assist Cotton.

Out in the parking lot, Ebens barreled toward Vincent. Before Vincent could run away, Nitz grabbed Vincent in a surprise bear hug from behind. Ebens slammed his Jackie Robinson "Louis-ville Slugger" baseball bat against Vincent's shoulder.

Vincent broke loose from Nitz's grip. He ran into the middle of the street.

He slipped. Cars honked and swerved around him.

Ebens charged after Vincent.

Cotton and Gardenhire held up their badges, shouting for Ebens to stand down. But Ebens didn't listen. "His eyes were glazed, he was in a heat of rage, and he had the bat up," Cotton remembered.

Ebens swung the bat again, striking Vincent in the shoulder and back.

"Mr. Ebens was standing over him with the baseball bat and he was just pounding him in the head like he was hitting a golf ball," Gardenhire said later in a newspaper interview. "He hit him four times. *Four* times. There was blood coming from everywhere. Out of his ears and everywhere."

"He was swinging that baseball bat as if he were going for a home run," Cotton agreed.

The blows shattered the Chinese jade pendant necklace Vincent always wore for good luck and protection.

Vincent was on his knees, his vision blurry.

Ebens swung the bat one last time, slamming it against the back of Vincent's skull.

*A home run.*

Officers Gardenhire and Cotton aimed their guns at Ebens.

"Back up! Back up!" Cotton shouted at the large crowd of bystanders who had had now gathered on the street.

Vincent was on the ground, struggling to get up. Cotton saw Ebens raise the bat again, breathing heavily. "Drop the baseball bat!" he shouted. Ebens didn't seem to hear him. Cotton cocked his gun. But too many bystanders were still blocking Cotton's view as Ebens struck Vincent again. "Get out of the way!" Cotton yelled.

Finally, the crowd dispersed. "And at this time, I had a clear shot."

Ebens saw the barrel of Officer Cotton's gun aimed right at him. He froze. What had he just done? Everything had happened so fast. He slowly put down the bat.

A horrified Jimmy Choi raced over to Vincent, who was struggling to get up. "Fight," Vincent croaked. *"Fight."* His pupils were fixed and dilated. His brain was already swelling. Blood poured from two open gashes on his scalp, the left side of his skull fractured. Abrasions and lacerations covered his shoulders and upper chest.

Vincent moaned. As Choi gently cradled his friend in his arms, Vincent's last words before slipping forever into unconsciousness were "It's not fair."

# Chapter 2
# MURDER CITY

In his eleven years as a firefighter and emergency medical technician with the Highland Park Fire Department, Sergeant Gerald Alan Thompson had never seen anyone beaten this badly with a baseball bat.

"I've seen a lot of violent death, but none exactly like that," Thompson said. "And, it was obvious, you know, that he'd been beaten—*beaten*—I mean, not just hit once in the head. He was beaten. He had broken bones all over. You know. Collarbone. Ribs. Skull."

On the night of June 19, 1982, Thompson was only three blocks away from the McDonald's where Vincent Chin lay dying when he received the emergency dispatch.

Thompson and the other EMTs arrived in an ambulance a few minutes later. Thompson took one look at Vincent and realized he didn't have much time left. "There was brains laying on the street. . . . Chin was obviously in a fatal condition. He wasn't dead yet. He was semiconscious, but from my experience of being on the street for so long, the man was a goner."

Meanwhile, Ronald Ebens tried to get Thompson's attention by pointing to his bruised lip. "Look what he did to me," Ebens said.

But Thompson didn't have time for Ebens and his puffy lip. He was more concerned with Vincent's head wound, as cerebral fluid spilled out of his fractured skull. "I had a critical patient laying on the ground and I couldn't really deal with both," Thompson said.

Meanwhile, Officers Michael Gardenhire and Morris Cotton had Ebens sit on the curb away from Vincent. Ebens stared at Vincent's body, still in a haze. "I'm sorry that this happened," he told both police officers. "[But] he shouldn't have done it."

As the other EMTs carefully lifted Vincent's body into the ambulance, Thompson turned his attention to Michael Nitz, who was still bleeding from the one-and-a-half-inch gash in his forehead from the earlier fight at the Fancy Pants Club. Thompson bandaged Nitz's wound, advising him that he would need at least two or three stitches.

He noticed Nitz was shaking with fright. "I can tell you this, he was scared, all right," Thompson remembered. "He knew he was in big trouble."

· · ·

Jimmy Choi sat by Vincent's side as the ambulance raced down Woodward Avenue, sirens blaring. "Come on, Vince, come on," he said as paramedics monitored his vitals. "Help is coming."

He overheard one of the paramedics say, "He's losing consciousness pretty fast."

Choi watched, helpless, as the paramedics began CPR on Vincent. "They started rapping . . . they started pumping his heart and all that," he said.

But Vincent was no longer responding.

"Don't lose consciousness," Choi begged his friend. "Hang in there."

. . .

Van Ong thought he had seen it all in his sixteen years of nursing. Born in Davao City in the Philippines, he had moved from his family's farm to Detroit in 1971 to become a nurse. Like Vincent, he had his share of experiences in racism, including a war veteran patient who took one look at Ong's face and said, "I killed a lot of you in Vietnam." Now thirty-six, he had worked his way up the ranks from staff nurse in 1973 to nurse manager in charge of the ER night crew. Theirs was a brutal shift, especially on the weekends, when it wasn't uncommon for them to deal with up to three hundred patients admitted during a twenty-four-hour cycle.

"I saw the dark side of the city," Ong said. "Every day, it was like the Vietnam War. I used to demand the hospital for combat pay."

"We used to call ourselves the Knife and Gun Club because we would have so many stabbings and gunshot victims," explained Laura Black, a young nurse who also worked at the hospital's intensive care unit at the time. "It was our way of coping."

By the time Sergeant Thompson's ambulance arrived at Henry Ford hospital, Vincent had fallen into a coma. By 10:21 p.m., when Vincent was admitted into the ER, most of his brain had ceased to function—he could only breathe and had some reflex movements of his left arm.

Ong ordered his nursing staff to begin the standard emergency procedure of doing compressions and hooking Vincent up to IV fluids to stabilize him.

Ong rifled through a bag of Vincent's personal belongings.

He pulled out Vincent's driver's license to use for identification in his patient report. He froze, staring at the handsome young man smiling at him in the license photo.

And then he glanced over at the same young man lying sprawled out on the ER gurney. Ong could barely recognize Vincent, now covered in blood and bruises. His head had ballooned to almost twice its size. He had been beaten beyond recognition.

. . .

While Van Ong and his nursing staff were tending to Vincent in the emergency room, Gary Koivu and Bob Siroskey desperately drove up and down Woodward Avenue, trying to find their friend. It was harder than it sounded—this was 1982, and cell phones didn't exist back then.

At first they thought Vincent and Jimmy had stopped by the liquor store for refuge. "I went there and asked if they have seen him and they haven't," Koivu said.

Frustrated, Koivu and Siroskey drove back to the Fancy Pants Club, hoping their friends had returned there. Again, another dead end. The parking attendant there told Koivu that Vincent and Jimmy had run off and never came back.

Koivu racked his brain, trying to figure out where else Vincent and Jimmy could have gone. He and Siroskey decided to stop by Vincent's workplace, the Golden Star Restaurant, hoping he had called a taxi and was already back there waiting for them. "That was the only place I could think of," Koivu said. "I just pictured him sitting in the Golden Star Restaurant and us walking in." In his mind, he could see Vincent teasing them: *"Where you guys been?"* Koivu imagined himself laughing and joking back, *"Looking around for you."*

But when they arrived at the Golden Star and asked if Vincent had come back, a waiter told them, "No, Vincent's in the hospital."

Not knowing what to expect, an anxious Koivu and Siroskey headed for Henry Ford Hospital. Soon friends and family members began joining them in the waiting room.

"It was pretty somber, and no one really said too much," Koivu said. "We waited all night. I was trying to get myself to prepare for the worst."

· · ·

Five percent.

That was Vincent's chance for survival.

A CAT scan revealed a large collection of blood covering most of the right side of Vincent's brain, with a smaller amount of blood pooling over the left side. Blood clots on both sides of his brain were causing dangerous levels of pressure, threatening to stop the flow of blood to the brain.

Even though the odds were stacked against Vincent, Dr. Jeffrey Crecelius, a twenty-seven-year-old neurosurgery resident, still had hope. "We tend to give a younger person every possible chance for recovery when they have injuries," Dr. Crecelius explained. "We felt that the only chance he had for recovery was to remove the blood clots and try to reduce the pressure."

Surgery began at one a.m. and lasted for five straight hours. Dr. Crecelius removed bones from both sides of Vincent's skull to get rid of the blood clots. Unfortunately, he discovered the right side of the brain was contused, or bruised. There was so much damage and swelling that he had to remove a small portion of Vincent's brain itself to relieve the pressure.

By six o'clock that morning, Vincent's condition remained the same as before the operation. Despite removing the blood clots, his brain continued to swell. Dr. Crecelius and his medical staff were unable to control the pressure.

Dr. Crecelius knew it was only a matter of time now before Vincent's brain would stop functioning entirely.

# Chapter 3
# "MAMA IS HERE"

Lily Chin liked to read before going to sleep. At ten o'clock that Saturday, she had just retired for the evening. She sat up in bed, reading the newspaper.

Only eight months had passed since her husband, David Bing Hing Chin, had died from kidney disease, and she still missed him deeply. So did Vincent, who would sometimes call out for his father before dinner, forgetting that David had passed. She looked forward to moving into a bigger house with Vincent and Vikki after their wedding.

Lily yawned. She glanced at the alarm clock by her bedside. Vincent had promised he would not stay out late. Maybe he was already on his way home, she wondered. Comforted by that thought, she folded up the newspaper and turned off the light.

Just as she was about to drift off to sleep, the doorbell rang. Lily smiled. "Vincent must have forgotten his keys again," she thought, amused.

But when she opened the door, it wasn't Vincent standing outside. It was Paul Ng, who owned the Golden Star Restaurant. He treated Vincent like his own son, even leaving him to manage the restaurant for the month he went home to China on vacation. So when Vincent had asked Ng earlier that night if he could leave early for his bachelor party, of course he said yes.

21

"Uncle Ping," Lily said, using a term of endearment and respect. "What happened? Why do you come so late?"

Ng entered and took Lily gently by the arm, leading her to the living room. He asked her to sit down. He had something to tell her.

Lily was suddenly wide awake. She sat down on the sofa, trying not to panic as Ng told her that Vincent had gotten into a fight. He was injured, but no one knew his condition. He said Danny, Vikki Wong's brother-in-law, would be stopping by shortly to take her to the hospital.

As Danny drove Lily to Henry Ford Hospital, Lily couldn't stop fretting about Vincent's wedding. "I was thinking, the wedding is only a week away," she said. "If Vincent is badly injured, he won't look good in the wedding. I wasn't really anticipating that he would die. I just thought maybe he had a hand or leg injury, nothing this serious."

They arrived at the hospital around eleven o'clock that night. Lily saw about a dozen of Vincent's friends pacing the hallway outside the operating room. The severity of her son's injuries began to sink in for her.

Danny, noticing her stricken expression, tried to comfort her. "Don't worry, Auntie," he said. "Vincent is a good person. Nothing bad will happen to him. Don't worry."

For the next eight hours, she sat in the waiting room.

"Vincent's mother was crying all through the night and I really didn't know what to say to her," Gary Koivu said. "I really wasn't sure how she felt about what's going on, hoping that she wouldn't blame me or us. She looked at Vincent as an angel, he was her only child. I knew it was really hard for her."

"Unfortunately, this violence wasn't unusual," Nurse Laura

Black said, recalling other similar head injuries from armed robberies and spousal abuse cases. "In terms of the injury itself, it wasn't unusual because of the violence. We *were* the murder capital. But this was so sad because the situation that surrounded it was unbelievable. His mom and fiancée were there at the hospital. Seeing them was pretty tragic. They were very quiet. They were trying to be very stoic about it, but you could feel that they were totally torn apart."

· · ·

When the sun rose at 5:55 a.m., Lily was still sitting in the hospital's waiting room. Although it was going to be another warm summer day in Detroit, the sky was gray and it was drizzling outside.

At seven, Dr. Crecelius approached Lily. She was surprised by how young he looked—he could have been one of Vincent's friends. She looked hopefully at Dr. Crecelius, but he shook his head. The young doctor explained that he and a team of neurosurgeons tried to save what remained of Vincent's battered brain. But the damage was too great.

"I ask how he is," Lily said. "The doctor says very, very bad. The brain all bad."

Dr. Crecelius took Lily upstairs to see Vincent, who was lying in a deep coma in the intensive care unit. The patients in ICU lay in beds packed next to each other, separated only with a curtain. There was not much privacy. Dr. Crecelius told Lily that Vincent's brain was dead—he was breathing only because the life support system was pumping oxygen into his lungs.

Lily's first thought upon seeing her unconscious son was that his beautiful, thick black hair had been ruined. He had just cut it for the wedding, too. She loved how neat his haircut was, how handsome he would look at the wedding.

And now his head had been shaved and wrapped with bandages. A railroad track of surgical stitches snaked out from under one bandage.

This was not the way Lily wanted to see her son for the last time. She and her husband had lost their first baby in 1949, one year after they had married in China and moved to America. Then, they discovered she was unable to have children. They decided to adopt. When Lily received a group photo of children from an adoption agency in China, her eyes were immediately drawn to a four-year-old boy named Jen, the only child smiling in the photo. She felt an immediate kinship to the child's open smile and friendly eyes. *He looks so smart and cute*, she had thought. He looked like he was smiling directly at her—as if he could see into her soul. She knew right away he was the one.

Lily showed the photo of the boy to her husband and said, "I like this boy." David agreed. They immediately began the paperwork to bring him to America. They gave him the American name Vincent, which means "to conquer" or "to win." The adoption process took one year, so by the time Vincent arrived in America in 1961, he was six years old. When Vincent met Lily and David Chin, the first words he said were, "Mommy! Daddy!"

"He was a terrific kid," Lily said. "He's always a good boy, even after he grew up. Even when he was twenty-seven, he never left the house without telling us first where he is going. During meals, he always greeted us first."

Meanwhile, Lily kept touching her son's face, hands, arms,

and feet. Why was his skin so cold? Nurse Black explained that the cold skin was an aftereffect of the anesthesia. Lily squeezed her son's hand and rubbed his arms and legs and feet, trying to warm him up.

"I kept saying, 'Mama is here, Vincent, Mama is here,'" she said. "But he didn't respond. I felt so hopeless. I just kept on crying and crying. I kept on saying, 'Vincent, Mama coming, Mama coming, you answer me, open your mouth. Open your eyes and see Mama,' No feeling, no feeling. I touched him many times. I broke down inside."

But as Lily held Vincent's hand, she realized—she could not afford to break down. She had to be strong for Vincent's friends.

Including Gary Koivu and Bob Siroskey, who returned to the hospital the next day after Vincent's surgery. They saw their friend lying in a coma in the ICU unit. "I remembered seeing his head bandaged up," Koivu said. "That was very hard to see."

"Is he going to be okay?" Koivu asked an attending nurse.

"It doesn't look good," the nurse told him.

"That felt like I was punched in the stomach when I feared the worst had happened," Koivu said.

For the last four days of Vincent's life, Lily and Vincent's bride-to-be, Vikki Wong, never left his side. "I was with him for four days," Vikki said. "Every day going there and seeing him. Just sit next to him. But he was unconscious."

But Lily refused to give up hope. "I am sometimes a stub-bornly strong person," she said. "So I kept telling myself, *Be strong, control yourself.*"

But it was hard to be strong when Dr. Crecelius delivered the grim news on the fourth day. Vincent was unable to breathe on his own. "His brain stopped functioning entirely," the doctor explained to Lily. He gently advised it was time to take Vincent off life support. Did he have their permission?

Lily paused, remembering how her son always wore his jade pendant for good luck and protection. Now it was her turn as his mother to protect him.

She said yes.

On June 23, 1982, at 9:50 p.m., Vincent died.

# Chapter 4
# FATHER'S DAY

While Vincent lay on the operating table at Henry Ford Hospital undergoing more than five hours of brain surgery, Ebens and Nitz were taken to the Highland Park police station.

Officer Cotton had Michael Nitz write a statement about what happened that night. Nitz wrote the following:

"We were at a bar. I was struck over the head with a chair and another guy started to throw punches after I was struck over the head. We chased out of the parking lot, and after that, I don't recall what else happened. This is signed by Michael Nitz. Signed witnessed by Patrolman Cotton, Badge number 28. 10:50 PM. 6–19–82."

Detective Donald Roberts, a nineteen-year veteran with the Highland Park Police Department, was at home when he received the call to report in as the officer in charge. Detectives didn't work after four p.m. on weekends, so he knew it was a serious situation.

At the station, it was chaos. "There was such a commotion going on," Roberts said. "They had several people from McDonald's in there. The officers were trying to get things straightened out. Mr. Nitz was there with his head bleeding."

Vincent Chin would turn out to be one of fifteen homicides in Highland Park that year. Despite Highland Park's small population of 28,000 residents, it had one of the highest per capita crime rates in the country.

When Roberts arrived, police had formally arrested Ebens and placed him in a jail cell. Nitz was on the phone with his mother, Juanita, asking her to take him to the hospital. Roberts proceeded to interview Vincent's friends, Choi, Koivu, and Siroskey.

Juanita soon arrived to take her son to the Bi County Hospital, where he received eleven stitches on his head.

Ebens spent the rest of the night in jail. Until that night, neither Ebens nor Nitz had ever been in trouble with the law or arrested.

Ebens had trouble sleeping. There were no blankets, no mattress, no pillows—just a steel cot. All he could think about were his children, his stepson Michael, and his ten-year-old daughter, who was asleep at home and had no idea what her father had just done.

"That was the first time I was in a jail cell," Ebens said. "I remember the next day was Father's Day, I remember that, I felt like a real jerk. Being in jail and knowing the next day was Father's Day."

The next morning, on Father's Day, as Dr. Crecelius was delivering the grim news to Lily Chin about Vincent's surgery, Roberts officially charged Ebens with second-degree murder, which meant that Vincent had been killed in the heat of anger. Second-degree murder is when a death is caused by "reckless conduct that displays an obvious lack of concern for human life."

A defense attorney showed up at the station to represent Ebens. He convinced Roberts to release Ebens without bond, which meant Ebens was free to go home. Roberts wasn't worried about letting Ebens go. "We checked the guy," he said. "He had no record. He worked at Chrysler, he owned his home. The attorney said he had known him for thirty years, a very respectable attorney. You don't figure anybody's going to take off on you on a deal like that. Which they didn't."

. . .

But Officer Morris Cotton couldn't believe it when Roberts told him that Ebens was free to leave. "He said it sounded like a fair fight," Cotton said, still shocked by the memory.

"Lieutenant, this was a prime example of lying in wait," Cotton protested to the detective. "They pulled up, hid behind a pole, and waited with a baseball bat. How was that self-defense?"

"Well, the guy threw a chair at his son at the club," Roberts replied.

"I don't know what happened at the club, but they had a chance to think about everything they were going to do since they left the club," Cotton said. "The Fancy Pants is a quarter-mile away. They had time to think about what they were going to do."

But Roberts told the young rookie that the men were still being released. If he and the other detectives found any other evidence that indicated foul play, they would put out a warrant for their arrest.

"I lock up people for marijuana, and they spend the night in jail," Cotton protested. "And you're letting this guy go?"

Roberts explained that Ebens was a foreman at Chrysler and was an "outstanding citizen."

But Cotton wondered what the detective really meant.

## Encounter

continued from page 12
to everyone in the office," coworker Bob Siroskey remembers. When he won an office pool, he invited everyone out for a few rounds on him.

Vincent had a promising future at Efficient Engineering Co., Inc., where he was a draftsman and a computer-terminal operator. He started there in December of 1980, and in two years earned four promotions. "Vincent wouldn't walk if he could run," recalls Gene Blair, his supervisor.

His friends remember him two ways. First, fishing. If he had a free Sunday afternoon, he'd drive up to Cass Lake with a 12-pack and anyone who wanted to come along. Second: reading. "He always had his nose in a book," says Jimmy Choi, who worked weekends with Vincent at the Golden Star restaurant. "He loved sagas, anything by Michener or Clavell."

Above all, of course, there was Vikki. "Vincent was devoted to her," says Marshall Chin, who was to be the best man at the wedding. "He was very excited about being married."

Vincent and Vikki had met at a dance four years earlier, when she was 20. What first attracted her, she said later, was his cheerful disposition. "Vince was a happy person—positive, always on the go. He had a lot of goals in life."

It was to be a big Chinese wedding—at least 400 guests. Vikki had two wedding dresses—traditional white for the ceremony, and a colorful Chinese gown for the reception. Gifts had begun arriving at his mother's home in Oak Park. Vincent already had paid for the honeymoon trip to Aruba, an island in the Caribbean.

May Chin, Marshall's wife, was to have been the bridesmaid. "I just remember the little things," she says. "Vincent was very good with kids. Very patient and gentle. He was very close to my two sons. They gravitated toward him. Most guys don't want to be around kids, but he always wanted to carry Brian. He's seven now and once in a while he asks, 'Is Vincent in heaven?' "

"I remember he always wished he'd had a brother," May Chin says. "It made us sick to hear that Vincent was alone and got into that mess. . .He didn't deserve to die, not the way he did. And the way the judge treated those guys, Ebens and Nitz, saying, 'These aren't the kind of people you put in jail.' I mean, Vincent's not the kind of guy you'd want to kill."

June 19, 1982, was a Saturday, cool and clear. Vincent was supposed to work at the Golden Star, but things were slow, and he asked Paul Ng, the owner, for the night off. Ng considered Vincent a second son; when he vacationed in China, he entrusted the restaurant to Vincent for a month at a time. Ng smiled and said okay.

Vincent went to his Oak Park home to change. That night, Lily Chin asked her son where he was going. He told her about the bar and that Gary Koivu, a childhood friend, would be driving. She was glad; she always worried when he drove. "This is the last time I'm going to the bar because I'm getting married," he said as he left.

She frowned. "Never say 'last,' " she admonished. "It is unlucky."

The Fancy Pants Club is brown and boxy. It sits behind a Burger King off Woodward Avenue in the heart of Highland Park. It has no windows. Just a small canopy and a doorman/bouncer to "watch your car" for $1. Inside, it is dark, cool, and red. The spotlights are red. The carpet is red. The tables are cheap. Large square slats of unframed mirrors line the walls and snake behind the stage to provide a rearview of the dancer. She wears high heels. The music is quasi-disco and loud. No alcohol is served, only Coke, Sprite, orange juice, and the like, for $1.50 a glass. But Vincent and his friends already had stopped at one bar, and, just for good measure, one of them carried a concealed flask of vodka.

When the bachelor party—Vincent Chin, Gary Koivu,

Bob Siroskey, and Jimmy Choi—arrived at the Fancy Pants that night, Vincent changed $50 into $1 bills for tipping. A few minutes later, Ronald Ebens and Michael Nitz entered. Ronald Ebens, then 42, was born in Dixon, Illinois, one of six children. He lived in the suburb of East Detroit with his third wife and two children, one of them his stepson, Michael Nitz. He liked bowling, basketball, hockey, and football. According to a psychiatric report prepared for the court, he "[had] been a frequent and excessive drinker for approximately 10 years. . .and may be chronically dependent on same."

The report also concluded that he had "above-average intelligence. . .extremely poor overall judgment, uncontrollable hostility, and a potential for explosive acting out."

On the night of June 19, the width of the stage at the Fancy Pants—about six feet—separated Ebens and Vincent. It evidently took only a few minutes for Ebens to say something to Vincent. Racine Colwell, a dancer at the club, heard only one remark: "It's

Officers Gardenhire [left] and Cotton at the crime scene.

because of motherf—— like you that we're out of work." Vincent may have said something about being Chinese, but that, of course, was not the point. The epithet Ebens used, perhaps more than any other, is particularly loathsome and provocative to the Chinese, who tend to take it literally. "That [kind of remark] is one of the things that Chinese are really leery about," says Jimmy Choi, "because we respect our mothers."

"I'm not a motherf——," Vincent retorted. "Don't call me a motherf——."

"I just don't know if you're a big f—— or a little f—— ," Ebens replied. According to witnesses, Vincent then got up and walked around the stage. Ebens rose and came to meet him. Vincent pushed Ebens. Ebens pushed back. Michael Nitz then charged over and helped Ebens pin Vincent against the wall. Ebens hoisted a chair to strike Vincent, but he deflected the blow. Within moments, Eddie Hollis, the club's bouncer, pulled them apart. "Let's get out of this place," Vincent said.

Nitz' head was bleeding, perhaps from being grazed

A feature article in the *Chicago Tribune* in July 1983 included a photograph of Highland Park police officers Michael Gardenhire and Morris Cotton at the exact site where Vincent Chin lay in a coma after being beaten with a baseball bat outside the McDonald's restaurant on Woodward Avenue. The two officers would later testify at the federal civil rights trial of *United States v. Ronald Ebens and Michael Nitz*.

"I locked up Black people for smoking marijuana, and they were letting the white guy go," he said. "It was devastating to see that. That really bothered me."

Cotton, however, wasn't surprised by the double standard. The twenty-four-year-old police officer was an African American who grew up in a racially divided Highland Park.

When he was a child and delivered newspapers before school, some white neighbors were surprised to see Cotton and would shout racist slurs at him. "You'd go to some folks' homes and get called names," he said. "They'd tell you to get off their property. You got used to it. It was acceptable back then. You couldn't really do a lot about it."

There was also tension between the Black community and the Highland Park Police Department. Cotton remembered being racially profiled when he was only nine years old. He and his twelve-year-old sister were coming home from church when the police stopped them. "They pulled their guns on us," he said. "I took off running and the police made my sister lie on the ground."

The tensions erupted on July 23, 1967, when Cotton was only ten years old. A police raid of an unlicensed, after-hours bar ignited a four-day rebellion known as the 1967 Detroit riots. Unemployment, poverty, racism, racial segregation, housing discrimination, and police brutality reached a boiling point in the city. More than two thousand buildings were destroyed, 1,189 people were injured, and forty-three people were dead. Both Governor George W. Romney and President Lyndon B. Johnson had to send in the National Guard as well as the U.S. Army's 82nd and 101st Airborne Divisions.

During high school, Cotton had discovered a passion and talent for both math and sports. He was a defensive back on the school's football team and an All-American high school wrestler. He won twenty athletic scholarships, including a full-tuition scholarship to Wayne State University. Given the violence he witnessed as a child during the 1967 protests, he was inspired to major in criminal justice.

While at Wayne State, Cotton impressed a campus police officer who suggested he apply for the police academy after graduation. Cotton not only enrolled at the police academy but also received his master's degree in liberal studies with a concentration in technology from Eastern Michigan University. Years later he would become one of the first African Americans to serve as chief of police at the Highland Park Police Department.

But on Father's Day in 1982, Cotton was still a rookie who had no choice but to follow his superior officer's orders. He let Ebens go.

. . .

Life continued for Ebens and Nitz. On the following Monday, they both went back to work, while Vincent's friends and family said their final good-byes to him.

On Wednesday, June 23, Lily Chin gave doctors permission to remove her son from life support.

Later that day, a friend called the Ebenses' home phone number.

Juanita was home while Ebens was at work. She answered the phone. The friend informed her that Vincent Chin had been taken off life support.

Juanita decided not to tell Ebens right away about what happened. "At that time, I didn't see any reason to call Ron at work because there really wasn't anything he could do," she said.

Ebens, who still played on a community baseball team, had a game scheduled for after work that day. Juanita heated up a late dinner for her husband when he arrived home later that evening.

As Ebens ate, his wife told him the news.

"Vincent died today."

• • •

Two days later Ebens and Nitz appeared before Judge Kalem Varian of the thirtieth district court for arraignment. They were charged with the second-degree murder of Vincent Chin.

Chapter 5

# "AS LONG AS WE HAVE EACH OTHER"

*Mrs. Lily F. Chin*

*and*

*Mr. & Mrs. Ping-Kuen Wong*

*Request the honor of Your presence*

*at the Marriage of their Children*

VINCENT

*and*

VIKKI

*On Monday, the Twenty-Eighth of June 1982*

The invitations to Vincent Chin and Vikki Wong's wedding had been mailed out months earlier, featuring swirling white calligraphy embossed against a rich red background.

In Chinese culture, the color red holds great significance. Red symbolizes good luck and happiness. At a wedding, the bride wears a red traditional Chinese qun kua ceremonial outfit.

Vikki Wong planned to wear two dresses for their wedding—

a formal white wedding gown for the ceremony and the qun kua for the reception.

She had met Vincent four years earlier at a dance, when she was twenty. Like Lily, Vikki noticed Vincent's trademark smile right away. "Vince was a happy person—positive, always on the go," she said. "He had a lot of goals in life."

"He was charismatic," said Vincent's longtime friend Denise Yee Grim, who had met him when they were teenagers. "He had the kind of gregarious personality that could woo all the girls." Grim laughed. "Which is why he got into trouble with his mom, because he would be dating all these girls."

Gary Koivu envied his outgoing friend's ability to bond instantly with anyone he met. "I was always the quiet one," Koivu said. "I never did say too much, and it was difficult for me to make friends. [Vincent] could walk into a place and get to know people real well. He's always the life of the party, he's always laughing and joking. Everyone will be talking to him. I kind of admired that. I wish I had the gift of gab."

But despite his outgoing personality, Vincent also had a quiet and romantic side. Before going to the Lawrence Institute of Technology to pursue an engineering degree, he dreamed of being a writer. When he wasn't studying for school or working at the restaurant, he could be found reading. An avid bookworm since grade school, he devoured historical novels by James Michener and James Clavell.

"He always had his nose in a book," said his friend Jimmy Choi, who worked weekends with Vincent as a waiter at the Golden Star Restaurant in Ferndale.

"He was a comic book geek," Grim added. As teenagers,

the two were enrolled in many Chinese cultural classes in Chinatown, including kung fu and Chinese dance. "We used to compare notes about comic books all the time, like 'Did you read the new Spiderman?'"

Lily, however, told her son that writing was a risky career. "I said, 'Vincent, you can't make money at that,'" Lily said.

Although Vincent eventually put aside his artistic ambitions for a more practical engineering career, he still enjoyed writing poetry. Especially when he met Vikki. He was smitten by the sweet-natured, beautiful young woman. She became his muse. He later surprised Vikki with a poem dedicated to her that appeared in the classified section of the *Detroit Free Press* on Valentine's Day 1979. "My love for you is like a fire," Vincent wrote. "The fire will last forever . . . as long as we have each other."

Koivu knew this girlfriend was special for Vincent. "I could tell they got along really well," he said.

To no one's surprise, Vincent and Vikki became engaged after one year of dating.

"Vincent was devoted to her," said Marshall Chin, whom Vincent asked to be his best man for the wedding. "He was very excited about being married."

Vikki proudly showed off her engagement ring to her friend, Leah Shafer, who worked with her at their insurance company in Farmington Hills. "She came to work wearing a very huge diamond," Shafer said. "For the better part of a year, they'd been looking for a house."

"We thought that was nice," Grim said. "Good for him! He's settling down."

· · ·

Perhaps one of the reasons Vincent wanted to settle down was the unexpected death of his father, David Bing Hing Chin. He had died on November 3, 1981, from kidney disease. "When his father died, Vincent began to worry," said his friend Jimmy Choi. "He didn't want to end up as a waiter or working in a laundry like his dad. He wanted to get ahead."

And Vincent did "get ahead." When he wasn't waiting tables at the Golden Star Restaurant in Ferndale on weekends, he worked full time during the week at Efficient Engineering Co., located in Troy, Michigan.

Vincent began as a computer technical operator but soon impressed his supervisor, Gene Blair, with his hard work and positive attitude. "Vincent wouldn't walk if he could run," he said. In less than two years, Vincent had earned four promotions. "There really wasn't anybody he didn't get along with," Blair said. "He started here working on the computer terminals, and then we put him on the drafting boards. He was extremely smart, and very energetic. I wish I had a room full of Vincent Chins. He had potential. He was on his way."

The hard work would be worth it—after the wedding, Vincent and Vikki would fly to Aruba not only for their honeymoon but for Vikki's twenty-fourth birthday on July 2. "Aruba!" said Paul Chin, twenty-six, one of Vincent's friends. "He was real excited about that."

Vincent was also excited to start a family with Vikki. After the honeymoon, they planned to continue searching for a bigger house. Lily would move in with them and help raise her future grandchildren.

May Chin, one of Vikki's bridesmaids, knew in her heart that Vincent would be a great dad. "Vincent was very good with kids," she reminisced. "Very patient and gentle. He was very close to my two sons. They gravitated toward him."

After his father died, Vincent presented Lily with a design he had sketched for his tombstone. It was a double serpentine-shaped headstone for both parents carved out of red marble. The family name CHIN was written in the center, with flowers flanking either side. Inscriptions were placed on the bottom right and left corners: BELOVED FATHER C. W. HING, 1905–1981 and LILY, 1920–. Above each name, Vincent had drawn a traditional Chinese lion. In China, stone lion statues often sat in front of the houses of royal families to protect them from evil.

"He said, 'Mama, I want you and father all together,'" Lily said. "'I draw these lions to give to father to watch the door.'"

. . .

Dozens of gaily wrapped wedding presents were arriving at the doorstep of Lily and Vincent's house in Oak Park. Some packages were postmarked from as far away as China. Theirs was to be a big wedding, with more than four hundred guests not just from all over America but also from Asia.

On the morning of June 29, 1982, Gary Koivu put on his formal suit. It was still fairly new because he had bought it last year for Vincent's father's funeral. He had planned to wear his one nice suit again for Vincent and Vikki's wedding.

But instead, he was now wearing it to another funeral . . . of his best friend.

Koivu missed Vincent every day. "I felt a great sense of loss," he said. "He was a good friend. And I'd known him for over twenty years, so we had a lot of history and we shared memories."

Koivu and Vincent became lifelong friends when they first met in first grade at Cortland Elementary School in Highland Park. "He's standing in front of the class, the teacher's introducing him, he looked so scared," he remembered. "Of course, a new school, a new country for him and it's sort of understandable. We became friends."

The two first graders walked back and forth to school together every day, past the giant elm trees that lined their street. In the early 1960s, Highland Park was the American Dream come to life, with Koivu and Vincent playing football on the front lawn while the local milkman dropped glass bottles of cold cream into the milk chute built into the side of Koivu's childhood home.

Koivu and Vincent were inseparable. They hung out together all the time, watching their favorite TV shows, playing board games, and reading *Superman* and *Archie* comic books on rainy days. They ran track and took violin lessons together. Koivu remembered going to Vincent's house for dinner and eating Chinese food for the first time in his life.

Although the two boys were best friends, they were what Koivu described as "opposites attract." "I was very quiet," Koivu said. "Vincent was outgoing." As they became teenagers, Koivu remembered Vincent as always "very friendly, always talkative. He liked to be around a lot of people, made a lot of friends, made a lot of girlfriends."

But whenever they went to the library together, Vincent could be just as quiet—if not quieter—than Koivu. Visiting the library was one of their favorite pastimes together when they were in the seventh grade. Koivu would check out the nonfiction books while Vincent would wander through the fiction section. Vincent was a bookworm, Koivu recalled. "He would take a couple stacks of novels, thick books," he said. "I'd help him carry them home. He read all through his life. You always see him with a book in his car, in his house . . . always reading in his spare time."

As young men, Koivu and Vincent remained close even though their lives were busy with work and dating. Vincent started working at the Golden Star Restaurant in Ferndale. Koivu would meet him at the Golden Star and have a beer at the bar while waiting for Vincent's shift to end so they could hang out.

On Sundays, Vincent would visit Koivu at his apartment on Cass Lake to go fishing in a rowboat. "We didn't catch much," Koivu remembered of their fishing days. "I think I caught a pike. We just enjoyed being out on the water." He remembered an impressed Vincent joking about how he wanted to take the fish home to cook it. "Whether we caught anything or not, we had fun."

Koivu never forgot the night when Vincent stopped by his apartment after his restaurant shift ended so they could hang out. They watched an old black and white movie on TV because Vincent was a fan of classic cinema. "We used to discuss old movies," Koivu said. "He enjoyed watching them. I fell asleep watching the movie."

The next day Koivu was amused to learn that Vincent had stayed awake to finish the movie so he could tell his friend what happened. "He told me the ending," Koivu said, smiling. "Things like that I missed. He's the only one that I knew who grew up with me and were still friends with."

Those moments of loyal friendship were what Koivu missed the most about Vincent. "I felt terrible," he said. "For someone that I knew for twenty years, was very close with, and had a lot in common . . . a part of me was lost."

. . .

At two p.m. on Tuesday, June 29, 1982, Lily Chin, Vikki Wong, Gary Koivu, and the other wedding guests attended Vincent Chin's funeral. He was laid to rest near his father.

At the time, the memorial headstone Vincent had designed for his father had not yet been completed. Vincent would never see the final version.

. . .

## DETROIT FREE PRESS
## FUNERALS TODAY
## JUNE 29, 1982

CHIN, VINCENT JEN—June 23, 27 years. Beloved son of Lily F. and the late Wing Hing. Funeral Tuesday 2 PM. at the Sawyer-Fuller Funeral Home. Interment Forest Lawn Cemetery. Visitation Sunday 3–8 PM and Monday 5–8 PM.

# Chapter 6
# "THE LITTLE YELLOW PEOPLE"

On Thursday, July 1, an article appeared on the front page of the *Detroit Free Press*. The headline read, SLAYING ENDS COUPLE'S DREAM. The photo showed Vincent Chin and Vikki Wong smiling for the camera.

The article caught the attention of Helen Zia. The thirty-year-old journalist was familiar with Detroit's reputation as "Murder City." But it wasn't the tragic headline that intrigued her. It was the photo of the young couple.

They were Asian.

In 1982 Detroit, Asians were a rarity. The city had a population of 1.2 million, of which 60 percent were Black and 40 percent were white. There were only 7,614 Asians—less than 1 percent of the city's population.

So Zia was shocked to see a front-page photo of a happy young couple in love who happened to be of Asian descent. Asian Americans were rarely covered in the local media.

"It was zero about Asian Americans ever," Zia said. "And suddenly to see this article and this picture of a Chinese American, his father and mother and bride-to-be and this story, and this was 1982 and the fact that he was killed? I had a visceral reaction."

People stand in line to apply for jobs at a Ford auto plant in 1977. When Vincent was killed in 1982, Detroit's unemployment rate was twice the national average. Anger and fear over the hundreds of thousands of layoffs in the auto industry soon transformed into anti-Asian racism as competition with Japan's import auto industry became a scapegoat for Detroit's economic woes.

Zia could not shake the uneasy feeling that Vincent's Asian heritage might have played a part in his violent death. After all, it was not uncommon to see American-made cars in Detroit sporting red-white-and-blue-colored bumper stickers with the words DATSUN. TOYOTA. NISSAN. REMEMBER PEARL HARBOR!

"It felt dangerous to have an Asian face," Zia later wrote in her memoir, *Asian American Dreams*. "Asian American employees of auto companies were warned not to go onto the factory floor because angry workers might hurt them if they were thought to be Japanese."

And Detroit was hurting. After the 1967 Detroit protests and the oil crisis and economic recession in the 1970s, Detroit's population plummeted as more than 300,000 people moved out between 1970 and 1980.

At the time, Zia covered the auto industry and labor move-ment for local magazines *Detroit Metro Times, Monthly Detroit,* and *Metropolitan Detroit.* But she had an insider's perspective that gave her an advantage over other reporters. During her first two years in Detroit, she had worked at Chrysler, like Ronald Ebens and Michael Nitz. If Zia, as an Asian American, was a rare sight in Detroit, she had been even rarer in the auto industry as one of the few Asian Americans who belonged to the United Auto Workers union at the time. "I definitely stood out," she said.

Zia had first moved to the Motor City in 1976 for an adventure. For most of her life, she had tried to be what she described as the "good Asian American child" by studying hard and staying out of trouble. After all, her Chinese immigrant parents had sacrificed everything to make sure their daughter had all the advantages they didn't. So Zia graduated from Princeton University in 1973 with a degree in public and international affairs and a minor in East Asian studies. She then spent a year working as a public affairs specialist at the U.S Department of State before attending Tufts University School of Medicine.

But by her second year of medical school, Zia realized, "I had made a terrible mistake." She missed her political activism days of college. She wanted to make a difference in the world. She decided to move to Detroit, birthplace of the automobile. "I was on a mission, a grand adventure," she wrote in *Asian American Dreams,* "to learn what it meant to be an American in America's heartland."

She drove from Boston to Detroit in her Chevy Vega with nothing other than a suitcase and one hundred dollars in her pocket.

Before she became a journalist, Zia's first job in Detroit was as a large press operator at a Chrysler stamping plant. For two years, she endured eight straight hours during her shift on the assembly line stamping giant sheets of steel into the shape of car hoods and fenders. The sound of gigantic twenty-foot-tall hydraulic presses slamming against metal reverberated like thunder throughout the two-story building.

"So we'd get a flat piece of steel, this thing went *bam!*" Zia said. "And it was metal on metal. I have hearing loss today partly because of it. You'd get little earplugs to wear, but it was the most incredible noise. Thousands of machines doing this all day long.

"Once I was working on a small press, and the machine came down on one of my fingers, and I still have nerve damage from it," Zia said. "But I was lucky I didn't lose my hand. You would never want to stick your hand in the press, if for some reason it malfunctioned, you'd be dead."

For many people, however, the risk was worth it. "These jobs paid a lot of money," Zia explained. "Full benefits. Just to give you a reference point, minimum wage at that point was $1.40, maybe $1.50 an hour. And these jobs paid ten dollars an hour for unskilled work. I had never had medical insurance my entire life, and for the first time I could go to the dentist to get my teeth checked."

This money allowed many autoworkers to feel confident about their job security despite what was happening in the outside world—a national recession, growing competition from import car companies, and an auto industry that was falling behind the times.

"The auto industry was totally wearing blinders," Zia said. "They continued making what would give them the best profit, these large clunky cars, without any attempt to invest in better technologies or whatever. And the lack of investment was very clear in the factory. These machines we worked on were dinosaurs of the industrial revolution. Most of these machines were the original machines that were forty or fifty years old."

As a result, the Big Three, in the early 1980s, were ill equipped to handle a dramatic drop in sales of their cars. Ford, GM, and Chrysler were forced to lay off thousands of workers, including Zia. Entire families' life savings were wiped out. People declared bankruptcy as they lost their homes and they became known as the "new poor."

Although Zia had experienced occasional racism while working at the plant, she had also forged strong friendships. "When I got laid off, I totally understood people's anguish," she said. "We would be in line in the dead of winter in Michigan, which was horrible, really awful, like being in Siberia, and we'd been standing in line for almost eight hours to get a paltry unemployment check."

Eventually, that anguish turned to anger as people tried to figure out the root cause of this problem. "These were good jobs," Zia said, "which is why people were so angry. It was because they lost everything. These are people who had really good incomes, they had second homes, they had two, three cars plus an RV. They had a future, kids they could send to college, and then they lost everything. *Everything.* You can't blame them for being super miserable."

But many people wanted to blame something—or someone— for their misery.

So in 1982 Detroit found a new enemy. Japan.

· · ·

Members of an autoworkers union chapter destroy a Japanese-made vehicle at a protest in 1981. News footage and media images of mostly white (and non-Asian) autoworkers destroying imported cars during the early 1980s disturbed the Asian American community, which feared this animosity would soon translate into an uptick in anti-Asian racism.

There was now a new "Big Three" threatening to take over America: Toyota, Datsun (now Nissan), and Honda.

These Japanese companies made more fuel-efficient cars. The cars were solidly built and, more important, *cheap*. They were more affordable than the expensive eight-cylinder gas-guzzlers made by Ford, GM, and Chrysler.

But for Michigan natives, buying a Japanese import car was considered treason in the state where Henry Ford had invented the automobile. It was anti-American.

In the early 1980s, racism against people of Japanese descent was at an all-time high in Detroit. "[Anti-Japanese] feeling in Detroit is running higher than I've seen it," said teacher and Detroit native Elaine Prout, who was also president of the local chapter of the Japanese American Citizens League. She recalled how another teacher snapped at her one day, saying, "Why don't you go back to Japan with the cars?"

Lawyer James Shimoura, who was born and raised in Detroit, was among the Japanese Americans who noticed an increase in racism against people who looked like him. "Italian Americans or German Americans don't suffer because of the imports of Fiats or BMWs," he said. "But because of our special visibility, due to physical appearance, we fall victim to the attitudes toward the Japanese nation."

Shimoura was an American citizen. "I was born here and raised in the Detroit area my entire life. Yet my Japanese friends and I have to defend ourselves. . . . I live in town here and I have a stake in the [economy] as much as anybody else. If Detroit prospers, I prosper."

Politicians soon joined in the fight against Japan. It didn't matter what party they were from or how liberal or conservative they were—both Republicans and Democrats were concerned by the competition from Japan. In just four years, more than 300,000 American autoworkers lost their jobs, their numbers falling from 750,000 in 1978 to 448,000 by 1982. As a result, people who did not consider themselves racist still used problematic and sometimes racist rhetoric to describe the situation.

During a December 17, 1982, session with the Committee on Commerce, Science, and Transportation, Senator Carl Levin (D-Michigan) used war metaphors to describe his frustration over the competition between the U.S. and Japan auto industries. "We are being shot at and shot up by the Japanese, who have the most protectionist economy in the world," Levin said. "But some of those who hold up the spectre of a trade war ignore that we already in the middle of such a war, but only the Japanese are shooting."

At a private Democratic Environmental Caucus meeting in March 1982 to discuss Japan's effect on the American auto industry, Representative John D. Dingell, Jr. (D-Michigan), described the Japanese car companies as "the little yellow people." When Representative Albert A. Gore, Jr. (D-Tennessee), the future forty-fifth U.S. vice president, and several shocked Democrats asked him to clarify what he meant by that, Dingell Jr. repeated, "The little yellow people. You know. Honda." After his controversial words became national news, the congressman publicly apologized, releasing a statement insisting that he "had never intentionally indicated any disrespect for the Japanese people or any other racial group."

During his 1980 presidential campaign, former California governor Ronald Reagan said, "Japan is part of the problem," adding that the "deluge of cars must be slowed while our industry gets back on its feet."

On March 8, 1982, in Detroit, House Speaker Thomas P. O'Neill, Jr. (D-Massachusetts), demanded an embargo on Japanese auto imports. "If I were president . . . I'd fix the Japanese like they've never been fixed." Other politicians compared the Japanese import car competition as "an economic Pearl Harbor."

Chrysler chairman Lee Iacocca warned that the Japanese were "in the backyard, taking over the country."

In addition to the anti-Japanese bumper stickers in Detroit likening the Japan trade war to Pearl Harbor, a new sign at the Chrysler plant parking lot read, 300,000 LAID-OFF UAW MEMBERS DON'T LIKE YOUR IMPORT. PLEASE PARK IT IN TOKYO.

By 1982, anything Japanese was a target in Detroit. But this "Jap bashing" made Zia and other Asian Americans nervous.

"There was a lot of hatred spreading against Japan and anybody who looked Japanese, so all of that innuendo had been booming in that echo chamber for five years," Zia said. "Every Asian American felt it. You had to watch your back, you had to be careful what car you were driving."

As Zia stared in shock at the smiling faces of Vincent Chin and Vikki Wong on the front page of the *Detroit Free Press,* she knew this was just the beginning of a much bigger story. So she carefully clipped out the article and placed it in one of her file folders.

"I knew there was something more to this," she said.

# "THEY KEEP THEIR HISTORY VERY QUIET"

A year passed, and Jarod had still not told his mom that he knew about Vincent Chin.

Instead, he looked up newspaper articles, documentaries, and news videos online. "I realized this was pretty important, historically," he said. "I should know more about this." He soon became an expert on Vincent Chin.

But when it came to information about his mom, let alone his whole family, Jarod was still in the dark. "They keep their history very quiet," he explained. "Vincent was never brought up to me by my parents when I was younger. They are very, very private about their past."

So Jarod was shocked, as he pored over old family photo albums, trying to find clues about his mom's life. He discovered she had moved to America from Hong Kong as a teenager. She fell in love with classic American '70s rock music. She had a happy, vibrant personality. And she had a flair for fashion.

"From the pictures I've seen, she seemed pretty outgoing," he said. "She definitely had feathered hair. She looked pretty stylish with her bell bottom jeans." In one photo, a young Vikki wore tinted sunglasses and stood proudly in front of her classic Camaro. "There are a lot of photos where I was like, 'Whoa, Mom looks cool!'" he said, laughing.

This Vikki Wong was not the mother Jarod had grown up with. "She has that conservative Chinese mom mentality where she wanted me to get a good job, good health insurance, don't do drugs, don't drink," he said. "She was very loving but also blunt."

For the first time, Jarod saw his mother in a whole new light. She hadn't always been the strict mother who constantly checked over his homework and pressured him to study hard. Instead, she was a charming, vivacious young woman who drove a cool Camaro, classic rock blaring from the speakers. She seemed like someone he would have liked to hang out with.

As Jarod learned more about Vincent Chin's death and the controversial verdict that polarized not just Detroit but America, he began to understand why his mother was so strict with him. She wanted to make sure what happened to Vincent didn't happen to him.

. . .

The more Jarod discovered about Vincent Chin, the more he realized how different Vincent was from his father.

Jarod's dad was born in San Francisco but moved to Houston at a young age. His family moved to Detroit when the Chinese restaurant boom exploded in the Midwest. Jarod's grandfather on his father's side, along with some family members and friends, opened a restaurant in Southfield where his father worked.

But although both Vincent and Jarod's dads worked in the Chinese restaurant industry, that was where the similarities ended. Jarod knew from the articles he had read that Vincent was far from shy. That he liked to go to parties and meet new people.

"My dad was completely 180 degrees different, just the complete opposite of Vincent," Jarod said. "He's a private person. Instead of going out all the time, my dad would rather be at home with friends and family."

Jarod peppered his relatives with seemingly innocuous questions, trying to find out whatever details he could about his parents' courtship. He found out that his dad used to work at a bar with Vincent, where many of their friends and family liked to hang out. In fact, Vikki's sister dated and later married the cousin of Jarod's dad. "From some of the stories I was told, it was a small crowd, a small group of friends," he said.

But unlike Vincent and his uncles, Jarod's dad rarely went out to parties. "He worked hard and saved a bunch of money," Jarod said.

From what Jarod could glean from his relatives' anecdotes, after Vincent's death, some cousins or maybe an aunt or uncle introduced Vikki to his future father. "I was putting all the pieces of the puzzle together," he said.

But so far the pieces did not add up to a complete picture.

PART TWO

# "IT'S NOT FAIR"

# Chapter 7

# "YOU MAKE THE PUNISHMENT FIT THE CRIMINAL"

"Guilty, Your Honor."

On March 16, 1983, Ronald Ebens and Michael Nitz stood in a courtroom in the Frank Murphy Hall of Justice in downtown Detroit. They had both just pleaded guilty to a charge of manslaughter and were awaiting their fate from the judge.

Nine months had passed since Vincent Chin's death.

During that time, the police and Wayne County prosecutor William Cahalan's office had charged Ebens and Nitz with second-degree murder, which in Michigan means an "unplanned, intentional killing" or a death caused by a "reckless disregard for human life." The theory was that they had killed Vincent on the spur of the moment in the heat of an argument. At a preliminary hearing in October 1982, based on the testimony by Gary Koivu, Robert Siroskey, and Jimmy Choi, Judge Thomas Bayles had suggested that Ebens actually should be charged with first-degree murder. But that did not happen. Far from it.

Because Detroit's court system was overloaded, lawyers and judges often took the shortcut of plea bargaining so they could focus on more serious crimes. "Plea bargaining is supposed to speed up justice . . . and keep courts from collapsing under the weighty volume of cases," explained *Detroit Free Press* reporters David Ashenfelter and John Castine in their 1983 six-part investigative series on manslaughter sentencing in Michigan.

In the Chin case, instead of increasing the charge against Ebens to first-degree murder as Judge Bayles had proposed, the prosecutors agreed to a plea bargain in which both Ebens and Nitz would plead guilty not even to second-degree murder, but to manslaughter.

According to the Michigan Penal Code 750.321, the felony of manslaughter was defined as "criminally negligent homicide"— the unintentional killing of another person resulting from recklessness or criminal negligence.

What made manslaughter different from murder was that the person had no intention of killing the other person. Accidents, poor judgment, and bad luck often resulted in manslaughter, from drunk driving to a fight that got out of control. Those convicted could be sentenced to up to fifteen years in prison and have to pay a fine of up to $7,500.

Ebens and Nitz agreed to plead guilty to manslaughter. This meant there would be no trial. Instead, a sentencing was set at the Wayne County Circuit Court.

On March 16, they stood before Judge Charles Kaufman. But no one had informed Vincent Chin's family about the hearing. As a result, Lily Chin was not at the courthouse that day. Even the prosecutor was not present to argue the state's case against Ebens and Nitz. It was not unusual for prosecutors to miss sentencings because of their busy workload. In fact, there was no law in Michigan at the time requiring the mandatory presence of a prosecutor during a hearing. Charles Marr, a spokesperson for Prosecutor Cahalan's office, later told reporters their office did not even have anyone available on that day to attend the hearing.

As a result, the only people standing in Judge Kaufman's courtroom on March 16 were Ebens and Nitz and their defense attorneys, Bruce Saperstein and Edward Khoury.

A Wayne State University Law School graduate, sixty-three-year-old Kaufman had served as a judge for eighteen years. A World War II air force navigator who had survived a prisoner of war camp in Japan, Kaufman was known for being lenient on first-time offenders with no prior records. His reputation for mercy gave a glimmer of hope for the nervous Ebens and Nitz.

Judge Kaufman had "perused" the transcript of the preliminary hearing from October 1982 before Judge Bayles, and he asked the defense attorneys to "refresh his memory." Not surprisingly, they took advantage of the absence of the prosecutor to put things in the best possible light for their clients.

"Your Honor, Mr. Ebens and Mr. Nitz were seated, and the victim walked up and punched Mr. Ebens in the mouth, initiating the physical assault," said Ebens's lawyer, Bruce Saperstein.

Nitz's lawyer, Edward Khoury, backed up Saperstein, adding that Vincent had "split his [Nitz's] head open with a chair."

Ebens told Judge Kaufman his side of the story. He and Nitz were sitting by the stage of the club when out of nowhere, Vincent Chin "came over, for what reason I still don't know, and struck me a blow in the mouth. And it upset me out of my chair." Ebens went on to describe how his mouth bled from Vincent's "sucker punch," and how his stepson also got hit in the head with a chair when he tried to hold Vincent back.

What Judge Kaufman didn't hear, however, and what he

apparently did not pick up from his "perusal" of the preliminary hearing transcript, were the very different accounts of Gary Koivu, Robert Siroskey, and Jimmy Choi, nor did he have access to the statements that the other witnesses had given to the police that also contradicted the accounts given by Ebens and his lawyers.

Contrary to Ebens's story that Vincent had come around the stage and hit Ebens in the mouth, some witnesses had told the police that Vincent and Ebens had met halfway around the club's stage before the fight began, and despite conflicting testimonies, no one could confirm that Vincent had indeed thrown the first punch.

There also had been differing accounts about what happened after the fight ended, and in particular, about whether Ebens and Nitz had jumped into the car to chase after Vincent, who had run away, or whether they were simply trying to get Nitz to the nearest hospital.

According to Ebens, it was a coincidence that they ended up driving past Vincent and his friend Jimmy Choi.

"During the melee inside, my stepson received a head injury plus I was bleeding from the mouth," Ebens told Judge Kaufman at the hearing. "And we left there with two intentions in mind: it really was to keep an eye out for them, plus going to get Mike medical attention because he needed stitches. And as we were going down Woodward, we noticed the two sitting out in front of McDonald's, laughing and joking with each other. We stopped. . . . I hopped out the back seat. I had the bat in my hand when I came out of the car. I came around the corner, and I yelled at Vincent and I struck him in the arm. He took off running. Jimmy Choi took off running down the street the other way. I don't know exactly where Mike came from, to be honest with you, but from that point on I don't remember what happened."

"[The killing] was not so much an act that was willful or with any specific intent to commit any crime, but a tragedy of major proportion," Nitz's lawyer, Edward Khoury, told Judge Kaufman.

Judge Kaufman did not hear the statement made to the police by one witness that Ebens and Nitz had allegedly paid him twenty dollars to help them find Vincent, which was not in the preliminary hearing transcript (since he had not testified) and which made Ebens's eventual encounter with Vincent sound less coincidental and more premeditated.

Ebens's lawyer, Saperstein, appealed to Judge Kaufman's compassion by reminding him that Ebens was not a hardened criminal.

"I'm confident that this would never happen again," Saperstein told the judge. "But normal people act strange when loved ones appear to be seriously injured, and that is what happened here, resulting in this tragedy. . . . With respect to punishment, Your Honor, Mr. Ebens is being punished every day of his life over this incident. He can't change that. He has to live with this."

When Judge Kaufman asked Ebens for his reaction to Vincent's death, Ebens replied, "Only that I'm deeply sorry about what happened. If there is any way I could change it, I sure would."

Judge Kaufman ordered a five-minute recess while he processed all the information.

When it was time for Judge Kaufman to deliver his sentence, he stated that his decision was based on both men's lack of previous criminal records. "They weren't the kind of people you send to prison," he would say later.

Judge Kaufman ruled that they would serve three years' probation and each pay $3,000 in fines and $780 in court costs.

Judge Kaufman believed his sentence was just. "We're talking here about a man who's held down a responsible job with the same company for seventeen or eighteen years and his son who is employed and is a part-time student. These men are not going to go out and harm somebody else. I just didn't think putting them in prison would do any good for them or for society. You don't make the punishment fit the crime; you make the punishment fit the criminal."

Even Ebens and Nitz were shocked by Judge Kaufman's ruling.

"I told my wife that morning she might as well put a stamp on my ass 'cause they were going to be sending me away," Ebens said. When Judge Kaufman announced his decision, Ebens said later, "you could have knocked me over with a feather."

*Probation. Three thousand dollars.*

That was it.

Judge Kaufman's sentence meant that Ebens and Nitz would never spend a single day in jail for killing Vincent Chin. They could go home.

They were free . . . for now.

## Chapter 8

# AN ASIAN AMERICAN DREAM DEFERRED

Lily Chin was confused.

"Three years' probation?" she repeated. "I don't know what probation means."

She had just come home from work when the phone rang.

It was Paul Ng. He had found out about Judge Kaufman's sentence.

"Uncle Ping, how come it's like this?" Lily asked.

Ng explained how Judge Kaufman believed his sentence was fair because Ebens and Nitz had no prior criminal records and came from stable working backgrounds.

Lily was furious. Her son also came from a stable working background. He had no prior criminal record either. But he hadn't killed anyone. So why were his killers set free? She wondered what would have happened if it had been the other way around—if two Chinese American men had beaten a white man to death with a baseball bat. Would the judge still take pity on them?

Although Lily wasn't sure how to answer that question, she knew what her father, Yee Char, would have said. *Yes.*

"My father warned me of a hard life in America," she said.

Growing up, her father had told Lily stories of hardship and

Lily Chin followed in the footsteps of her great-grandfather, who was among the 20,000 Chinese immigrants who helped build the transcontinental railroad, by moving to America to make a new life for her new family—including her adopted son, Vincent.

bigotry that her great-grandfather endured in America during the latter half of the nineteenth century. He was one of the thousands of Chinese immigrants who had come to America a century earlier, after gold was discovered in California in 1848. Famine and war had torn apart the Guangdong Province, where the Chin family lived. Families were desperate for work. The Chinese viewed America as their 金山 (Gam Saan), meaning "Gold Mountain."

Lily's great-grandfather never found gold. Instead, he ended up working for very little pay on the transcontinental railroad. The work was not only physically difficult but also dangerous. Chinese railroad workers would drill a hole into mountainous rock, pour black dynamite powder into it, then light a fuse. They had only a few moments to run as far away as they could before the flame made contact with the powder, causing a detonation.

It was a crude and unpredictable process that killed many men. The Central Pacific Railroad Company did not consider Chinese lives equal to the lives of their white workers. Better to risk the life of a "Chinaman" rather than their more valued white counterparts, the company bosses reasoned.

No one knows exactly how many Chinese men were killed from these explosions, but there are estimates of over fifteen hundred unnamed deaths. This horrific toll soon led to the racist expression *a Chinaman's chance in hell,* meaning "no chance at all."

Still, Lily viewed America as her Gold Mountain. As a young woman during World War II's Second Sino-Japanese War (1937–45), she had hidden with her family in the mountains outside Canton and watched as air raids devastated her city. When the war was over, she didn't trust the new Communist leader, Mao Zedong, who was fighting to establish the People's Republic of China. For Lily, America represented freedom and equality.

Vincent's father, David Bing Hing Chin, felt that hope as well when he left China for America at age seventeen in 1922. He lived in Seattle and New York before settling down in Detroit. He became an American citizen and enlisted in the army during World War II to fight for his new home.

After the war ended, he wanted to marry and start a family. He received many letters and photos of prospective brides in China. But it was Lily's photo that caught his eye—he was drawn to her quiet smile and expressive eyes. It turned out his mother and Lily's grandmother lived in the same village in Guangdong Province. It was as if they were destined to be together.

David returned to China to meet Lily. They wed in 1946 and moved to America in 1948, one year before the Chinese Communists assumed power, cutting Lily off from her family for many years.

David and Lily first moved into an apartment in Highland Park, coincidentally less than a mile from the McDonald's on Woodward Avenue where Vincent would be beaten with a baseball bat. But in 1949 Highland Park was still a prosperous middle-class neighborhood. "Highland Park was high class back then," Lily said.

But Lily's life was anything but high class. The high-wage auto plant jobs were out of reach for poor Chinese immigrants who could not speak English. So from seven a.m. until midnight, Lily and her husband worked in a basement laundry, starching, ironing, and folding more than a hundred shirts a day, at twenty-two cents per shirt. They were lucky if together they made a total of one hundred dollars a week.

"Some of them got jobs in the auto plants but I think for the most part, it was in the service industries around all of the higher-paying work in Detroit," said Helen Zia. "Primarily for Chinese, it was laundries and restaurants."

The first year was hard for Lily, isolated in a neighborhood where she and David were the only Chinese people for miles. They rode the bus on Sundays to downtown Detroit's Chinatown district, where they would stock up on groceries and occasionally treat themselves to a movie.

While they worked long hours in the steamy basement laundry, the white children in the neighborhood rode by on their bicycles. Sometimes they would stop and press their faces against the window. Lily, who loved children and wanted to start a family of her own, would smile at them. But they did not smile back.

"They made ugly faces at us," she recalled, heartbroken. "They stuck out their tongues and made as if to slit our throats." Lily remembered how the children would pull their eyes back in an exaggerated slanted motion. She knew what that meant—they were making fun of her race. "I guess when the kids walked past our building, seeing us working at the basement sort of made them see us as prisoners," she said. Lily realized her father was right. Like her great-grandfather, she was not truly welcome here. The basement laundry was no longer a prison. *America* had become her prison.

But when Lily and David adopted Vincent in 1955, she felt the first stirrings of freedom. Unlike Lily, who had a difficult time adjusting to her new life in America, her six-year-old son seemed to fit in right away. His smile charmed everyone who met him. Vincent had a cheerful disposition and an ability to make friends on first sight. She called him her "gentleman" because he was always combing his hair and wearing a tie to school.

And now her son was not only dead, but his killers had been set free.

Lily remembered how, almost a hundred years earlier, her great-grandfather, along with other Chinese laborers, had risked his life, transporting and setting off volatile dynamite to blow up tunnels through solid mountain rock.

She thought about how the white railroad company bosses had viewed him and these other "Chinamen" as less than worthy, as less human. She wondered—did the courts see her son as less than worthy, too? Was his life worth only $3,000?

*Something is wrong with this country,* she realized.

Lily decided she would not give up. She would fight back. She reached for the nearest pen and piece of paper. She began to write.

"This is injustice to the grossest extreme. I grieve in my heart and shed tears in blood. My son cannot be brought back to life, but he was a member of your council. Therefore, I plead to you. Please let the Chinese American community know, so they can help me hire legal counsel to appeal, so my son can rest his soul."

As Lily wrote, she had no idea that this letter, which she would later mail to the Detroit Chinese Welfare Council, would be as powerful as the dynamite her great-grandfather had lit in the dark tunnels of the California mountain range, ready to explode.

Chapter 9

# "THIS IS HOW FAR WE'VE COME IN TWO HUNDRED YEARS?"

"The dead man threw the first punch."

The words stopped Helen Zia cold. She was in the middle of a break at work at *Metropolitan Detroit* magazine, coffee in hand, when she saw the front-page story in the Friday, March 18, 1983, edition of the *Detroit Free Press*. The headline blared, 2 MEN CHARGED IN '82 SLAYING GET PROBATION.

A shocked Zia read the opening paragraph: "Two men charged with beating a man to death two days before he was to be married have been sentenced to probation by a Wayne County Circuit Court judge, who said the dead man threw the first punch."

Her heart sank as she remembered the article she had clipped nine months earlier. The newspaper photo of the smiling Vincent and Vikki on the front page had haunted her since then.

And there was one sentence in the article that raised red flags for Zia.

"The dead man threw the first punch."

Suddenly, in a simple turn of phrase, Vincent Chin had gone from victim to villain.

At thirty-one years of age, Princeton graduate and former autoworker Helen Zia found her voice as a writer and activist, protesting the killing of Vincent Chin and helping to organize the American Citizens for Justice (ACJ).

Why did it matter that Vincent might have *started* the fight? Zia wondered. Was that enough of a reason to let his two killers walk free with a $3,000 fine each and three years of probation for beating him to death with a baseball bat?

As a journalist, Zia knew she had to remain impartial and hear all sides of the story before drawing any conclusions. But images from history textbooks she had studied in college, about the history of Asian immigrants in America, kept flooding her brain.

How a frenzied mob of five hundred white men had lynched and murdered eighteen Chinese immigrants in a Los Angeles Chinatown on October 24, 1871, after a white man was accidentally killed in gun crossfire during a dispute between two Chinese men.

The unknown death toll of hundreds of Chinese laborers forced to transport volatile sticks of dynamite during the building of the transcontinental railroad in the nineteenth century because white laborers' lives were considered too valuable to put at risk.

How 120,000 Japanese Americans had lost everything when their own government forced them from their homes and imprisoned them during World War II in "relocation centers" (later referred to as "internment camps" and "concentration camps").

And now in 1983 Detroit, images in the news of American white autoworkers literally bashing Japanese import cars with sledgehammers and shouting racist slurs.

Given this history, Zia could not shake her instinct that race was behind Vincent Chin's death.

"It was total shock and outrage," she said. "The thought that kept coming to me all day long is 'This is how far we've come in two hundred years?' This is how we get treated in America. This is how far we've come?"

. . .

Helen Zia wasn't the only person outraged by Judge Kaufman's lenient sentencing.

Two young lawyers, Roland Hwang and James Shimoura, had also noticed the photograph of Vincent and Vikki on the front page of the *Detroit Free Press* the previous July.

Like Zia, both men had been surprised to see a photo of two young Asian Americans featured so prominently in the local newspapers.

"Asians were pretty much an oddity because we were so small in number," Roland Hwang said.

And the then-thirty-three-year-old Hwang would know. Born in Detroit, he was one of the very few Asian American students at Brady Elementary School. The only time he ever saw other Asians was on weekend trips to the Chinese grocery store in Detroit's Chinatown.

The majority of Chinese immigrants living in Chinatown were working class. Many of them hailed from South China and worked in laundries and restaurants. But Hwang came from an upper-middle-class family. His father, a mechanical engineer with Ford Motor Company, had originally emigrated from China to Detroit as a college student, graduating from the University of Michigan in 1944 and 1948 with both bachelor and master's degrees in mechanical engineering. His mother attended Eastern Michigan University.

Hwang's family eventually moved to Livonia, a suburb just outside Detroit. At his high school of over 2,500 students, he was one of only five Asians, two of whom were foreign exchange

Attorney and American Citizens for Justice (ACJ) member James Shimoura, twenty-nine, born and raised in Detroit, came from three generations of Japanese Americans, starting with his grandfather, who arrived in America in 1911 and was famous for knocking on the door of Henry Ford's mansion to ask for a job. He later became an apprentice chemist for the Ford Motor Company.

students from Thailand and Korea. There were a few Arab American students, maybe one African American student, he remembered. "Livonia in the 1960s was pretty white."

In fact, Livonia was so white that before the Hwang family moved into their new house, a neighbor went door to door to ask, "'What do you think about this Chinese family living here?'" Hwang said. "There was no violence, but she was checking with everyone to make sure it was okay to have a Chinese family living in Livonia. This happened in 1962."

Like Hwang, James Shimoura, twenty-nine years old at the time, had also dealt with a lot of racism while growing up Detroit. "When I was in the seventh grade, a kid shoved my face into a drinking fountain and cracked my front tooth," he said. "*Chink* and *Jap* were pretty interchangeable, and I got into a couple of fights along the way."

The irony was that Shimoura's family had longer roots in America than many of the white kids who bullied him. His grandfather was famous for knocking on the front door of Henry Ford's mansion in 1911 to ask for a job.

"They thought he was looking for a job as a gardener or cook," Shimoura recalled. "He said, 'No, I want to work on cars.' So he actually got to meet Henry Ford, got hired and ended up becoming an apprentice chemist."

Both Hwang and Shimoura's experiences with racism helped form their racial consciousness and identities as they also became active in high school and college with Asian American student groups. Hwang would later become president of the Detroit chapter of the Association of Chinese Americans.

As a teenager, Shimoura belonged to the youth organization of the Japanese American Citizens League. In the 1970s he helped write and deliver letters on behalf of the league to demand individual reparations for the 120,000 Japanese Americans who were illegally imprisoned during World War II.

So when Hwang and Shimoura read the *Detroit Free Press* article in March 1983 about Judge Kaufman's lenient sentence of probation for Ronald Ebens and Michael Nitz, memories of racism during their Detroit childhoods flooded back to both of them. Because they were both lawyers, the leniency of Kaufman's sentence also shocked them.

"I was pissed," Shimoura said. "I suspected racism. It was a real visceral reaction, this anger that somebody had gotten beaten with a baseball bat and died and then they walked. I've had clients who were picked up for nonpayment of child support who spent more time in jail than Ronald Ebens."

"When Kaufman issued his probation and fine, it caused an outrage," Hwang said of the immediate reaction in the Chinese American community.

. . .

There was outrage, but there were also tears. Even though almost a year had passed since Vincent's death, it was hard for Gary Koivu to move forward. Out of nowhere, at the most random moments, an image of his friend would appear in his mind. When they first met in the first grade. When they watched NFL football games on TV on Sunday afternoons together. When they went fishing at Cass Lake. "Still hurts just talking about it," Koivu said. "Left an empty hole in my heart."

For the past eleven months, Koivu had tried his best to not dwell on what had happened. He worked hard at his job at a wholesale clothing outlet. He still went fishing at Cass Lake. "I just stayed by myself and got on with life," he said.

But Koivu never forgot the morning of May 18, 1983, when he picked up the newspaper on his way to work and saw the headline 2 MEN CHARGED IN '82 SLAYING GET PROBATION.

"I looked at the headline, and it was like a punch in the gut," he said. "I wasn't really too knowledgeable about court cases and sentencing and stuff like that, but I was shocked. How could you kill someone like that and not do any jail time? I was brought up to know that if you did something wrong, you had to pay the price."

. . .

Vikki Wong agreed with Koivu. In a rare public statement, she told *The Detroit News* that she did not believe Judge Kaufman's rationale behind the lenient sentence—that Ebens and Nitz deserved probation instead of jail time because they had no prior criminal records.

"I have never committed a crime in my life," Vikki said. "Does that mean I could kill and get away with it? They ruined my life, my future. How can you commit murder and get away with nothing? It's not fair. All I can do now is scream to myself, for him and for me."

. . .

"You can kill a dog and get thirty days in jail, ninety days for a traffic ticket," an angry Henry Yee told *The Detroit News*. "This was premeditated. They had to go to the car to get that baseball

Henry Yee, owner of the popular Chinese restaurant Forbidden City and known as Detroit's "Unofficial Mayor of Chinatown," helped to organize the first meetings to protest the 1983 probation sentencing of Ronald Ebens and Michael Nitz. These meetings would lead to the creation of the ACJ, which raised awareness of Vincent's killing and led to the first federal civil rights trial for an Asian American alleged to have been killed on the basis of race.

bat. The Chinese community, especially the younger generation, want to see justice done. Now what can we do?"

Sixty-three year-old Henry Yee was a well-known Chinese American businessman in Detroit and owner of the popular

Forbidden City Chinese restaurant, in the heart of Chinatown. He was often referred to as the "Unofficial Mayor of Chinatown" for his charisma and sharp business networking skills.

Yee had persuaded Vincent Chin and other younger Chinese American men to join the Chinese Welfare Council, of which he was a prominent member. Yee and the older generation wanted to add fresh blood to the rapidly aging association.

Detroit's Chinatown began as a working-class neighborhood founded by immigrant merchants. The first Chinese immigrant to arrive in Detroit was Ah Chee, in 1872. He set up a laundry business in Chinatown's original location on Third Avenue, between Michigan and Howard streets. Its first Chinese restaurant opened in 1905. By the 1920s, Chinatown had blossomed with three hundred laundries and thirty-two restaurants.

But by the 1980s, Chinatown had fallen onto hard times. Barely half a dozen Chinese restaurants remained, along with just a handful of stores. Meanwhile the Chinese population boomed out in the suburbs, thanks to the 1965 Immigration and Nationality Act, in which the U.S. government could no longer put a limit on the number of Chinese and other Asian immigrants allowed to move into the country. This new federal law nullified the earlier Chinese Exclusion Act of 1882, which was the first U.S. law to prevent immigration to America on the basis of a person's race.

As a result, the new wave of Asian immigration after 1965 consisted of educated professionals, such as scientists, professors, lawyers, and engineers. These newer Asian immigrants stayed far away from the working-class roots of Detroit's Chinatown, choosing to live in Michigan's suburbs. Many of them worked as engineers for the Big Three automakers. As a result,

Detroit's Chinatown population began to age and die out. The mom-and-pop curio stores and Chinese restaurants began to fold, due to declining business.

Meanwhile, a culture gap formed between the suburban Chinese teens who only spoke English and the Chinese-born Chinatown kids. The Chinatown teenagers viewed their suburban counterparts as "snobs," while the suburban teens dismissed them as "T.C."—"Typically Chinese."

Henry Yee, however, wasn't having it. He had fought too long to keep Chinatown alive to let racism and socioeconomic divisions destroy it. He saw great potential in Vincent—a working-class Chinese adopted child who climbed up the ladder from waiter to a draftsman at an engineering firm. Vincent was the future of Chinatown—someone who could bridge the social divide between town and country, perhaps someone who could even one day become the next Unofficial Mayor of Chinatown.

So when Yee received Lily Chin's letter asking for help, her words touched his heart: "This is injustice to the grossest extreme. I grieve in my heart and shed tears in blood. My son cannot be brought back to life . . . help me hire legal counsel to appeal, so my son can rest his soul."

Yee knew he couldn't waste another minute. He, along with Chinese Welfare Council president Kin Yee (no relation), immediately called everyone they knew in Chinatown, including Roland Hwang, who was president of the Association of Chinese Americans.

"We've got a problem," Kin Yee told the young lawyer. "And we need help."

Chapter 10

# "WE MUST LET THE WORLD KNOW THAT WE THINK THIS IS WRONG"

The room was silent save for one sound.

Lily Chin's sobbing.

It was March 20, 1983, just four days after Ronald Ebens and Michael Nitz's sentencing. A small group of twenty or thirty Asian Americans crowded the back room of the Golden Star.

The Golden Star was a popular restaurant in Ferndale that specialized in traditional Cantonese cuisine, because the majority of Chinese immigrants in Detroit came from Guangdong Province. The restaurant was known for its festive atmosphere, with its dragon-imprinted red velvet flocked wallpaper and famous drinks like the flaming volcano rum "Scorpion" bowl.

But in the back room, the mood was muted and solemn. Traditional Cantonese dishes like lo mein and char siu bao sat on the table, largely untouched and growing cold. Everyone was still too shocked—and angry—to have much of an appetite.

In the room were some of Michigan's top Asian American lawyers, journalists, and activists. It was no coincidence that the meeting had been arranged at the Golden Star. Vincent Chin had worked here as a waiter on weekends. Meeting there felt like the right thing to do, as if in tribute to Vincent's spirit.

Most of the lawyers at the Golden Star meeting were very young. James Shimoura was one of the oldest, at twenty-nine years of age. "The entire Asian bar was there," he said. "People were really upset. I was pissed, too."

Helen Zia was also at the meeting, taking notes to write a story for her magazine. But she felt her heart sink as one specific word was uttered over and over by Hwang, Shimoura, and the other lawyers in the room.

*Nothing.*

The lawyers explained to Zia and everyone in the room about the double jeopardy rule—how a defendant cannot be tried twice for the same crime. Ebens and Nitz had not actually been tried, but by pleading guilty to manslaughter, they had in effect been found guilty of that crime just as though they had been tried and found guilty by a jury. They could not be prosecuted again in a criminal court of law for killing Vincent Chin. The criminal case was over. It pained Hwang and Shimoura and the other lawyers to explain this, but the law was the law.

"I thought this was a really big story, an important story that the world needs to know about," Zia said. "And all the lawyers said, once the sentence is rendered, there's nothing we can do. They all stood up, one by one, in a line and kept saying, 'There's nothing we can do. There's nothing we can do. There's nothing we can do.' You could feel the energy in the room getting totally deflated until it was silent except for Mrs. Chin sobbing. You could hear and feel all of her grief in the echoing of, 'There's nothing . . . nothing . . . nothing.'"

The pen felt heavy in Zia's hand as she wrote the words "There's nothing we can do."

That's it? she thought to herself. Is this how it's going to end? *Nothing?* She was frustrated by the tunnel vision of these lawyers, whom she felt were too boxed in by legal technicalities and logic and were unable to see the forest for the trees.

Just then Lily Chin finally spoke up. "These men killed my son like an animal," she said. "But they go free. We must tell the people, this is wrong."

Lily's plea inspired Zia's activist zeal from her Princeton University days. She realized she could no longer sit by and be a witness. She had to do something. She put down her pen and addressed everyone: "We must let the world know that we think this is wrong."

"I stepped out of being a silent journalist," Zia later said. "I raised my hand and I said, 'You know what, we might not be able to change the judge's ruling, but we have to let people know this is not okay. We have to let people know that we as Chinese Americans—as Asian Americans—that it's not okay to kill us and go unpunished. This is not okay.' And so by saying that, you could really feel the energy in the room shift."

Zia's words inspired Hwang and Shimoura as well. Sure, there was nothing they could do as lawyers. But as Asian Americans—*as people*—maybe there was something they could do.

To this day, Zia never takes sole credit for starting the fight for justice for Vincent Chin. "I don't want to single myself out or pat myself on the back," she said. "But what I actually do say, when I tell students and young people this story today, is that I don't think raising my hand and saying that was such an extraordinary thing. It's the kind of thing every one of us, every human being, has the ability to do."

So on March 20, 1983, Helen Zia, Henry Yee, Kin Yee, Roland Hwang, James Shimoura, Lily Chin, and the other couple of dozen Asian Americans sitting in that back room of a modest Chinese restaurant agreed that this was not okay. They would no longer be silent.

And soon the whole world would listen.

# "ARE YOU GONNA LET HIM CALL YOU THAT?"

Jarod was twelve years old when someone called him "Chink" for the first time in his life.

But he had no idea what the word meant.

Having grown up in a mostly white suburb in Michigan, Jarod didn't have much exposure to other Chinese or Asian Americans. So when a seventh-grade boy called him a "Chink" in the gym locker room, Jarod was just confused. He had never heard that word before.

But Jarod's friend, who was white, had definitely heard that word before. And he knew what it meant.

"Dude, he called you a Chink!" Jarod's friend said, upset. "Are you gonna let him call you that?"

"What does that mean?" Jarod asked.

After his friend told him it was a racist slur against people of Asian descent, Jarod immediately got into a fight with the other boy. The other students and a teacher had to break it up.

Afterward Jarod told his dad about what happened at school. "Brush it off next time," his dad advised. "Don't get into a fight about it. You're better than that."

Jarod realized his parents had never talked to him about racism. They never prepared him for what would inevitably happen as he grew older. "I learned about racism through friends," he said.

Jarod wanted to know more about how his parents had dealt with racism when they were growing up, but they refused to discuss it with him. "They never shared their personal experiences with me," he said. "Vincent was never brought up to me by my parents when I was younger. They are very, very private about their past. My dad will open up here and there about his past, which seemed to be a normal upbringing in America. But those traumatizing moments were never brought up to me, so when I found [out] about Vincent Chin on my own, I was in shock."

Years later Jarod would wonder if his dad had warned him never to fight because of Vincent Chin. But he decided not to ask them. If his parents had refused to talk to him about racism and their connection to Vincent Chin after all these years, why would they talk now?

PART THREE

# JUSTICE FOR VINCENT CHIN

# Chapter 11
# THE WARRIOR

Liza Chan felt trapped. She had just turned thirty, and she hated her job. She was the lowest-ranked lawyer at a small general civil practice firm in Southfield, a suburb just outside Detroit. She spent long hours either writing endless legal briefs or rushing about the hallways of the courthouse, trying not to trip in her heels as she clutched a giant pile of documents in her arms.

"The practice of law was nothing close to what I had imagined what and how it would be," she later wrote in her memoir, *My Impossible Life*.

Chan had always imagined herself as a warrior. Growing up in Hong Kong, she was enamored with 武俠 or wuxia, the martial arts heroes featured in action adventure movies set in ancient China. Her favorite toy was a plastic sword. She envisioned herself as a woman warrior, ready to defend her family at all costs.

This warrior fantasy consumed Chan's life, especially because she had a rare spinal cord condition that often affected her health. She strongly believed that she had been a warrior in a past life. When she left Hong Kong in 1972 to attend Barnard College of Columbia University in New York City, she signed up for archery, fencing, and horseback riding classes.

But Chan quickly realized she lacked the physical stamina for these rigorous sports. She soon suffered chronic fatigue, burning chest pains, and other mysterious ailments. In 1981 she would be diagnosed with glomerulonephritis, a disease that damaged her kidneys, and with vaculitis, which caused her immune system to attack her own organs.

After graduating from Barnard in 1976, Chan moved to Detroit to attend Wayne State University Law School. That was where she discovered her passion for justice. *This* was her true calling as a warrior! "I was no longer 'in combat' literally, but yet, I somehow ended up being an attorney, sparring and dueling in court all the same," she wrote in her memoir.

While living in Detroit, Chan socialized with an LGBTQ group called Women Together at a local church. But Chan, who was a lesbian, did not reveal her sexual orientation publicly because of her status as a foreign student living in the United States on a temporary travel visa known as the H-1B. In the 1970s and '80s, immigration regulations were very restrictive, discriminatory, and homophobic—if you were outed, you could be deported. (The 1990 Immigration Act finally eliminated the exclusion of immigrants based on their sexual orientation.)

So Chan focused all her energy on becoming a full-time lawyer in Michigan. She passed the state bar exam and was admitted to practice law as a licensed attorney on November 24, 1980.

But it was her international background that intrigued senior partner James A. Hiller, who hired her on the spot at her job interview to be a law clerk for his general civil practice firm in Southfield. She and another law clerk were assigned legal research duties and often had to drive across Michigan to various courthouses to file pleadings on cases. One lawyer, Daniel J. Hoekenga, who specialized in public sector law, took

Chan under his wing by reviewing her legal briefs and letting her accompany him in the court whenever he had to deliver an oral argument.

Although Chan admired Hoekenga, she soon grew disillusioned with her career choice in law. She felt restless having to spend most of her time sitting in an office writing tedious legal briefs. Even though she had envisioned herself as a warrior in the courtroom, she often became tongue-tied and nervous when speaking publicly.

Chan began to wonder if she had chosen the "wrong" profession. "But it was too late . . . to push the 'reset' button," she wrote in her memoir. She had to keep her job at the law firm, or she would lose her temporary status and be forced to return to Hong Kong.

So when Henry Yee called Chan to invite her to the meeting at the Golden Star Restaurant to discuss the probation sentencing for Ronald Ebens and Michael Nitz, Chan hesitated. She had not heard of the Vincent Chin manslaughter case.

Chan remembered meeting Yee at a Lunar New Year's banquet at his Forbidden City restaurant a couple of years earlier. But this meeting at the Golden Star sounded like trouble. Asian Americans protesting the politics behind a manslaughter case? The last thing she needed was to be associated with a bunch of rabble-rousers and risk losing her temporary visa status. She decided to play it safe. So when Yee asked if Chan would attend the Golden Star meeting, she said no.

The next morning Chan was back at her office, writing yet another endless legal brief, when her mentor, Dan Hoekenga, stood in her doorway. He held up the *Detroit Free Press* front-page story about the Vincent Chin case. He was furious that Judge

Kaufman had given three years' probation to the killers. "What are you going to do about this?" he asked.

Chan was shocked as she read the article. She regretted not attending the meeting the previous night. She immediately called Henry Yee, who told her that he and Helen Zia planned to meet with Judge Charles Kaufman to discuss his sentence. But they had no legal counsel. None of the lawyers at the Golden Star meeting had volunteered to help, out of fear of jeopardizing their jobs over such a controversial case.

And that was when Chan realized, *This is what I've been training for my whole life.* "I'll meet with Kaufman," she said to a grateful Yee.

As Chan gathered her papers, preparing to research the case, she finally felt like a warrior about to head into battle.

Chapter 12

# AMERICAN CITIZENS FOR JUSTICE

Mable Lim's feet ached.

The sixty-three-year-old grandmother and her husband, Ray, had spent the entire day driving all over the Detroit area and hand-delivering press releases about the Vincent Chin beating death to the local news media outlets.

But Mable Lim was far from exhausted. Instead, she was excited to help raise awareness about Vincent Chin. She was shocked by the news that Ronald Ebens and Michael Nitz had been given three years' probation for fatally beating Vincent. "It was certainly unfair," she said. "We had never heard of such a thing. That's no way to treat a human being."

In the seventy-two hours since the meeting at the Golden Star Restaurant, Helen Zia had worked nonstop to create these press releases for Mable Lim to deliver. It was tedious and time-consuming work.

Personal computers were still a thing of the future, so Zia pounded out the press releases on the keys of her manual typewriter. "I wrote my stories out in longhand, then I would type them on my light blue Smith Corona typewriter," she said.

She used a pair of scissors and a bottle of glue to cut and paste the text into an eye-catching design. She then took this master document to a local copier and print shop to make several hundred copies.

And that was where Mable Lim and Ray came in. The elderly couple piled boxes of these press releases into their car. They drove—and sometimes even walked—all over the county to deliver them.

Lim was used to volunteering. She was an active member of the Association of Chinese Americans, a nonprofit group founded in Detroit in 1972 to promote the general welfare of its community with outreach and educational programs.

So when Lim heard about the beating death of Vincent Chin, she wanted to help Zia and the others in any way she could. She knew Vincent's mother, Lily, who attended the same church. After she learned Judge Kaufman had given the killers only three years' probation each, Lim wondered if racism had played a part in that lenient sentencing.

Growing up, Lim remembered how the other children would make fun of her and her siblings on the school playground, calling her everything from "Ching Chong" to "Chinaman." This racism bothered Lim, who was born in Detroit in 1920. This was her home. She was a proud and loyal Detroiter whose Chinese immigrant family ran a laundry business in the city. When she was only ten years old, Lim helped her family by ironing customers' clothes and mending socks.

Lim later graduated from Northern High School in 1938 and majored in sociology and government at Wayne State University. After college, she found a job at Detroit's civil service commission where she worked with tax assessors. She met her future husband, Ray Lim, at the Central Methodist Church in downtown Detroit.

As a young married couple in the early 1950s, the Lims had a hard time finding any white landlords who would rent to them because of their race. "We were trying to find a place to live, so we'd read the newspaper and then you call up the ad and answer it," Lim said. "And then you'd go there and they would say, 'Oh our place is rented.' And I would say, 'I just called twenty minutes ago.' I felt the prejudice." Mable and Ray realized they would never be able to rent from a white landlord. Instead, they managed to find a Chinese family who owned a duplex and let them rent the upper floor.

When asked if she ever fought back against the racism she encountered when she was younger, Lim shrugged. "I accepted it," she said. "You're used to being excluded and treated differently. It's part of growing up." For example, when a white restaurant owner refused to serve her and her husband, they left quietly without complaining. "You know you're different," she said. "We knew they wouldn't serve us. We just walked out."

But when Lim read about the Vincent Chin manslaughter case and the probation sentencing, she realized she couldn't walk away this time. She had to help somehow. So she volunteered to help deliver Helen Zia's press releases to the media. "I would take the press releases to the papers, like the *Detroit Free Press* and *The Detroit News*," she said. "We were the messengers."

And everyone heard the message. As a result of growing public dissent and Zia's press releases, Judge Charles Kaufman's office was flooded with hundreds of angry phone calls from the public.

On March 31, 1983, more than one hundred Asian Americans from all over the Wayne County area met in the cold and drafty meeting room at the Chinese Welfare Council building in Detroit's Chinatown. They included members from a variety of groups, including the Chinese Engineers Association, the Detroit Buddhist Church, and the Organization of Chinese American Women.

Although the room bore the flag of the Republic of China, the people attending were not just of Chinese descent. Lawyer James Shimoura and several others from the Japanese American Citizens League were present, along with concerned citizens of Korean and Filipino descent.

During the meeting, the group decided they had to form an official organization to protest Judge Kaufman's probation sentence. They agreed that *all* Asian Americans, not just Chinese Americans, would band together to fight for Vincent Chin's justice.

After a long debate about what to call themselves, the group settled on a simple name.

American Citizens for Justice.

"The American Citizens for Justice (ACJ) believes that all citizens are guaranteed rights to equal treatment," Zia wrote in the group's official mission statement. "When the rights of one individual are violated, all of society suffers as a result."

In other words, the ACJ was not just fighting for Vincent Chin. It was fighting for *all* Americans.

Chapter 13

# "THEY WILL NEVER BE THE SAME"

Even though Ronald Ebens was a free man, he felt like a prisoner in his own house.

Twelve days after Judge Kaufman's sentencing, Chrysler officially fired Ebens from his job as a general foreman at its Warren Truck Plant because he now had a felony conviction and a criminal record.

With no job, Ebens had nothing to do and nowhere to go. He mostly sat in the house, the curtains drawn, watching TV while his wife, Juanita, continued to work. "There hasn't been any life," he said. "You can't go anywhere without getting permission. You couldn't go if you wanted because you can't afford to go. You spend time worrying about where your next dollar is gonna come from the pay the bills. If you've worked your entire life since you're seventeen years old, like I have, and supported yourself, then all of a sudden you lose that capability, it's quite a shock to your system."

At forty-three, this was not where Ebens had thought he would be, facing a future scraping by with whatever low-wage jobs he could find.

He was born one of six children on a rural farm in Dixon, Illinois, about one hundred miles outside Chicago. As a child, he woke up at dawn every day before school to help milk the cows. His family grew crops of soy, alfalfa, and corn.

After high school, Ebens served for two and a half years in the Army Air Defense School. When he completed his service in 1965, he started work at a Chrysler plant in Belvidere, Illinois. He made a minimum wage of $1.25 an hour. He was assigned to assemble and wire the dashboards into the cars on the assembly line. Although he never went to college, his quick thinking and gregarious personality impressed his superiors, who promoted him to foreman. "I worked on the line for three months and they made a supervisor of me," he said. "I took over a group of 50 people in it; and I just progressed from there." When he moved to Michigan a few years later, he quickly worked his way up to superintendent.

After joining the ranks of management, Ebens was able to invest some of his savings into a bar he named Ron's Place in Detroit. He maintained an amicable relationship with his first wife and their child. Along with Juanita's son, Michael, he and and Juanita had one child together, a bright eleven-year-old daughter who worked hard at her newspaper route and classes.

But sitting in the darkened living room, the curtains drawn, Ebens grew depressed and had suicidal thoughts.

His friends were worried—it was unlike him to withdraw from everyone. They missed his larger-than-life personality and his quick laugh.

"We used to have a lot of fun," said family friend Sylvia Wulbrecht.

Sylvia and her husband at the time, Jim Wulbrecht, were shocked when Ebens was arrested for killing Vincent. They were equally shocked by the allegations of racism after Ebens and Nitz were found guilty of manslaughter. This was not the Ron Ebens they knew. They believed this was a tragic bar brawl that had gotten out of control.

"They had all been drinking," Sylvia Wulbrecht insisted. "And what happened was unfortunate. It was unfortunate for everyone."

"When Chin did die, I know Ron was totally upset that day," remembered Richard Wagner, who had worked with Ebens at a Chrysler auto plant in Illinois years earlier, before they both decided to move to Detroit. "You couldn't even talk to him. He was choked up, he couldn't talk, he didn't know what would happen from that point on, and he was very concerned over what the path forward would be."

Jim Wulbrecht noticed how withdrawn Ebens had become since the sentencing and growing media notoriety. "He's a lot less trusting of people," he said. "But those of us who are his friends and have remained his friends through all this find that the core of the man hasn't changed. He's still the same kind of person he was before. It's just that it's more difficult for him to find a way of expressing the feeling now. It's tough. Very tough."

And the core of Ebens, according to his friends, was his generosity. "If you wanted to call him for anything, you could," Jim said. "He wouldn't have any difficulty in finding the time to help you out. And he gave of himself. He still does that."

Friends gave examples of Ebens's random acts of kindness, from helping a neighbor fix his car to surprising an elderly woman by using a snowplow to clear her driveway after a snowstorm. When Jim was laid off by Chrysler, Ebens was the first one to lend him money. Jim never forgot it. "He just dug in his pocket and said, 'Just take this,'" he said. "That's the way he was."

Sylvia was frustrated by the media's portrayal of Ebens, which she felt did not tell the whole story. Although she mourned Vincent Chin's death and condemned Ebens and Nitz's crime, she also felt conflicted. She agreed that Ebens and Nitz deserved their guilty conviction of manslaughter. But she insisted he was not a racist villain but a man who had behaved badly and made a fatal mistake. She believed Ebens's remorse was genuine.

"Ron has to live with it every day," she said. "No matter what he did, it wasn't right. When Vincent was in the hospital, he wanted to go, but because of advice from his lawyers, he stayed away. He wanted to go to the funeral—he was devastated. And because he was told, 'No, don't do that,' then it was all taken the wrong way. Like he didn't care. Like he was an insensitive person. Well, he's not an insensitive person. Not at all."

· · ·

Ebens's stepson Michael Nitz had also withdrawn from society. He quit playing with his amateur baseball league. He stopped hanging out with his friends at their favorite bars.

"He just changed," said Nitz's friend Debbie Walker. "He was somebody, a young man that liked life, and he's just more introverted now and it's sad."

Like the Wulbrechts, Walker was shocked to learn of Vincent Chin's death at the hands of Nitz and his stepfather. In early July 1982, she was at a friend's house when she noticed a newspaper lying nearby with the front-page headline SLAYING ENDS COUPLE'S DREAM.

"I thought it must be someone else with the same name," she

said. "I kept reading and reading and I just can't believe it because they are not like that. I just figured there has to be a mistake, or that maybe there was bias. It's just impossible. There's no way that it could be Ron and Mike, they are not like that. I don't think Mike's ever been in a fight before, not in Wisconsin, not in Michigan. He's not that way, not at all."

But the public scrutiny and media notoriety caused the already-shy Nitz to retreat even further from everyone close to him. Walker and other friends noticed he had become anxious and even paranoid. "He's just scared to talk to any of his old friends because he thinks everyone is against him," Walker said.

Nitz's paranoia worsened to the point that it affected his everyday behavior. "When he came in to see me at work, he's always looking over his shoulder," Walker said. "I started feeling sorry for him. He was like really nervous, said he's only staying for a little while, just needed to see a friendly face. He only stayed for a little while and he leaves. He didn't want to stay long and someone recognizes him and they start saying some shit to him."

But Nitz's fears were not unfounded. Ever since he and Ebens were found guilty of manslaughter, harassment had started. Late-night phone calls from strangers shouting obscenities at them, and even death threats. Sylvia Wulbrecht remembered Juanita breaking down at the calls.

Even Ebens's and Juanita's eleven-year-old daughter was not immune. She had to change her newspaper route after neighbors recognized her and asked, "Oh, are you the daughter of that killer?"

· · ·

Veteran *Detroit Free Press* columnist Nickie McWhirter had little sympathy for Ebens's difficult life, because Vincent was dead and he was not. On March 25, 1983, she penned an angry column with the headline A LESSON—AND A LICENSE—THAT KIDS SHOULD NEVER GET.

This crime, McWhirter wrote, was "no act of self defense. It was a willful act of mayhem which resulted in the death of an innocent person. It deserves punishment, and for other reasons than simple retribution."

She criticized Judge Charles Kaufman for saying, "I just didn't think that putting them in prison would do any good for them or society," in defense of his probation sentencing for Ebens and Nitz.

"With due respect for your high office, Your Honor, you are quite mistaken," she wrote. "By not putting these admitted manslayers in prison you have done terrible wrong to society, to the respect society has for your office and to the public perception of justice and fair play."

McWhirter also accused Kaufman of insulting the memory of Vincent Chin, along with his family and friends. But she didn't stop there: "You have raised the ugly ghost of racism, suggesting in explanation of your sentence that the lives of the killers are of great and continuing value to society, implying they are of greater value than the life of the slain victim, upon which you put a price of $6,000, total. How gross and ostentatious of you; how callous and, yes, unjust."

Walker and their other friends, however, believed Ebens and Nitz were being punished enough.

"Mike loved life before and so did Ron," Walker said. "And they will never be the same."

Chapter 14

# "WE DROPPED THE BALL"

Helen Zia and Liza Chan couldn't take their eyes off it.

There, behind Sergeant Detective Donald Roberts's desk, was the baseball bat. It was the same Louisville Slugger that Ronald Ebens had beaten Vincent Chin with—a thirty-four-inch, flame-tempered bat with Jackie Robinson's signature etched along the side.

The bat had an index card tied around it with a white string. The card identified it as evidence in the Vincent Chin manslaughter case.

This was no longer a baseball bat. This was a *weapon*.

And it was just sitting there, as if discarded, in the middle of the busy Highland Park Police Department. In fact, in the ensuing months, Detective Roberts would pose with the baseball bat for newspaper interviews, saying, "Some heavy sucker, eh?"

This type of carelessness no longer surprised Zia and Chan. For the past few weeks, the two women, along with other members of their newly formed American Citizens for Justice, had been researching the Vincent Chin case. Chan had even volunteered to work for free, on a pro bono basis.

But as they worked on reconstructing what happened on the night of June 19, 1982, they discovered that many things had slipped between the cracks. "It soon became clear that there

were failures at every step of the criminal justice process," Zia wrote in her memoir. "The police and court record was slipshod and incomplete."

Zia and Chan learned that the police did not interview key witnesses, including employees of the Fancy Pants Club. For example, police never contacted Angela "Starlene" Rudolph, a Black dancer who worked at the Fancy Pants on the night

A July 1983 article in the *Chicago Tribune* featured a photograph of Highland Park detective Donald Roberts posing in his office with the actual baseball bat used to beat Vincent Chin to death.

of June 19 and witnessed the fight between Vincent, Ebens, and Nitz.

After Vincent Chin died, Rudolph and the other dancers expected the police would visit the club to ask questions about what had happened that night. But no one ever stopped by.

"We were all surprised that they didn't come to us and ask us what happened," she said. "All the dancers were shocked."

But Detective Roberts insisted he had done his due diligence with the investigation. He told a *Chicago Tribune* reporter the day after Vincent was beaten that he had called the club and spoken to the manager. "I told him about the incident, and said you can get a hold of the bouncer or anybody in there that knows anything about it, have them come in and talk to me, call me. He said okay. That's the last time I heard from him."

*Detroit Free Press* reporter John Castine, who covered the Vincent Chin case, felt Detective Roberts should have tried harder to pursue these witnesses.

"There were mistakes in the criminal justice system," Castine said. "The police investigation was poor. Sergeant Roberts said to me, 'Well, I called the Fancy Pants and said is anyone willing to be interviewed? No one called back.' Come on. That's not gumshoe work."

But Castine also wondered if the news media should have also covered the story more thoroughly before Judge Kaufman's sentencing in 1983. Perhaps that would have had an effect on Ebens and Nitz's fates.

"We dropped the ball," he said, noting that the only coverage of Vincent Chin's death was the initial July 1, 1982, *Detroit Free Press* story by Brian Flanigan. Castine described it as "the sob story about how Vincent Chin was about to be married and gets beaten to death."

But after that one story, there was no more media coverage until Nickie McWhirter's angry *Detroit Free Press* editorial in March 1983, when Judge Kaufman sentenced Ebens and Nitz to probation instead of jail time.

Castine regrets that the local press ignored the Vincent Chin case for almost a year until the sentencing. "If we had followed that story more closely, if the [*Detroit*] *News* and the *Free Press* had been inside the courtroom? They're aware when we're there. They're aware when the Fourth Estate is watching. But everybody walked away from that case, and just let it go through the courts. We never double backed in checking. This is a murder you should've wanted to know more about."

. . .

It wasn't just that the police and the press failed to follow up on Vincent Chin's killing. The fact that the Wayne County prosecutor's office was not present during the sentencing of Ebens and Nitz meant Judge Kaufman could rely only on the defense attorneys to answer his questions about the case. Zia and Chan discovered witness testimonies collected by the police on the night of June 19, 1982, that contradicted the accounts given by the defense lawyers and Ebens himself to Judge Kaufman.

For example, during the sentencing, defense attorney Edward Khoury claimed his client Michael Nitz's head had been split open with a chair that Vincent slammed at him. But eyewitness testimony collected during the preliminary hearing a year earlier stated that it was Ebens who had first picked up a chair.

And Ebens's defense attorney, Bruce Saperstein, had told Judge Kaufman that it was Vincent Chin who started the fight. "Your Honor, Mr. Ebens and Mr. Nitz were seated, and the victim walked up and punched Mr. Ebens in the mouth, initiating the physical assault," he said.

Witnesses, however, claimed otherwise. One friend insisted

Vincent had *not* punched Ebens in the mouth—instead, he allegedly shoved Ebens in the chest. Another witness remembered both Ebens and Vincent standing up and meeting each other halfway in the club. Regardless of the various versions, one thing was clear—no one saw who threw the first punch.

In addition, there were conflicting accounts of where Ebens and Nitz were planning to go once they got in the car after getting kicked out of the club. Were they pursuing Vincent? Or did they just coincidentally run into Vincent on their way to the hospital so Nitz could get stitches for his head wound, as his defense lawyers claimed?

Zia and Chan found out about a witness named Jimmy Perry who had been walking down Woodward on the night of June 19. He had told Detective Roberts that Ebens and Nitz had offered him a twenty-dollar bill to help them find Vincent Chin, and that Perry joined them in the car and had been with them when they found Vincent and Jimmy Choi sitting outside the McDonald's. Although Officer Morris Cotton said that he knew Jimmy Perry from high school and considered him a trustworthy source, Detective Roberts had questioned Perry's credibility. Although Perry's statement had been submitted to the prosecutor's office, no one pursued Perry for further questioning.

This oversight bothered Chan, who felt Perry's testimony could have been a "missing link" in the case. When interviewed by reporters, Chan bristled, noting that Roberts "[took] the defendants' word for it that they were going to the hospital and bumped into [Vincent Chin] and beat him up savagely and killed him. I mean, *really.*"

. . .

Given the many problems with how the Vincent Chin case was handled, Liza Chan was determined not to leave any stone unturned in her investigation. She visited the Fancy Pants Club. She drove several blocks around the area, trying to retrace Vincent Chin's steps as he ran away from Ebens and Nitz on that fateful night. She reached the McDonald's where Vincent had been beaten and pulled into the parking lot.

"I walked around the premises, imagining myself . . . in front of the restaurant, anticipating to hail my buddies driving by with the car," Chan wrote in her memoir, *My Impossible Life*.

While Chan was sitting on the curb in front of the McDonald's, she looked over at her parked car. She had recently celebrated her new job as a lawyer by buying a Toyota Supra sports car. And here it was, parked in the middle of the Motor City.

What was she thinking? She had seen reports on the news about how angry unemployed autoworkers had smashed Japanese import cars with sledgehammers to vent their frustrations over the economy. How drivers had reported strangers leaving racist notes on the windshields of their Japanese import cars. Chan suddenly became nervous, realizing she had "bought the 'wrong' car at the 'wrong' time."

Two weeks after Chan's visit to McDonald's, Zia and Chan found the most powerful evidence yet. Like Angela Rudolph, Racine Colwell had been working at the Fancy Pants Club on the night of June 19. The police had never contacted her for a

# First a bat, then a gavel dent dream

**CHIN, from Page 1A**

shattered in a Woodward Avenue street fight, then in the marble and oak-paneled courtroom of Judge Kaufman.

*A new life in America*

Lily Yee married Hing Chin in China in 1947 after World War II when he returned from the United States. She said Hing Chin emigrated to Seattle in 1922. He served in the U.S. Army during the war, but because he was in his 30s, he was sent to Michigan to work in a munitions factory, she said.

Hing Chin brought his wife to a land where they said everyone was respected, was equal under the law.

Never having had children of their own, the Chins adopted Vincent from China in 1961, when he was six and they lived in Highland Park.

**AT AGE 62,** Lily Chin is employed at a

Free Press Photo by DAVID C. TURNLEY

**Dancer Racine Colwell in the Fancy Pants Club:** "Never once did I know him (Chin) not to be laughing. And (until that night) I didn't know he ever got mad."

A *Detroit Free Press* clipping from May 1983 shows Racine Colwell, a twenty-four-year-old employee of the Fancy Pants Club. Colwell had no idea she would soon be in the national spotlight for her key witness testimony in *United States v. Ronald Ebens and Michael Nitz*, the country's first federal civil rights trial in connection with the death of an Asian American citizen.

witness interview. She told a private investigator hired by the ACJ that she overheard Ebens say, "It's because of you little motherfuckers that we're out of work."

To Zia, Chan, and the ACJ, the words "It's because of you," spoken in early 1980s Detroit, where xenophobia against Japan had risen due to the competition from Japanese import car companies, were racially charged. Although Vincent was of Chinese and not Japanese descent, according to many white people, he was still an "Oriental." (Back in the 1980s, it was common and considered acceptable to refer to Americans of Asian descent as "Oriental." Today this word is a racist slur.)

Chan remembered how nervous she felt to have parked her Japanese import car at the McDonald's crime site. And now this—testimony from Colwell about Ebens allegedly accusing Vincent of being part of the reason why Detroit was in decline.

And with Colwell's testimony, Zia and Chan now had evidence that Vincent might have died simply because he was Asian.

Chapter 15

# A MAN OF THE LAW

Judge Charles Kaufman's phone was ringing off the hook. Again.

Ever since he sentenced Ronald Ebens and Michael Nitz, his office had been flooded with angry letters and phone calls condemning his decision.

The outrage shocked him. "In all my years, I have never received such vilification," he told *The Detroit News*. "This was just another case. This wasn't anything unusual. This kind of thing happens regularly."

Kaufman believed his sentence was fair. Not only did Ebens and Nitz have no previous convictions or criminal records, but the Michigan Supreme Court had recently approved a sentencing guideline program for judges to base their decisions on. According to these guidelines, Ebens and Nitz, if found guilty of manslaughter, were eligible to serve anywhere between zero and thirty-six months in prison. In fact, it wasn't unusual for manslaughter cases to result in probation. In 1983, Ebens and Nitz were among 58 out of 209 defendants convicted of manslaughter in Michigan to receive probation—about just over one-quarter of all cases that year.

So as far as Kaufman was concerned, justice had been served for Vincent Chin's killers.

But the media frenzy and public outcry over his sentence

Judge Charles Kaufman, a World War II veteran and a prisoner-of-war survivor known for his often-liberal viewpoints, was shocked and hurt at being accused of racism for his sentence of probation and a $3,000 fine each to Ronald Ebens and Michael Nitz for the beating death of Vincent Chin. Although he agreed to reconsider his sentence, Judge Kaufman would eventually stick to his ruling, saying there was no legal basis to reverse it.

bothered the judge, who was known for his politically liberal viewpoints and his compassion.

In the early 1960s, Kaufman was one of a group of lawyers who had created the Fund for Equal Justice, which provided legal assistance for civil rights activists, prisoners, women's organizations, and marginalized and financially disadvantaged individuals. This group also gave financial aid to students of color, including Asian Americans, who wanted to attend law school. Many lawyers and judges who had worked with Judge Kaufman in court described him as "impartial, intelligent and fair."

"He is a man of the law," insisted Edward Khoury, who had been assigned as Michael Nitz's defense attorney. "He is one of the best judges in my view and he has followed the law, despite public pressure."

But Frank H. Wu, a lawyer and author who has written and spoken about the Vincent Chin case over the years, believed Judge Kaufman actually "violated" the rules. "When Judge Kaufman said, 'You don't make the punishment fit the crime; you make the punishment fit the criminal,' he uses that to excuse their behavior," Wu explained. "But in assessing guilt or innocence, you're not supposed to do that. You're supposed to look at just that specific act."

Meanwhile the revered elder Detroit Chinatown spokesman and the first ACJ president Kin Yee slammed Judge Kaufman's decision to give Ebens and Nitz probation, saying it was no more than "a $3,000 license to commit murder, provided that you have a steady job or if you are a student."

Vincent's death struck Yee hard. He had been one of the guests invited to Vincent and Vikki's wedding. "The hall was already set," he said. "We had our invitations, and some of our friends had already delivered their wedding presents, and we were looking forward to that wedding. And after that happened, instead of going to the wedding, we went to his funeral."

Yee's grief and anger over Vincent's killing inspired him and the ACJ to collect tens of thousands of signatures for a petition demanding the judge reconsider his decision. "It has aroused the anger of the Asian community by recalling the days of 'frontier justice' when massacres of Chinese workers were common-place," he said.

In addition, the ACJ requested the services of former Mich-igan Supreme Court justice Thomas E. Brennan, who agreed to help them as legal counsel. Along with Liza Chan and her law firm, the ACJ released reports listing all the errors they had discovered in their own investigation of the original case. They requested a public hearing to air their concerns.

"We have asked Judge Kaufman, on his own motion, to review the record and take notice of the substantial material errors and take all appropriate and necessary action to rectify the record," Chan told reporters.

Kaufman wasn't afraid of this hearing. He stood by his deci-sion. "If I had to do it over, I'd do the same thing," he declared. "I believe it was the right decision."

· · ·

On Friday April 29, 1983, about one hundred people crowded the Wayne County courtroom. The hearing started off on an awkward note when Judge Kaufman met Kin Yee and immedi-ately asked, "Do you speak English?"

Although angered by Kaufman's question, Yee wasn't entirely

surprised. Many Asian Americans were often asked if they spoke English or where they were "really" from, even if they were born and raised in America.

For Yee, the question *Do you speak English?* evoked the stereotype of the Asian as a "perpetual foreigner," even though Yee was an American citizen. But Judge Kaufman was unaware that his question about Yee's English fluency was loaded with cultural baggage.

To add insult to injury, Kaufman did not realize Kin Yee was one of the elder statesman in Detroit's Asian American community. Yee had moved there from Hong Kong in 1940 when he was only fifteen years old. His family had set up a laundry business in Detroit's Chinatown. He worked long, hard hours after school to help his father iron shirts. "Seeing how hard my father had to work . . . I make up my mind that if I could help it, myself and all my children would never have to do the same thing again," he said.

Yee was true to his word—he later married and had five children, all of whom graduated from college. So when he heard about Judge Kaufman's sentence of probation for Ebens and Nitz, he questioned whether racism played a part in his decision. "One of his remarks that the killers are gainfully employed and they would not be doing the same thing again and that's why he was only giving them probation, we felt that a Chinese life was worth a lot more than that," Yee said. "A Chinese life was worth a lot more than the three thousand dollars and the probation."

And now this—Kaufman asking if Yee even spoke English.

Kaufman, however, insisted to Yee and the others that he was not racist. "He told us that he was involved with civil rights work in the early 1940s," Yee said. "He was trying to convey to us that he wasn't prejudiced. Now I'll let you be the judge of that."

. . .

Others in the Asian community believed that Kaufman harbored an anti-Asian bias because of his experience as a prisoner of war in Japan during World War II. But according to Kaufman, nothing could be further from the truth.

A native Detroiter, Kaufman had been attending Wayne State University's law school when World War II broke out. He left to serve in the Army Air Force as a bomber pilot and navigator. He flew twenty-seven missions before being shot down by the Japanese on his last one.

For eighteen months, Kaufman lived as a prisoner of war at Omori, the main camp located on a man-made island in Tokyo Bay. The prisoners worked almost twelve-hour days, seven days a week, loading and unloading cargo from the docks and working in the coal yards, mines, and warehouses to help the Japanese war effort.

Prisoners lived in separate cells, each one about six by eight feet in size, made of plywood and tarpaper. They slept on straw and grass mats on the ground. They survived on a half bowl of rice each day. As the war worsened for Japan, cattle feed and even straw were mixed into the rice. Protein was rare, except for the intestines of an occasional horse killed during an air raid battle. Starving prisoners were so desperate that they even ate maggots.

The average American POW lost at least sixty pounds or

more during his stay at Omori. Kaufman was one of them, going from 160 pounds to ninety-two pounds. The slightest infraction, like not folding your bedsheets properly, would result in a severe beating from the guards, from being stabbed with sticks to being clubbed in the knee. Fleas, parasites, malnutrition, and infections led to Kaufman and the others suffering from boils, hepatitis, jaundice, dengue fever, dysentery, malaria, beriberi, and other diseases. More than 60 percent of prisoners in Kaufman's camp died from starvation and disease.

For Kaufman, surviving meant using his smarts. He quickly learned enough of the Japanese language to be an unofficial interpreter. He used his law school training and negotiation skills to convince the Japanese guards to give him and his fellow inmates more food, clothes, and even tools to mend their shoes.

Kaufman never forgot his eighteen months as a POW. He knew how prison could change a person's life forever. That was why he often gave probation to first-time offenders in hopes of rehabilitating them. "I'm one of the few judges to know what it's like to be in prison for a long time," he said.

"He has a more liberal philosophy," agreed lawyer Miriam Siefer, who would later become Michael Nitz's defense attorney, "and maybe a more realistic philosophy of what happens to people when they get sent to prison and whether or not our prison system is rehabilitative." She explained that Judge Kaufman was always looking for alternatives in his quest for rehabilitating criminals. "I think he's not as law and order as some of the other judges on the bench."

So when Judge Kaufman reviewed Ebens and Nitz's case, he truly believed that it was a drunken bar brawl that had turned into a tragic and fatal accident. He did not think either man intended to kill Vincent, at least based on the partial information he had been given at the time of the original hearing. As a man of the law, Judge Kaufman focused on the legal definition of manslaughter. These two men had beaten Vincent "too severely in careless reckless disregard of human life which is what manslaughter is," he concluded. "And that's what they were found guilty of and that's what I predicated my sentence on. Had it been a brutal murder, of course these fellows would be in jail now."

• • •

The judge firmly denied all accusations of racism, including speculation that his POW experience may have influenced his probation decision. "It was a bad experience, but it doesn't affect any of my feelings against any group of people," he said.

Helen Zia, meanwhile, wanted the media spotlight off Judge Kaufman.

"Judge Kaufman has never been accused of racism by our organization," she wrote in a letter to *The Detroit News*. "Even though it was reported in *The Detroit News* that the judge was held in a Japanese prisoner of war camp, we have not speculated on his feelings toward Asian people."

Instead, Zia wanted the focus to return to the case itself. "We're not out for revenge," she said. "We feel the [sentencing hearing] was not tried properly." She believed Judge Kaufman would change his mind about the sentences he had handed down once he heard all the facts that were not presented at the original hearing.

• • •

Over a hundred Asian Americans of all ages march outside the City-County Building in Detroit on April 29, 1983, to demand that Judge Charles Kaufman reconsider his original sentence of probation for Ronald Ebens and Michael Nitz in the beating death of Vincent Chin.

The crowd that packed into Judge Kaufman's courtroom on April 29, 1983, included members of the ACJ and Vincent's mother, Lily. Reporters from *The Detroit News,* the *Detroit Free Press,* and other media outlets were also present.

For an hour, Judge Kaufman and the crowd listened as Liza Chan and Daniel Hoekenga presented their motions on why Kaufman should consider a resentencing of Ronald Ebens and Michael Nitz in the manslaughter case of Vincent Chin.

Hoekenga argued that Judge Kaufman's original sentence was based on inaccurate and incomplete information. The defense attorneys had said Vincent allegedly started the fight. Because no prosecutor was present, there had been no one to contest that claim. As a result, that was the only information Judge Kaufman had had to go on. He was given an incomplete picture, and therefore his decision was not fair.

Ebens and Nitz were not at court that day. But their defense attorneys, Bruce Saperstein and Edward Khoury, fought on their behalf.

"I did not misconstrue facts in this case," Saperstein said, declaring he stood by his word from the original hearing. Both attorneys agreed that Judge Kaufman's original sentence from March 1983 was "fair and reasonable."

But Chan and Hoekenga refused to back down. Hoekenga raised his voice, waving his arms in the air to emphasize his points. "Talk about a crime," he said. "We have a man beaten to death with a baseball bat . . . and that man [Ebens] walks the streets and Vincent Chin is in the ground. We ask that these men be put behind bars."

As Hoekenga spoke, people in the courtroom cheered loudly.

"Our motion is not prompted by a desire for revenge . . . but

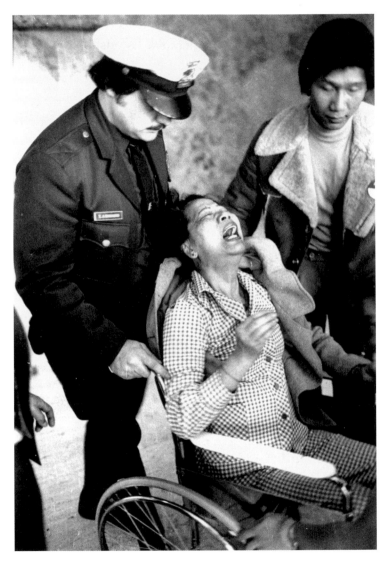

After Judge Charles Kaufman agreed in April 1983 to reconsider his original sentence of probation for Ronald Ebens and Michael Nitz, a relieved Lily Chin was overcome with emotion and nearly fainted. Friends and family escorted her home in a wheelchair. Over time, photos like this, showing Lily in mourning, drew public sympathy and support for her family's cause. Defense attorneys for Ronald Ebens and Michael Nitz feared these images would make it difficult to find an impartial jury for the trial.

because we believe errors in fact were presented to the court at sentencing," Hoekenga concluded amidst applause from spectators.

Judge Kaufman waited for the crowd to quiet down. As silence settled over the courtroom, he finally spoke. "This is a very emotional and volatile issue," he said.

To Chan and Hoekenga's relief, Kaufman agreed to review their arguments in order to determine if he needed to resentence Ebens and Nitz.

The ecstatic crowd cheered again before heading out to the City-County Building to chant protest slogans and talk to the media.

Lily Chin was so overcome by the hearing that she nearly fainted. Helen Zia and some of the ACJ members gently escorted her out of the building in a wheelchair. "The emotions caught up with her," said one protester who attended the hearing. "She was taken home for rest."

In the meantime, Chan and Hoekenga felt cautious but hopeful about Kaufman's agreement to reexamine the case.

"I feel very positive," Chan said. "This is a case we feel should be corrected. I'm glad the judge feels it is serious enough to study further."

Ultimately, Judge Kaufman's son Richard, also a Wayne County circuit judge, felt his father's harrowing experience in the Japanese prisoner of war camp influenced him to reconsider his original sentence. "It bothers him," he said. "He feels there's no way for him to ever explain to people everything that will allow them to make a fair judgment. It wrenches him, especially when he is accused of having no feeling for Vincent Chin."

And now Judge Kaufman had to decide Ronald Ebens and Michael Nitz's fates . . . again.

Chapter 16

# "TIME TO TALK ABOUT RACE"

On the night of June 19, 1982, when Officer Morris Cotton was filling out his police report about the killing of Vincent Chin, the form contained only two boxes to mark the victim's race.

White.

Black.

Cotton had no choice but to check the "white" box.

In 1982 the topic of race in the United States centered on white and Black. Asian Americans and others were often not even considered part of the conversation. In fact, several politically liberal organizations shared this narrow view of racism. At the time, even the Michigan chapter of the American Civil Liberties Union believed civil rights laws did not apply to Asians and other people of color.

In other words, when it came to civil rights and race, Asian Americans were considered "white."

Helen Zia and other members of the ACJ were outraged at being considered white. As far as they were concerned, Asian Americans did *not* share the same privileges as white people, from Zia being called "Chink" on the school playground to Roland Hwang's white neighbors questioning his family's presence on their street because they were Chinese.

On April 15, 1983, after Judge Charles Kaufman sentenced Ronald Ebens and Michael Nitz to three years of probation, the ACJ held its first news conference at the Detroit Press Club. Given the growing notoriety of the Vincent Chin case, newspaper reporters, photographers, and TV broadcast news crews packed the room.

"It was big news to see Asian Americans coming together to protest injustice," Zia remembered. "To the reporters and the people of Detroit, Asian Americans seemed to emerge from nowhere. Our task, and mine in particular, was to educate them quickly, in sound bites, about Asian Americans."

The ACJ's efforts to educate Americans about anti-Asian discrimination caused some soul-searching among Detroit's media news outlets.

" 'Real Americans Buy American' continues to be one of the more popular sayings gracing the large chrome bumpers of cars in Detroit," wrote Matt Beers for *The Detroit News*. "The case of Vincent Chin has peeled back those slogans, showing that what makes them cling to the chrome is a powerful and ugly undercurrent of racism. It's a revelation that Detroit will not soon forget."

The ACJ gained the support of many diverse groups, including local churches and synagogues, the B'nai B'rith organization, the Spiritual Assembly of the Bahá'ís of Detroit, the Association of Italian Americans, the Latino Americans for Social and Economic Development, the American Arab Development Foundation, the Detroit chapter of the NAACP, and the Detroit Area Black Organizations group. Several local and national politicians such as the president of the Detroit City Council and U.S. representative John Conyers (D-Michigan) also pledged their support.

Roland Hwang and James Shimoura credit this multicultural

coalition for helping to open doors for the ACJ. Prosecutor William Cahalan "wasn't interested in meeting a bunch of Asian American lawyers and community activists," Hwang said. "It took people like Horace Sheffield, head of the Detroit Area Black Organizations, and other groups, like the Anti-Defamation League, to be added to the chorus. They were instrumental in getting us an audience with the prosecutor."

"We owe a big debt of gratitude to the African American community because they paved the way," Shimoura added.

Other groups within the Asian and Pacific Islander community also spoke out, including the Japanese American Citizens League, the Korean Society of Greater Detroit, the Greater Detroit Taiwanese Association, and the Filipino American Community Council. Back then, these groups mostly kept to their own communities. Until Vincent Chin. Now they were all banding together for one cause—justice for Vincent Chin.

The ACJ's efforts to raise awareness about Asian American civil rights also caught the attention of Congressman Norman Mineta (D-California), who had been imprisoned as a child with his family during World War II at the Heart Mountain relocation center.

"All Americans—Asians and non-Asians alike—should work to gain justice in the Chin case," Mineta said in an official statement. "And we must all work to prevent violent bigotry from striking again. This country depends upon our success."

At the time, Asian Americans made up only 1.5 percent of the U.S. population (3.5 million out of a total of 226.5 million, according to 1980 Census Bureau statistics). They were scattered across America, with the largest concentrations located in New York and California.

Despite Michigan's small Asian population, more than two hundred members of the ACJ crowded the cafeteria at the Ford Motor Company world headquarters in Dearborn on a Sunday night in early May. A representative from the U.S. Department of Justice explained how difficult it would be to get a federal civil rights investigation of the Vincent Chin case.

"The FBI would need to show that there was a conspiracy to deprive Vincent Chin of his civil rights," remembered Zia. There would also need to be public support for an investigation. "The strong public outcry would also be a factor in its decision to investigate."

But that was easier said than done. At the time, Detroit's Asian American community was very conservative. Many hesitated to "rock the boat" and draw attention.

That silence was partly the result of surviving not just decades but centuries of oppression of Asian immigrants in America.

"A lot of people of my generation felt that if we kept our nose clean, got our education, didn't stir up trouble, and built up our careers we would disappear into the white mass and become incognito," said Kaz Mayeda, a Wayne State University biology professor and member of the Japanese American Citizens League.

During the ACJ meeting, an older Chinese American engineer with GM asked Zia if it was "necessary" that they even talk about race when it came to Vincent Chin. Many people voiced fears of retribution if they spoke out about Vincent's death as being racist. Would they then become targets themselves?

Zia was discouraged by the crowd's hesitation and fear.

Then a computer programmer stood up. "I've worked hard for my company for forty years," he said, his voice rising in anger.

"They always pass me over for promotion because I'm Chinese. I have trained many young white boys fresh out of college to be my boss. I never complain, but inside I'm burning. This time, with this killing, I must complain. What is the point of silence if our children can be killed and treated like this? I wish I'd stood up and complained a lot sooner in my life."

That opened the floodgates. One by one, people stood up, telling their stories of discrimination, from being called racist slurs on the street to being told to "go back to Japan."

David Hwang, a research engineer who had worked for Ford for thirty-six years and had reserved the cafeteria for that night's meeting, also spoke up. "We want to win this case, and we want equal justice for all, including all Asian Americans," he declared.

Zia and the others realized they had spent years suppressing their anger over experiences of racism. If they chose to remain silent now, they would be just as complicit in Vincent's death. They had to speak out.

"It was time to talk about race," Zia said.

Chapter 17

# "WE WANT JUSTICE"

## WE WANT JUSTICE!

## IT'S NOT FAIR!

## $3000 FOR A LIFE?

## A JOB IS A LICENSE TO KILL?!

## CHIN UP FOR JUSTICE!

The signs were everywhere.

Precisely lettered. Clear, easy-to-read typeface. All the signs uniformly sized as if they had come fresh off a factory assembly line.

Which they practically had. A "demonstration committee" of Asian American engineers and scientists who worked at the General Motors Technical Center spent hours crafting these signs for the upcoming protest rally being organized by the ACJ.

"They joked that this would be the most precisely planned demonstration in history," Helen Zia said.

"All the protest signs you saw were made by engineers over at GM," said James Shimoura. "They kind of snuck in and stole all the wood and paper from the tech center. They took time off from work to meet and make the signs and brought a whole bunch

# RALLY ON MAY 9TH!
## JUSTICE FOR VINCENT CHIN!

On June 19, 1982, Vincent Chin, a draftsman and an honor graduate of Control Data Institute, who worked to support himself and his mother, went to a bar with three friends to celebrate his upcoming wedding. Ronald Ebens, one of the defendants at the bar, accosted him with racial slurs and obscenities, saying, "It's because of you motherf------s that we're out of work." A scuffle occurred. Subsequently, Chin was chased and briefly escaped. But the defendants continued to search for him for about 20 minutes, ambushed him, and he was brutally clubbed to death with a baseball bat.

What did the defendants get for this heinous and utterly repugnant crime? Three years probation and a fine of $3780!! It was so unfair!! So insulting!! Fellow Citizens, it means a life is worth no more than $3780!! Do you accept this price tag? If not, let us unite to express our outrage.

JUDGE GRANTS LICENSE TO KILL ASIAN PEOPLE; SAYS "JUSTICE HAS BEEN SERVED"

To justify his ridiculous sentence, Kaufman cited the backgrounds of the 2 killers, saying, "Ebens has held the same job for 17 years, while Nitz was working and going to school." We say, so what? What if the killers had been unemployed, or black, or Hispanic? Would they go to jail then? And what if the victim had not been Chinese? Would his life be worth more than $125 per month?

PROSECUTOR CAHALAN SCREWS UP; NOW HE SAYS "I'M SATISFIED"

The prosecutor's office bungled this case from the start; they failed to fully investigate the crime and interview key witnesses. They settled for a charge of 2nd degree murder, even though Judge Bayles later said the charge clearly should have been 1st degree murder. Then Cahalan settled for a plea-bargain down to manslaughter, an offense that includes auto deaths, etc.! Now Cahalan is trying to cover-up his incompetence, and says he's satisfied with the way his men handled the case.

NO MORE FREEBIE MURDERS! NO MORE ATTACKS ON ASIANS!

Kaufman and Cahalan were elected to protect the interests of "The People", but all they're protecting is their own jobs. Their self-serving incompetence lends support to racist views that blame Asian people for the country's economic depression. Each and every human life is worth more than $3780!

Join us in our fight for human rights. You can help us by contacting your state and US representatives. Tell them how you feel, and ask them to instruct the US Department of Justice to file a civil rights suit against Ebens and Nitz. Or contact William Bradford Reynolds, Asst. Secretary of the Dept of Justice, Pennsylvania Ave., Washington, DC 20530.
for further information contact:
American Citizens for Justice, c/o ACA, PO Box 37343, Oak Park MI 48237

# RALLY: MONDAY, MAY 9TH
## 11 A.M., KENNEDY SQUARE
### DOWNTOWN DETROIT, WOODWARD & MICHIGAN AVENUES

A flyer alerting the public to the May 9, 1983, rally for justice for Vincent Chin. Long before personal-use laptops, smart phones, and social media existed, members of the ACJ worked long hours into the night handwriting and typing up fliers to be distributed physically on foot.

of engineers from the tech center. I remember they were sitting around trying to come up with nifty phrases to put in there."

"The debate was whether the signs would be bilingual or not," added Roland Hwang. The engineers ultimately decided to write English-only protest signs to combat the stereotype of the Asian American as the "perpetual foreigner." They arranged for protesters to carry American flags as well. They even decided to wear their business suits while marching to present a professional image.

"Early in the decision process, there was a debate as to whether or not to be typical Asians," Shimoura said. "Be passive. Write letters. Be polite about it versus being vocal in the streets with protest, and making a case in the media. In the end, the decision was made to go public. We felt we had to fight and let everyone know the anger and the sense of injustice we had suffered."

· · ·

On Monday, May 9, 1983, at eleven a.m., more than five hundred Asian Americans crowded Kennedy Square in downtown Detroit. Many wore red and white buttons that said JUSTICE FOR VINCENT CHIN.

Confused customers stood outside the locked doors of Chinese restaurants. Because Vincent had been a waiter, Detroit Chinese restaurants shut down during the busy lunch hour so their waitstaff could participate in the march. "It's like when police officers show up for one their fallen," explained Hwang.

"Vincent was one of theirs, a waiter," Shimoura added. "He was a part of the family."

On May 9, 1983, more than five hundred Asian Americans marched through the streets of Detroit in protest of Vincent Chin's killing, waking up not just the city but the entire country to the existence of a growing Asian American community that refused to be ignored any longer.

Zia praised the restaurant owners' courage for shutting down. "Most restaurants are hand to mouth," she said. "They would lose all of their income for an entire day whether they were the owners or the waiters. People saw this as a matter of life and death. Not just for themselves but for their children and for future generations. That's what compelled them to speak out, to shut down their restaurants for the day, so that they and their cooks and waiters and grandmothers could go to these demonstrations."

The protesters, however, were not just of Asian descent. Photojournalist Corky Lee, who documented the event, recalled seeing people of all backgrounds. "This was a huge outpouring of diverse people," he said. "African Americans, Pacific Islanders, and Caucasians." When Lee asked an elderly Filipino man why he was protesting, the man replied, "If we don't stand together, we'll always be divided." Van Ong, the nurse who tended to Vincent in the ER on the night of June 19, 1982, was also among those Filipinos who marched in the demonstration. "That's when I started questioning the justice system here," Ong said. "How can somebody be found not guilty when somebody is six feet below the ground?"

The rally began with the crowd singing the national anthem, followed by a prayer from Father Carl Sayers of St. Stephen's Episcopal Church. Many organization leaders gave speeches in support of the protest, including Horace Sheffield, officials from the Detroit branch of the NAACP and the National Conference of Christians and Jews, Detroit councilwoman Maryann Mahaffey, and a representative from the office of Congressman John Conyers.

It was a clear, cool, and sunny day for the march, the temperature hovering around sixty-five degrees Fahrenheit. Zia shouted "Justice for Vincent Chin!" into her bullhorn along with the hundreds of protesters as they walked from Kennedy Square to the Murphy Hall of Justice to the City-County Building, which housed all the criminal and circuit courts. "We symbolically hit all the courts," Shimoura remembered.

Parker Woo was one of the many Asian Americans who rushed over to Kennedy Square during their lunch breaks to participate in the demonstration. The twenty-nine-year-old Detroit native's family was in the local food business. Woo also had a personal connection to Vincent and Lily Chin, both of whom had worked at his family's restaurant in Oak Park.

So Woo had been shocked when he first heard about Vincent's death and the lenient sentence of probation given to Ebens and Nitz. It reminded him of his own experiences with racism growing up in Detroit. He remembered being harassed by other students at school when he was a child.

"They'd use their fingers to stretch their eyes out," he remembered. "They'd ask if we used chopsticks or if we spoke English. *Chink* was so common we kind of ignored it."

To honor Vincent, Woo wrote Vincent's last words, "It's not fair!" on his protest sign. As he shouted, "Justice for Vincent Chin!" with the crowd, his blood stirred not only with anger but with pride. "I'm not afraid to fight," he said. "You have to be willing to fight when you see something wrong."

The large crowd of Asian Americans marching down the streets of Detroit ranged in age from babies in strollers to students and young adults like Parker Woo to the elderly, including Mable Lim and her husband, Ray. "It was a tremendous rally because it was the first time that the Asian community was in a united effort like this," remembered Lim. "That was terrific."

Shimoura was inspired by the fact that many of the people who showed up to protest the Vincent Chin case had never protested before in their lives. "The thing that was amazing about the case was that people who had never been to a protest rally in their entire lives . . . showed this sudden outburst of energy and commitment to see that justice was done," he said.

For Mable and other members of the older generation, protesting in public was taking a huge step. "We've never had any demonstration of Asian Americans because from the very beginning of our background, our peers have always taught us to be very low key and not to participate in activities, or even in politics," she explained. "So the Asian Americans had always been in the background and reluctant to speak out."

Now Mable and her husband found themselves marching past the Renaissance Center, the muscular skyline of Detroit in the background, toward the federal courthouse, to demand justice for Vincent Chin. "This was different," she said. "This was the first time that we felt we have an opportunity to express ourselves to speak out as Asian Americans."

And the country took notice. "People had never seen this before," said Frank H. Wu, also a Detroit native. "People in Detroit, in Michigan, in the Midwest, in America and anywhere in the world had not seen Asian Americans marching, giving speeches in Hart Plaza, holding rallies, carrying signs, displaying anger publicly, writing letters to the editor and being angry. That was so different than the stereotype of Asian Americans at the time. People tend to leave Asian Americans out of the story of civil rights."

The march ended at the steps of the U.S. District Court for Eastern Michigan. Kin Yee stood in front of the imposing gray building, with the words THE UNITED STATES OF AMERICA carved in stone above his head. "Eyewitnesses have come forward to confirm something that we suspected all along: that Vincent Chin was brutally slain as a result of a racial incident," Yee said, reading from a prepared statement for the ACJ written by Helen Zia. "This misguided view encourages attacks on Asian American people and it must be fought against by all who cherish justice and have respect for human dignity."

And then a hush fell over the crowd as an emotional Lily Chin stood before them. She wore a red and white JUSTICE FOR VINCENT CHIN button on the lapel of her blue jacket. "Ladies and gentlemen, I want to thank you for your support," she said, her voice shaking as she held back tears. "I want justice for my son Vincent. What happened to him could happen to any of us. We must work hard to win justice for all. I hope no other mother will have to go through my suffering of the last year. Thank you again."

The protest rally ended with the crowd singing the famous civil rights hymn "We Shall Overcome." Yee and the ACJ then officially hand-delivered a petition with three thousand signatures to U.S. Attorney Leonard Gilman, demanding a federal intervention into the Vincent Chin case.

· · ·

After its successful demonstration, the ACJ reached out to other Asian American and Pacific Islander communities across the country to set up similar rallies for the week of June 19, 1983, to commemorate the one-year anniversary of Vincent Chin's death.

"A lot of us were really inspired," said Francis Wong, an activist and musician who attended a protest march in San Francisco in June 1983. "At a very visceral, gut-level feeling, there was a connection. That was really something to see. I don't know if we've really seen something like that since."

Stewart Kwoh, a thirty-three-year-old lawyer in Los Angeles, helped raise awareness about the Vincent Chin case on the West Coast. In 1983, having specialized in civil rights law, Kwoh cofounded the Asian Pacific American Legal Center, which provided legal services for the Asian American community with an emphasis on advocacy and civil rights. When he first read about the Vincent Chin killing in a May 1983 *Los Angeles Times* article, Kwoh immediately called the ACJ to volunteer his help with any civil rights legal counsel they might need. He took the first flight to Detroit meet with Liza Chan and other ACJ members, and he even visited the Fancy Pants Club and McDonald's locations for his own research.

When it came to civil rights issues, it wasn't unusual for Kwoh to jump into the middle of the action headfirst. He was inspired by his paternal great-grandfather, the first Presbyterian minister in China, and his activist mother, Beulah Quo, who was one of the first Asian American actresses in Hollywood. He graduated with a law degree from UCLA in 1974. Although he was a top student who aced his exams and was selected to write for the *Law Review,* he decided to take a less glamorous career in the world of community and public service. He established legal aid programs in Chinatown and Little Tokyo in downtown Los Angeles to help low-income youth. "I followed my path, so to speak," he said.

Kwoh also believed the ACJ should pursue civil rights as an alternative if Judge Kaufman decided not to resentence Ebens and Nitz. "It was pretty clear that federal prosecution made the most sense," Kwoh said.

· · ·

On June 19, 1983, national TV news broadcasts featured images of Asian American protest marches across the country, from New York to Chicago to Los Angeles and San Francisco, demanding justice for Vincent Chin.

Veteran news anchor Dan Rather discussed how the Vincent

Chin case had gone national during a broadcast of the *CBS Evening News*. "The killing didn't attract much attention outside the Detroit area," he said. "Then a sentence was handed down . . . and there was an explosion of outrage and a sense of betrayal."

Jesse Jackson, the Black civil rights activist, minister, politician and two-time candidate for Democratic presidential nomination, became a prominent ally and supporter for Vincent Chin and the ACJ. "These attacks on Asian Americans are no different than the atrocities of the Ku Klux Klan against Blacks in the South," he declared.

Angelo N. Ancheta, a legal scholar specializing in civil rights, later said the Detroit march for Vincent Chin served as a wake-up call for Asian America. "It was a major turning point," Ancheta said. "It was a signal that we needed to get more engaged in pan-Asian activities nationally. This was affecting everybody across the country."

But before 1983, the concept of an Asian American civil rights movement and even the terms *Asian American* and *Pacific Islander* were rarely spoken by anyone other than college students and activists. The phrase *Asian American* was actually first used in 1968 by University of California, Berkeley graduate students Emma Gee and Yuji Ichioka. They established a group called the Asian American Political Alliance to be inclusive for people of all Asian descent. They are credited with coining the term *Asian American*. This term has evolved over the years to be more inclusive. For example, the White House would later rename "Asian-Pacific Heritage Week" (originally established in 1978) to "Asian-Pacific American Heritage Month" in 1992 to "Asian American and Pacific Islander Heritage Month" in 2009.

Although the term *Asian American* had been in use since

1968, Americans of Asian descent in 1983 still tended to identify according to their country of heritage, be they Chinese American, Japanese American, Korean American, and so on.

Until Vincent Chin. His death inspired Chinese, Japanese, Korean, Indian, Filipino, and other Americans of Asian and Pacific Islander descent to unite in one cause. Justice for Vincent Chin meant justice for *all*.

"Since Vincent's death, we let the whole world know that we're not so easy to be brushed off," Kin Yee said. "We had to be contended with."

Chapter 18

# MRS. CHIN
# GOES TO WASHINGTON

Lily Chin could not stop crying. She sat by ACJ president Kin Yee's side as reporters, photographers, and news camera crews crowded the storefront in Detroit's Chinatown. The ACJ was holding a press conference there to comment on Judge Kaufman's final decision.

It was June 3, 1983, three weeks after the Detroit rally and just a couple weeks before the one-year anniversary of her son's death. The day before, Judge Kaufman had announced that he would not change his original sentence of probation for Ronald Ebens and Michael Nitz.

Kaufman did not take his decision lightly. He considered the ACJ's concerns to be "real and sincere." But after extensive research and serious reflection, he concluded there was no legal basis to reverse his original sentence.

"While sympathizing with the family and community of the victim, it is the obligation of the court to decide the matters submitted in accordance with the mandates of law," Kaufman wrote in his seven-page opinion. Even though the prosecutor was not present at the original hearing, Kaufman observed that "the prosecutor appears at sentencing less than one percent of the time." He stated that "no error" was made and that Ebens

Free Press Photo by LIZ KELLY

Liza Chan, left, Kin Yee and Lily Chin at Friday's press conference: "A miscarriage of justice."

# Another Chin case appeal

By JOHN CASTINE
*Free Press Staff Writer*

A group of Chinese-Americans seeking prison terms for the killers of Vincent Chin said Friday they will ask the Michigan Court of Appeals to overturn the defendants' sentences of probation and fines.

Kin Yee, president of the American Citizens for Justice, and the group's attorney, Liza Chan, said Wayne County Circuit Judge Charles Kaufman "compounded a miscarriage of justice" by not reversing the probation sentences he gave to Ronald Ebens, 43, and Ebens' 23-year-old stepson, Michael Nitz, last March.

Kaufman ruled Thursday that there was no legal ground to change his sentences.

"He (Kaufman) completely failed to recognize what we have here, which is a gross misappraisal of the court of all the facts," Chan said at a news conference in a vacated storefront in Detroit's Chinatown. "This set this case apart from any other cases. It's not a question of legal niceties."

Chan also said she believed Kaufman did not reverse his decision because "of a little bit of pride."

Yee said Kaufman "would have been one of the judges that go down in American history being the first one to (reverse a sentence because of a misrepresentation of facts at the sentencing.)"

Vincent Chin's 62-year-old mother, Lily Chin, sat by Yee's side, crying at times.

**CHIN, 27, OF OAK PARK,** died June 23, 1982, four days after he was chased by Ebens and Nitz, then beaten with a baseball bat on Woodward Avenue in Highland Park. The three had quarreled in the Fancy Pants Club, an establishment with nude female dancers.

The East Detroit men were originally charged with second-degree murder. But Ebens pleaded guilty, and Nitz pleaded no contest to manslaughter in a bargain with the Wayne County Prosecutor's Office. Manslaughter allows a sentence from probation to 15 years in prison.

No prosecutor attended the sentencing, and Yee's group claims defense attorneys Ed Khoury and Bruce Saperstein persuaded Kaufman to give their clients probation by saying Chin "threw the first punch." The attorneys deny they made any misrepresentations to Kaufman.

Attorney Liza Chan (left), ACJ president Kin Yee, and Vincent's mother, Lily Chin, shown here in a *Detroit Free Press* article from June 1983, defied racist stereotypes of Asians as passive and unwilling to "rock the boat."

and Nitz's sentence of three years of probation for manslaughter would remain unchanged. Reversing his original sentence of probation would be illegal, he said. "If people feel no one should get probation for manslaughter, then they should go to the legislature to change the law."

Liza Chan expressed her frustration at a press conference, condemning Kaufman's final decision as a "miscarriage of justice." His decision, she believed, was influenced by "a little bit of pride."

Edward Khoury, the defense attorney for Michel Nitz, disagreed. He described the judge as a "principle guy." "He's not going to subvert the law in response to public pressure," he said.

In a scathing editorial for *Pacific Citizen,* James Shimoura blasted Judge Kaufman's refusal to change his original sentence as "systemic failure."

"[They] chose to ignore the wider problem the case symbolizes," Shimoura wrote. "The facts surrounding Vincent Chin's senseless death bring into focus the continuing problem of racism in America in 1983, particularly against Asian Americans. . . . The burning hatred and scapegoating of our country's economic problems, against Asians, was brutally illustrated. Vincent Chin was attacked and killed because he was an Asian American."

The ACJ and the Asian American community, however, weren't the only ones outraged by Judge Kaufman's final decision. Highland Park judge Thomas Bayles, who had presided over the preliminary hearing in the case on October 5, 1982, expressed deep regret. He believed the Vincent Chin case proved the system was broken.

"I think there's [enough] fault to go around," Bayles said in a moment of soul-searching. During the preliminary hearing the previous fall, Bayles felt the charge of second-degree murder should have actually been first-degree murder. "Even in my court. Perhaps I should have said, 'I'm going to delay this thing and give you an opportunity to recharge the man.' I take the blame. Perhaps I should have done that. Perhaps I should have stopped the proceedings. I didn't do that. So I can say the blame goes right down the line. I'm perhaps as much to blame as the [sentencing] judge [Kaufman] is in this whole thing. The whole process fails, we fail everybody because we're maybe more interested in getting through a number of cases than we are in doing all of them right."

• • •

For Lily Chin, June 2, 1983, was a huge setback. The law had decided *again* to let Vincent's killers remain free. But she refused to let her grief overwhelm her. She had promised to love and protect her son—and she would do so even in his death.

Lily Chin proved to be more than just the "grieving mother" of Vincent Chin: she became an activist, speaking out for justice for his killing. Lily's fight won over many supporters, including Reverend Jesse Jackson, the civil rights activist and two-time candidate for the Democratic presidential nomination, who would accompany Lily at various speaking engagements, including this June 1984 event in San Francisco. (Jackson is seated directly behind Lily at the podium, along with Helen Zia to her right.)

Vikki Wong also wanted to fight back. But Lily wanted to protect Vikki, who was still mourning the loss of her fiancé. She feared the media scrutiny and invasion of privacy would not only overwhelm Vikki but also prevent her from fully processing her grief. So she advised Vikki to stay silent for now, and she would speak for all of them. Lily promised to be Vikki's voice in the fight for Vincent's justice.

Vikki agreed. "This controversy just goes on and I don't want to say any more about it," she said in one of her last media interviews in 1983. "It still hurts me very much."

In the meantime, the general public saw Lily only as the grieving mother. The news media published mostly photos of Lily in tears. "Many people only saw Mrs. Chin through the media, in her terrible grief and sadness, over the tragic death and injustice of her beloved son, Vincent," Zia said.

For Zia and other members of the ACJ, that image was far from accurate. To them, Lily was strong. She had guts. This was the same woman who demanded that everyone fight back for her son when they were ready to give up on that March night at the Golden Star Restaurant.

"I never heard Mrs. Chin complain about her life," Zia said. "Not once. She wasn't a victim—she was a doer and a fighter in every way."

But Lily also had a gentle side. Zia remembered how despite her anger and grief, Lily always welcomed ACJ members into her home with a warm smile: "She had a backbone of steel and a heart of gold—she was generous and giving."

Lily made sure no one went hungry at her house. She would whip up a feast of dim sum and pastries, using fresh vegetables from her garden and even grinding her own meat. She made sure everyone's plate was full as they pored over court briefs and debated into the late hours about their legal options for Vincent's case.

When she wasn't cooking, Lily was always making gifts for everyone. "And could she ever knit!" Zia said. "She could knit a vest or a sweater in a day or two—a scarf, in a blink! She was always making something to give to someone."

Like Roland Hwang. "She knit me a hand-knit sweater which I have to this day," he said. He smiled, remembering how Lily had even played matchmaker with a few of the younger ACJ members, like trying to set up the twenty-nine-year-old bachelor Shimoura with dates.

"I think her favorite hobby was matchmaking," Zia agreed. "She was always trying to find matches for the single, unmarried people she met."

Lily's fondness for Hwang, Shimoura, Zia, and Chan, all in their late twenties to early thirties, was also because she missed her own family. Recently widowed and still grieving the loss of her son, Lily developed a close bond especially with Chan and Zia. "Liza Chan spoke Toisanese, which made it easier to converse with Lily," Shimoura said. "And Helen was like an adopted daughter of Lily."

"Mrs. Chin was everyone's mother, grandmother, sister, auntie," Zia said. "She paid special attention to the small children of so many of the ACJ volunteers who were young parents back then."

Chan never forgot how kind Lily was not just to her but also to her girlfriend at the time, Bev. Although Chan had still not come out publicly as a lesbian, Lily never badgered her about being single. Chan realized Lily might have suspected she and

Bev were partners in a committed relationship at the time. "She simply accepted us as a pair," Chan remembered.

But Lily wanted to do more than make dim sum and knit sweaters. She wasn't just a grieving mother. She was an angry mother.

"I'm Chinese," she told the press when asked about Judge Kaufman's final decision. "This happened because my son is Chinese, not American. If two Chinese killed a white person, they must go to jail, maybe for their whole lives. But only the skin's different. The heart (of a Chinese) is no different from an American's. I don't understand how this could happen in America. My husband fought for this country. We always paid our taxes and worked hard. We never had any trouble. Before, I really loved America, but now this has made me very angry. Something is wrong with this country."

Lily's fury and willingness to speak bluntly about what happened to her son defied the racist stereotypes of Asian women as quiet and submissive.

"She was very observant and sharp; she knew what was going on around her," Zia said. "She read the *Detroit Free Press* and *The Detroit News*—in English, of course. She also read the Chinese language newspapers. She was very up on current events. And she knew everything that was happening with her son Vincent's case."

· · ·

On June 23, 1983, the one-year anniversary of Vincent's death, Asian Americans across the country paid tribute to him. In Detroit, one hundred people gathered at the Central United Methodist Church to pray for the Chin family.

146

Two thousand miles away, in Los Angeles, more than three hundred Asian Americans rallied outside City Hall to hear Mayor Tom Bradley's speech to end "racial scapegoating." In San Francisco's Chinatown, protests and parades with Chinese lion dancers and firecrackers lit up the streets. Future U.S. senator Barbara Boxer, then a member of the California House of Representatives (D-California), demanded a federal investigation into the Vincent Chin case.

Many people now believed Vincent Chin's civil rights might have been violated. This opened up the possibility of a federal indictment because Ebens and Nitz could not be tried twice for the same crime of manslaughter.

The Civil Rights Act of 1964 ended segregation and outlawed discrimination based on race, color, religion, sex, or national origin.

The Civil Rights Act also stated: "All persons shall be entitled to the full and equal enjoyment of the goods, services, facilities, privileges, advantages, and accommodations of any place of public accommodation, as defined in this section, without discrimination or segregation on the ground of race, color, religion or national origin."

In other words, the Civil Rights Act protected people from discrimination not only in school and the workplace but also in any place of "public accommodation." These places included everything from hotels to restaurants to movie theaters, sports arenas, concert halls, and whatever else could be considered a "place of exhibition and entertainment."

Like the Fancy Pants Club. It was a place of exhibition and entertainment open to the public. It was open to everyone. It was not just a club—it was a place of public accommodation.

Which meant Vincent had every right to be there.

This was no longer a local case about a wrongful death in the state of Michigan. This had become a potential federal crime in which two white men might have violated the civil rights of an Asian American citizen. There had never before been a criminal civil rights case involving an Asian American citizen.

On June 29, 1983, Zia, Chan, Kin Yee, and Lily, and Robert Wu, national president of the Organization of Chinese Americans, met with Assistant Attorney General William Bradford Reynolds at the Department of Justice in Washington, D.C. Reynolds was head of the department's civil rights division. They demanded a federal investigation of the crime.

Reynolds was used to fielding requests for civil rights investigations. That year alone the Justice Department would receive 10,500 complaints. The FBI investigated 3,200 of those complaints. Vincent Chin's case would be one of them. Reynolds ordered the FBI office in Detroit to open up an investigation to find out if the attack had been racially motivated. He described the case as "a brutal incident that was treated with apparently way too light a sentence."

Reynolds credited the recent protests across the country with alerting the Department of Justice about the Vincent Chin case. In fact, he confirmed that this case had generated more letters than any other case he had received at the DOJ. "I don't know of a case that has generated as much interest or as much correspondence," he said.

For Reynolds, the Vincent Chin case also had a familiar ring to it. In November 1980 in Kansas City, Missouri, Raymond Bledsoe, who was white, beat Stephen Harvey, a Black jazz musician, to death with a baseball bat. Bledsoe was acquitted of state

**6A** DETROIT FREE PRESS/THURSDAY, JUNE 30, 1983 ● ●

# U.S. likely to probe Chin death

By PAUL MAGNUSSON
Free Press Washington Staff

WASHINGTON — The government's chief civil rights enforcement official hinted strongly Wednesday that federal authorities would intercede in the case of the two men given sentences of probation for the 1982 baseball bat slaying of Vincent Chin in Highland Park.

Assistant Attorney General William Bradford Reynolds, head of the Justice Department's civil rights division, told Chin's 62-year-old mother, Lily, Wednesday he considered the case "a brutal incident that was treated with apparently way too light a sentence," according to a Justice Department spokesman.

Under Justice Department guidelines, Reynolds may choose to bring before a federal grand jury a case involving violations of U.S. civil rights laws, even if the defendant's case has been tried in a state court.

**REYNOLDS HAS** done so only twice — more recently in the case of a black musician in Kansas City who also was killed with a baseball bat. The killer was found innocent by state courts, but was later sentenced to life in prison by a federal court, said a Justice Department spokesman.

UPI Photo

**Lily Chin with Assistant Attorney General William Bradford Reynolds in Washington on Wednesday.**

The spokesman quoted Reynolds as saying "This is an equal candidate for that kind of approach."

The FBI is doing a "comprehensive investigation" of the Chin slaying, the Justice Department said. The FBI probe began after the sentencing was protested in several cities. Some protesters

charged the defendants got a light sentence because the victim was of Chinese ancestry.

Michael Nitz, 23, and his stepfather, Ronald Ebens, 43, pleaded guilty to manslaughter in the slaying of Chin, 27, of Oak Park. They could have received up to 15 years for manslaughter, but were instead sentenced to three years' probation and fined $3,000 each by Wayne County Circuit Judge Charles Kaufman.

Reynolds said, "I don't know of a case that has generated as much interest or as much correspondence.

"If the facts bear this out and the legal technicalities permit, this would be something the federal government ought to leave as it has been left."

Reynolds also called the FBI investigation "a high priority case" and said he hoped to decide whether to bring the matter to a grand jury before the end of the summer.

## Help for teen parents

NEW YORK — (AP) — About 700 teen parents will start receiving educational and job counseling, family planning help and other services this summer as part of a two-year program, a foundation official says.

A *Detroit Free Press* article covering the June 29, 1983, meeting between Lily Chin, members of the ACJ, and Assistant Attorney General William Bradford Reynolds at the Department of Justice in Washington, D.C. This meeting would be followed by a grand jury indictment against Ronald Ebens and Michael Nitz for two counts of violating Vincent Chin's civil rights, the first-ever race-based civil rights case brought on behalf of an Asian American.

murder charges. But the Department of Justice later indicted him for depriving his victim's civil rights because he was killed in a public park—just as the ACJ was claiming Vincent had been prevented from being at the Fancy Pants Club, another public place. Bledsoe was found guilty of these federal charges and sentenced to life in prison. Reynolds told Lily and the ACJ that Vincent Chin's case was "an equal candidate for that kind of approach." He considered the Vincent Chin killing to be a "high priority case."

The next day newspapers featured a photograph of Reynolds shaking hands with Lily Chin. In the photo, Reynolds is smiling. Lily is not. Although they are shaking hands, Reynolds's hand is shaped like a fist. Lily grips his hand tightly, as if she is holding onto a lifeline.

This was the new Lily Chin. No longer teary-eyed, this new woman showed a steely determination in her eyes. "Mrs. Chin is a model for Asian Americans," wrote the editorial staff of *Asian Week*. "Like a lot of our mothers, she is an immigrant with limited English. Suddenly a widow with no children, she dared to stand up and fight for justice."

Lily continued to speak out about her son's death. She flew as far as California to give speeches at various Asian American community organizations. She was interviewed on several national TV news broadcasts, including the number-one syndicated daytime talk show, *The Phil Donahue Show*. "We are all citizens," she told Donahue. "We are only the skin type different. But the heart is the same." Her appearance caused a sensation, flooding the TV show with thousands of sympathetic letters from across the country.

"Vincent Chin's mother, Lily Chin, an immigrant from China who spent a lifetime of hard work in restaurants, laundries, and factories, became the moral conscience of this national campaign," Zia said.

Barely a month after her trip to Washington, on September 1, 1983, the Justice Department announced that a special federal grand jury in Detroit would officially review Chin's slaying.

Mrs. Chin had gone to Washington, and Washington listened.

. . .

On November 2, 1983, a federal grand jury indicted Ronald Ebens and Michael Nitz with interfering with Vincent Chin's right to use and enjoy a place of public accommodation on account of his race and with conspiracy.

Three women spoke out about this decision—and their opinions could not have been more different.

"We feel this is sort of the first step in possibly seeing justice," Helen Zia declared. "It's sort of a culmination of eight months of hard work trying to convince the Department of Justice and the American people that not only was a murder committed, but it was a serious violation of Vincent Chin's civil rights."

"It's all politics and you know it," Juanita Ebens said, speaking on behalf of her husband. "We have nothing to say to the press. We will not try this case in the newspaper. That's what they've done."

And although Lily Chin felt there was "still hope for justice in this land" because of the federal indictments, she found little joy in the process.

"I'm grateful and hopeful," she said. "But happy I am not. My son is gone forever."

# "IN THE SPOTLIGHT"

Jarod loved *Teenage Mutant Ninja Turtles*. As a child, he watched the cartoon every chance he could get. He loved sketching the cartoon turtles all over his notebook.

His mother noticed Jarod had a talent for art. A once-aspiring artist herself, Vikki encouraged her son to keep drawing. The two would sit and draw for hours at the dining room table, surrounded by stacks of sketching paper and colored pencils, markers, and crayons.

"When I was younger, my fondest memories I have with my mom is just her sitting with me and drawing," Jarod said. "I was really good at drawing at a young age. We just sat and would draw cartoons together forever."

Jarod noticed that his mother was also a talented artist. "My mom was really good at drawing," he said. "I remember trying to get as good as my mom when it came to drawing."

Although Jarod's art talents blossomed in high school, his parents were afraid he would not make enough money as an artist. Vikki pressured her son to major in business in college. "But I shortly realized after enrolling in the business school that I was not really good at math," he said. "I was bombing a lot of classes. I got a little depressed and homesick."

And then Jarod remembered those quiet afternoons when he was a child, sketching cartoon characters with his mom in the dining room. "I decided to transfer to the art department, and I loved it," he said.

After graduating from college, Jarod had trouble finding a steady job as a graphic designer. Desperate for work, he accepted a job at a photography studio. Although he had no experience, Jarod quickly discovered he had a natural talent for photography.

"Photography was the last thing I thought I would do as a creative outlet, but I fell in love with it and kept pursuing it," he said. "I loved being out there exploring and getting lost and meeting people and understanding the world through photography."

Jarod's parents soon realized their son had a gift when he began winning awards for his work. In 2016 he was a finalist for the Outwin Boochever Portrait Competition at the Smithsonian's National Portrait Gallery. He also won a $10,000 emerging artist grant that year for his photo series *Maybe I'll See You There,* documenting the rise and fall and rebirth of Detroit for the Photo District News' annual Exposure Photography Award. "That's when they knew I was good," he said.

After Jarod learned about his mother's connection to Vincent Chin, he became distracted. He started taking more pictures of Vikki instead of Detroit. It was as if he were unconsciously documenting his own mother, trying to uncover her hidden history.

At first Vikki cooperated by posing for some portraits. But she grew increasingly uneasy as Jarod kept taking photos of her. "My mom kept protesting, 'I'm old, I'm in my pajamas, stop taking my picture,'" he said. "She became more uncomfortable with me taking photos."

Jarod wondered if there was something more behind her

discomfort. And then he remembered the first photo of twenty-four-year-old Vikki with Vincent that had flashed across his computer screen the year when he had Googled *Vincent Chin*.

His mother had already been in the spotlight. If Jarod could easily find images of his mother online, so could she. And so could everyone else. The last thing she wanted was to be the focus of attention again.

Jarod realized that while he was trying to capture his mother's image, she just wanted to disappear.

# PART FOUR

# UNITED STATES VS. RONALD EBENS AND MICHAEL NITZ

# Chapter 19

# THE DEFENDERS: MIRIAM SIEFER AND FRANK EAMAN

Miriam Siefer's favorite activity as a child growing up in Detroit was to spend hours in the Detroit Public Library. She read everything from Nancy Drew mysteries to her favorite book, *Charlotte's Web*. "I was a bookworm," she said.

Siefer attended a racially diverse high school in Detroit. As a teenager, she had a multicultural circle of friends. After the 1967 Detroit protests and fires, she remembered seeing abandoned houses in the city. "I became aware that the American promise wasn't for everyone," she said.

That awakening inspired Siefer to pursue a career in law. "I was drawn by the injustices and the civil rights movement of the early 1960s," she said. "At Michigan as an undergrad, I was politically active with the other students. I knew I wanted to do something in social justice."

So Siefer majored in sociology at the University of Michigan and then received her law degree at Wayne State University Law School.

While at law school, Siefer realized the best way she could help fight for social justice was by becoming a public defender.

"I had a desire to really help those who could not afford counsel," she said.

After graduating in 1975, Siefer clerked for a small law firm. She also taught at the criminal clinical program at Wayne State University Law School while moving up the ladder to become a federal public defender. She had been at the federal public defender's office for only two years when the Vincent Chin killing happened.

"I remember being aware of the whole case," she said "It received quite a lot of publicity. I did not think it would end up on our doorstep."

Siefer was assigned, along with Kenneth R. Sasse of the federal defender's office, to represent one of the men painted as a villain by the media—Michael Nitz. Although saddened by the death of Vincent Chin, Siefer noticed that certain inaccuracies had been published in the news. "It was always about two unemployed autoworkers. That was an urban myth," she explained. "Mike Nitz worked at a furniture store."

In addition, she believed the seamy details of the case led to its sensationalism in the press. "It was a fight at a strip bar in a seedy part of the city," she said. "They had too much to drink and were fighting over the affection of one of the strippers.

"Sometimes the media gets it wrong because they don't see all the evidence," she said. "It can shape the opinions of your jurors before you step into court. We had to take extra measures to get a jury who was going to be impartial and not be influenced by what they read or had seen. The media surrounding it changed the nature of the case to fit the times."

Siefer, however, was acutely aware of the growing tension in Detroit over the competition from Japanese automakers.

"There's no question about it, that discrimination was going on," she said. "Given that Detroit is—or used to be—the car capital of the United States, possibly the world, people are more sensitive to foreign imports."

She was also sympathetic to the Asian American community for organizing and bringing awareness about anti-Asian racism in Detroit. "This case was used as a symbol to bring people together, to let people know, in the rest of the country, that this was not right."

But as Siefer researched her new client Nitz and the case, she started to grow concerned. "All of a sudden they found themselves as symbols and scapegoats regarding Asians in their own country. But I think what happened is the case grew bigger than the actual facts."

Siefer knew this was a tragic case. But she had to put aside her personal feelings and focus on representing her client. "You have to see beyond the publicity and really understand the motivations of all the parties before you begin to pass judgment," she said. "That's true in any situation. Don't jump to immediate conclusions. Delve into the facts of an issue before you make up your mind."

And as Siefer dug into the facts of the case, a new truth emerged for her. Yes, Nitz and Ebens had committed a horrific act of violence that led to an innocent person's death. But had they violated Vincent's civil rights?

The answer for her was no.

"It was not a civil rights case at all," she said. "In that sense, Ron Ebens and Michael Nitz were also victims."

· · ·

Frank Eaman never forgot the day in 1963 when he and a friend and their teacher marched in a civil rights demonstration down the streets of Dearborn, Michigan. He was a senior in high school and one of the few white students to take part in the march.

"As we marched along the street, I saw my high school classmates over there in knots jeering and spitting on us, yelling in obscenities and bad racial terms," Eaman remembered. "It was a very bad and frightening experience."

But Eaman continued to march. Later that night the phone calls began. Strangers called his family's house at all hours of the night to scream and harass them for participating in the march. They were forced to change their phone number.

Eaman, however, did not let the racist harassment silence his passion for civil rights. In fact, the racism inspired him to fight back by becoming a defense lawyer. "I stood up for the rights of everyone because when you defend someone's rights in a criminal case, you're defending everyone's rights," he said.

His decision wasn't surprising. Eaman hailed from a long line of defenders who had championed equal rights for everyone. In 1940 his grandfather Frank Eaman quit his lucrative career as a lawyer to become Detroit's police commissioner. His sweeping reforms included opening the doors for Black police officers. Newspapers dubbed his reign the "Eaman Earthquake."

"Our grandfather was an inspiration to us all," Eaman said. "He was an honest man and had a lot of integrity and fought hard for what was right."

Growing up, Eaman remembered hearing stories from his grandfather about how "he used to get a death threat a day." So when strangers harassed Eaman's family after he marched for civil rights as a teenager, he remembered his grandfather's advice.

"I knew most people who did that type of harassing behavior were not legitimate threats," he said. "It was upsetting to get them, and I'd rather not have to deal with that kind of thing. But they were cowards, or they wouldn't make these anonymous phone calls, so I wasn't afraid."

After he became a criminal defense attorney, Eaman was fascinated by the Vincent Chin case. He was aware that racism was not limited to the Black and white communities. "I always knew that Asian Americans faced discrimination," he said.

So he faithfully watched the news coverage of the case. "I saw the storyline develop slowly in the news," he said. "There were a lot of rallies and publicity. I noticed at a rally somebody gave a speech and said Ronald Ebens was an autoworker, and that autoworkers hate all Asians, and that's what he did, he just hated all Asians. And I thought, well, that's an interesting theory. I wonder if there's any evidence to support that."

When American Citizens for Justice first formed, Eaman thought they had "good motives," too. "They wanted to illuminate discrimination against Asian Americans," he said. "They wanted to use the case as a vehicle to educate people about violence against Asian Americans and anti–Asian American feelings."

But after Eaman was assigned—along with David M. Lawson, a lawyer who worked at a private firm—to represent Ebens and researched the case in depth, he began to have doubts about how Ebens was being portrayed in the media.

"There's nothing in Ebens's background, nothing that his friends ever told us or even the FBI, that he even has any animosity toward Asian Americans," he said. "Yet he stands as the symbol or the scapegoat for Asian American violence. No one ever stopped to consider who Ron Ebens was . . . and the fact that he might get twenty-five years in jail. And they were doing it to someone who really didn't have any ill will against the Asian American community."

When Frank Eaman and Ronald Ebens had their initial meeting, Eaman said he never forgot Ebens's despair. "When Ron Ebens first came in to see me, I had the feeling I would be meeting someone who is like a hunted animal. And that's in fact what he was, a man . . . who was looking for a place of shelter, that someone could help direct everything back to sanity because he had watched his whole world come down around him."

Despite his compassion, Eaman still knew that what Ebens had done to Vincent Chin was wrong. Period. "He let himself get out of control, and as a result, a young man was dying. He had a hard time accepting that."

But Eaman also believed Ebens was not guilty of racism. "He's not guilty of doing this because of racial animus or racial feelings or racial bias or racial prejudice," Eaman said. "It so happens that the person he was involved with was Chinese."

Eaman soon found himself being harassed again. But this time, it wasn't a racist white crowd spitting at him for marching for civil rights. It was a diverse group of people of all races and ethnicities who felt he was defending the "bad guy."

Eaman remembered his grandfather's story about receiving a death threat every day for trying to do the right thing. He realized he *was* following in his grandfather's footsteps.

"I think that lawyers have an obligation to defend the unpopular defendant and take on cases that the general public may hold you in scorn for taking," he said. "But that's part of the job that we have to do. I'm not embarrassed or ashamed that I defended Ron Ebens in this case. That's the kind of case that we have to take on. Because if lawyers turn down a case because the defendant was unpopular or held in public scorn, then how would that person ever get anyone to represent them?"

Although Ronald Ebens was facing federal charges of violating Vincent Chin's civil rights, Eaman believed that by representing Ebens, he was still standing up for civil rights. "My representing Ron Ebens in this case was supporting civil rights and was speaking out to maintain fair enforcement of the Civil Rights Act," he said.

Chapter 20

# THE TRAILBLAZER: THE HONORABLE ANNA DIGGS TAYLOR

"A steel fist in a velvet glove."

That was the expression people used to describe the Honorable Anna Diggs Taylor, the judge who would preside over the Vincent Chin case in federal court.

"She was very gracious, unfailingly courteous to people," remembered John Mayer, a former court administrator. "I remember a couple of personnel situations that she handled and they could have been ugly. Because of her graciousness, she was not soft in dealing with these situations, but sort of like the old saying 'a steel fist in a velvet glove.' She was very good at what she did."

Judge Anna Diggs Taylor drew her gracious strength from having attended segregated schools while growing up in Washington, D.C., in the 1930s and '40s. She then attended the private Northfield School for Girls in East Northfield, Massachusetts. In 1946 Northfield was one of the very few private schools in the country that accepted Black students. After graduating from Northfield in 1950, Taylor attended Barnard College of Columbia University. In 1957, she was one of five women to graduate with

Judge Anna Diggs Taylor, the first Black female judge to be appointed to the federal bench in Michigan, was known for her crusade in 1964 Mississippi to help register Black voters. In 1984 she found herself presiding over a groundbreaking civil rights case: the first federal civil rights trial arising out of allegations that an Asian American had been killed solely because of his race.

a law degree from Yale Law School. She fought for civil rights during the 1960s.

So when the now fifty-one-year-old judge was preparing for her latest trial, *United States v. Ronald Ebens and Michael Nitz*, she was more than ready for what was to come, given her life experience.

Especially her experience from twenty years earlier, when she had been a young lawyer on her way to Philadelphia.

But this Philadelphia wasn't the site of the Liberty Bell—it was a small city in Mississippi.

She had just given birth to her first child, but she had still insisted on traveling to offer the legal services of the National Lawyers Guild to a group of white and Black civil rights workers who had been jailed for registering Black voters in Mississippi. Taylor and her first husband, Democratic congressman Charles Cole Diggs, Jr., were passionate supporters of civil rights. In fact, he was the first African American to represent Michigan in Congress.

When they arrived in Mississippi on June 21, 1964, the temperature had reached a blistering one hundred degrees Fahrenheit.

But it wasn't just the weather that was boiling over. An angry mob of white people harassed Taylor and her colleagues outside the Neshoba County Courthouse. "They were shouting the worst of insults," Taylor remembered. "The sheriff offered no help at all, but it was the residents who paid an awful price for merely trying to register to vote. They were the true heroes."

Taylor feared for her life as the crowd surrounded them. "We were afraid we were going to be killed," she said.

Taylor's terror was justified. It turned out she had arrived on the same day that three young civil rights activists—Andrew Goodman, twenty, and Michael Schwerner, twenty-four, both white, and James Chaney, Black and twenty-one—had gone missing. They had been part of the activist group canvassing Mississippi to help register Black voters.

When Taylor interviewed Neshoba County sheriff Lawrence Andrew Rainey about the missing activists, he refused to answer her questions.

It was later alleged that Sheriff Rainey might have already known about the disappearance of the three young men, whose bodies were found two months later buried in an earthen dam just outside of Philadelphia. (Rainey would later be acquitted on charges of civil rights violations.) They had been shot by members of the Ku Klux Klan.

Despite the death threats against her, Taylor spent that summer of 1964 in Mississippi, offering legal advice to the other civil rights activists.

Taylor said the crusade to help register Black voters in Mississippi in 1964 was "a watershed for equal rights in the United States." She downplayed her role, however, saying she was a "small part" of a large movement. "It was important to me to have been there and seen firsthand the wrongs being done. No one felt safe. But unless the work was done, by all the attorneys who went down there, nothing at all would have changed."

In 1979, President Jimmy Carter gave her a lifetime appointment as federal district judge to the U.S. Sixth District Court, which covers Michigan, Ohio, Kentucky, and Tennessee. Taylor became the first African American woman to serve as a federal district judge in Michigan.

She knew this was a historic moment. "I think for some of my white colleagues, the federal court is still sort of a social club and Black judges and female judges have too often been isolated," she said.

Taylor believed it was important for her to give back to the local community. "Black judges have an important role, especially in staying close to their communities," she said. And she was true to her word, volunteering at the Community Foundation for Southeast Michigan, teaching as an adjunct labor law professor at Wayne State University, and participating on the gender, racial, and ethnic fairness task forces for the Sixth Circuit court.

"She was gracious," said criminal defense attorney Bill Swor, who had been on many trials with Taylor. "She was considerate, and she gave everyone who appeared in front of her respect. Everyone felt that they had been given a fair hearing, and she genuinely tried to honor the spirit as well as the letter of the law."

In June 1984, twenty years after her summer in Mississippi, the Honorable Anna Diggs Taylor found herself in the spotlight again with another civil rights case. But this case was different. It was the first case to be prosecuted under the 1964 Civil Rights Act statute providing federal penalties for civil rights violations against an Asian American.

Chapter 21

# THE JURY: "YOU MUST KEEP AN OPEN MIND"

Juror number forty was scared.

She was one of 158 people being interviewed during the week of June 5 for a possible spot on a twelve-person jury.

Because the Vincent Chin case had been covered by the national media for the past two years, more than 90 percent of potential jurors knew about it. When polled, only eight people had never heard of Vincent Chin.

The lawyers for the trial knew they had their work cut out for them. They had to interview all potential jurors before choosing twelve jury members and four alternates to hear the case. And there were six lawyers present, which meant there would be a lot of questions. U.S. Attorney S. Theodore Merritt and Assistant U.S. Attorney Amy Hay were appearing on behalf of the United States. Miriam Siefer and Kenneth R. Sasse, of the federal defender's office, represented defendant Michael Nitz. And Frank D. Eaman and David M. Lawson were defending their client, Ronald Ebens.

The protests and demonstration rallies across the country made many jurors nervous. Including juror number forty. She worried about the media and possible protesters harassing jurors outside the courtroom.

"If they know I'm going to be on the case, and they're going to be following me to the garage or wherever I'm parking, I'm concerned about my safety," she said.

She wasn't the only one. "It's beginning to boil even now," said another potential juror. "I would be afraid afterwards if our names were released, if there would be any harassment of the jurors. It makes me fearful. It makes me a little upset, not knowing."

"This is an unusually publicized case," agreed Judge Anna Diggs Taylor. She told potential jurors that as a safety precaution, federal marshals would escort jurors back and forth to their cars at the end of each day. As for their privacy, although the court would not release the names or addresses of the jury, she could not guarantee what the media might be able to dig up on their own.

During the screening process, nearly half of potential jurors were dismissed for health or economic hardship issues. Judge Taylor also dismissed eleven jurors who declared they had already made up their minds about the case including one juror who admitted, "I have formulated some pretty strong opinions on that case. . . . I wouldn't be able to set aside what I already know about the case. That would be tough for me to do."

The nature of the Fancy Pants Club, which featured nude dancers, also concerned some potential jurors. They worried about not being able to remain impartial during the testimony of three dancers. "The fact that she is a nude dancer could affect my judgement," said one potential juror, who was excused.

The R-rated nature of what was said at the club also proved

to be an obstacle for some people. "I don't like vulgar language or to listen to it," one potential juror said.

"Would you be unable to evaluate the case if there was profane and vulgar language?" Judge Taylor asked.

"Yes."

The judge excused the potential juror.

Jurors were asked about their knowledge of and relations with the Asian community.

"Do you have any strong opinions about Japanese automobile imports which would cause you to judge this case more heavily in one way or the other?"

"Mr. Ebens and Mr. Nitz are white and Mr. Chin was Chinese. Even though they were people of different races who were in a dispute, are you able to keep an open mind as to whether Mr. Chin was killed because of his race or these events occurred because of race?"

During the first day of jury selection, a dozen Asian Americans were present in the courtroom. Including Helen Zia, who was not happy when the defense started asking potential jurors questions like "How many Asian friends do you have?" and "Would you feel any pressure from your Chinese friends?" She was grateful when Judge Taylor stopped that line of questioning.

In fact, Zia estimated that out of the jury pool, "15 to 20 percent of the persons who went through the courtroom questioning were Black or Hispanic." No people of Asian or Pacific Islander descent were being considered for the jury, she observed.

So Zia and the American Citizens for Justice arranged to have at least two trained court watchers attend the trial on a daily basis to observe and take notes. Although there were no

Asian Americans in the jury pool, they were out in force in the courtroom.

• • •

As a result of the ACJ's daily presence in the courtroom, potential jurors were asked if that might pressure their decision to convict or not to convict. When one woman expressed fear that the ACJ and other protesters might harass her, Zia wondered if that reaction might stem from racism. "The killers [and their families] were there in court the whole time. . . . She did not feel threatened that those men might do something to her," she said.

In addition, during the early 1980s, recent wars with Asian countries still remained fresh in many people's minds, from the 1941 Pearl Harbor bombing to the 1950 Korean War and the Vietnam War, which had ended less than a decade earlier.

When one potential juror said he had a brother-in-law who served in the Vietnam War, prosecutor Theodore Merritt asked, "Was there anything about that experience that you think might color your fair judgment in this case?"

"No," the potential juror said.

Some potential jurors wondered if their relationships with Asian Americans could possibly influence their judgment. One woman who worked at Henry Ford Hospital admitted she had signed a petition that was circulated by a group of Chinese American doctors and staffers protesting Judge Charles Kaufman's original probation sentence for Ebens and Nitz.

And two people had actually gone to high school with Vincent Chin. "He was in my graduating class," one of them said. "I have been following it closely on the news and TV. I feel very strongly about the two men getting off as they did. I feel I would not be impartial."

Another obstacle for finding an impartial jury was the violent nature of the crime itself. Many jurors had trouble separating the images of Vincent's brutal beating death from the more abstract concept of his civil rights being violated.

"I can't bury the emotion that I would feel," one potential juror confessed.

"I just feel like no one has got a right to take anyone's life," another person declared. "I was brought up that way. I don't know if I'll be fair about it or not. I don't know how to answer that."

Many jurors also could not let go of their sympathy for Lily Chin's loss. "The boy that died was killed with a baseball bat," one person said. "I thought it was a terrible way to die, being hit with a baseball bat. I also felt pity to his mother. It is a terrible loss."

One potential juror, who was also a mother, especially identified with Lily. "When I saw the victim's mother on TV . . . because I have a son, I felt very bad for the woman," she said. "It's very hard to take that and push it aside."

"Of course, a mother who has lost her son is very tragic," agreed Judge Taylor, herself a mother. "But the question is whether you could decide certain questions which would be presented to you based upon the evidence which would be presented to you and follow the constitution?"

"I think so," the potential juror said.

Ultimately, the lawyers and Judge Taylor settled on a final

jury of five men and seven women plus two alternate jurors. Out of fourteen people selected, three were Black, eleven were white, and none were Asian.

. . .

On June 12, 1984, the jury for *United States v. Ronald Ebens and Michael Nitz* was sworn in.

Judge Taylor reminded the jury that the defendants, Ronald Ebens and Michael Nitz, were presumed innocent until proven guilty. "Your purpose as jurors is to find and determine the facts," she said. And although she was the presiding judge, she told the jury that they too were judges—"You are the sole judges of the facts."

"You are to perform this duty without bias, or prejudice as to any party," she said. "The law does not permit jurors to be governed by sympathy, prejudice, or public opinion. . . . In fairness to the parties of this lawsuit, you must keep an open mind."

Chapter 22

# THE OPENING
# STATEMENTS:
# "THE BURDEN OF PROOF"

On June 13, 1984, the federal civil rights trial *United States v. Ronald Ebens and Michael Nitz* began with a question.

Why?

No one in the courtroom questioned *who* killed Vincent Chin. They were sitting right there at the defendants' table. Ebens and Nitz had already been found guilty of manslaughter.

But what was the actual motivation behind the killing? Was Vincent Chin's death the result of a drunken barroom brawl gone too far, as the defense maintained? Or was it, as Department of Justice prosecutor Theodore Merritt, asked, a case of "ugly racism which turned violent?"

· · ·

In their opening statements, Merritt and his co-counsel, Amy Hay, declared that the witnesses' testimony, especially that of Fancy Pants Club dancer Racine Colwell, would prove that Ebens and Nitz had targeted Vincent because of his race.

"On June 19, 1982, a brutal crime was committed on the streets in Highland Park," Merritt said. "On that night, the defendant, Ronald Ebens helped by his co-defendant, Michael Nitz, repeatedly beat with a baseball bat, a Chinese American citizen of the United States by the name of Vincent Chin. And beat him so bad that he died four days later from massive head injuries. And the evidence will prove that Vincent Chin died at the hands of these defendants, because he was a Chinese American."

But the defense disagreed.

"The burden of proof is on the government to prove not only that Ronald Ebens and Michael Nitz were responsible for the death of Vincent Chin, but to show that they killed Vincent Chin because of his race," said David Lawson, one of Ebens's defense attorneys. "Now, we do not believe that the evidence will support the prosecution's charges. . . . We do not believe that the prosecution will prove beyond a reasonable doubt that Mr. Ebens acted because of Vincent Chin's race. We believe the evidence will show this was not a civil rights case, but a fight between angry and intoxicated men that ended in the death of one of them."

In fact, the defense believed this federal civil rights trial was a "media event" and a desperate act of retribution. Lawson claimed that Judge Charles Kaufman's original probation sentence from March 1983 "set off a chain of events that resulted in this trial today." He accused Vincent's friends, family, and community members of trying "to come up with some evidence that would turn this homicide into a federal matter."

Kenneth Sasse, who served as Michael Nitz's lawyer along with Miriam Siefer, claimed that the civil rights charges were the result of the "vivid imagination" of lawyer Liza Chan and Vincent's friends.

Although Vincent Chin and Ronald Ebens came from different worlds, they shared similar characteristics. They were described as hardworking men with steady jobs who loved their families. The younger Michael Nitz was also depicted as a hard worker and a small-town boy who grew up playing baseball.

The lawyers for both sides agreed that the three men went to the Fancy Pants Club to have a good time. Vincent was there to celebrate his bachelor party. Ebens and Nitz showed up to blow off steam after a long day of work.

But that's when their stories veered off into different directions.

Merritt claimed that Vincent's "last fling" with his best friends was ruined by Ebens's "barrage of obscenities and racial insults."

Defense attorney Sasse, however, explained that Ebens was a "factory man" where swearing was commonplace. "He's worked in the factory for years, where he was used to using words like that."

Prosecutor Merritt stood firmly by his belief that Ebens and Nitz violated Vincent Chin's civil rights. "When you have heard all the evidence, ladies and gentlemen, I'm confident that you will return a verdict of guilty as to both defendants on both counts," Merritt said.

Lawson, however, asked the jury to be impartial during the trial. "The only thing that we ask you to do is listen carefully to the testimony," he said. "And to keep an open mind until you have heard all of the evidence."

Over the next two weeks, the jury would hear evidence that told two sides to the same story. Which side would they believe?

Chapter 23

# THE BACHELOR PARTY: "WE ARE JUST HERE TO HAVE A GOOD TIME"

Unlike the other witnesses, Gary Koivu had known Vincent Chin for most of his life. Theodore Merritt described him to the jury as Vincent's "lifetime buddy."

Which was why Koivu felt nervous as he sat down in the witness stand to be the voice for his friend who could no longer speak for himself.

Looking back, the shy Koivu regretted not speaking up more in court. "I wish I could have elaborated more," he said in an interview years later. "Maybe the jury would get more of a picture of what really happened. But I just wanted to get out of there."

On the witness stand on the second day of the trial, Koivu described Vincent to the jury as "happy and relaxed" as they drove to the club to celebrate his bachelor party. "He was having a good time," Koivu said.

"Would you say he was drunk?" asked prosecutor Amy Hay, who was in charge of the initial witness examination.

"It was obvious he had been drinking, but he didn't appear staggering, or slurring his speech," Koivu said. "He was pretty much in hand."

Koivu later confirmed for the defense team that he did not hear Ebens say any racist or ethnic slurs. But he remembered Vincent saying to Ebens, "Don't call me a fucker, I'm not a fucker."

"I looked across and there was a man sitting on the other side of the stage," Koivu said. "I put my hand on Vincent's arm and said something like forget it. I looked across at Ebens and he said something like, 'I'm not sure if you're a big fucker or a little fucker.'" Koivu then testified that Vincent had walked over to Ebens and shoved him in the chest. "And Ebens shoved back and they both started swinging and punching until when the third man joined in the fight."

Koivu recounted that Vincent challenged Ebens to another fight in the parking lot after they had all been kicked out of the club, but he said they did not expect Ebens and Nitz to pull a baseball bat from their car trunk. After Vincent and Jimmy Choi ran away, Koivu testified that he and Bob Siroskey grabbed a tire iron from their car to protect themselves.

"I heard shouts coming from the car," Koivu said. "'We're going to get your friend, and you're going to need more than a tire iron when we get your friend.'"

The defense team was skeptical of Koivu's testimony. They wondered if he had been coached by lawyer Liza Chan. A year before the trial began, in May 1983, Chan had had Koivu, Bob Siroskey, and Jimmy Choi meet to discuss what happened on the night of Vincent's death.

"What was the purpose of that meeting?" Lawson asked.

"Well, she wanted to get an idea of what happened, just to get the flavor of the night, to get an idea of what happened," Koivu said.

But Lawson wasn't buying it. He had a transcript of a

recording that Liza Chan had made of the meeting that night. "Isn't it true that the purpose of the meeting was so you could get your stories together, so that there wouldn't be any conflicts in testimony that would be coming up?" he asked.

"No," Koivu said. "She was aware that people see different things in a different way. We told her what we saw or what we heard, the way it was."

Lawson, however, called Koivu out for expressing concern to Chan about their meeting in the first place. "Did you not express a concern that when you met to get your stories together, that you did not want your testimony to sound rehearsed, that you were concerned about it being too accurate, that it matched too well?"

"In a way," Koivu admitted.

"Well, can you answer, yes or no?" Lawson pressed.

"I estimate I may have said that," Koivu replied. But he still insisted there was no collusion and that he was not lying on the stand. "I'm pretty sure my testimony is as accurate as anyone else's."

Lawson then grilled Koivu about whether he had heard Ebens say any racist or ethnic slurs at Vincent. "Now, [Vincent] did not say 'Don't call me a Chink,' did he?"

"No," Koivu said.

"And you did not hear him say, 'Don't call me a Nip or Jap,' or anything like that?"

"No," Koivu said, adding that Vincent was upset at being called the obscenity "motherfucker."

During his final moments on the witness stand, Koivu answered questions from Nitz's lawyer Miriam Siefer about his relationship with Vincent. These personal questions were the most difficult ones for Koivu to answer because he was a private person and was still grieving the death of his childhood friend.

"Mr. Koivu, you knew Mr. Chin a long time?" Siefer asked.

"Yes," Koivu said.

"You went to school together?"

"Right."

"For a period ten years, you probably saw him every day of your life?" Siefer asked.

"Not every day," Koivu replied.

"Close to it?" Siefer pressed.

"For the first few years." ·

"Very close friends?" Siefer wondered.

"Yes."

"And certainly since this event of June 19, you have been following the news stories regarding this case, is that accurate?"

At this point, Koivu knew the purpose of Siefer's questioning. She was trying to hint to the jury that perhaps Koivu's close friendship with Vincent may have influenced the accuracy of his testimony. But he had no choice but to answer the question honestly. "Yes."

Siefer turned to Judge Taylor. "I have no further questions, Your Honor."

· · ·

On June 19, 1982, twenty-two-year-old Robert Edward ("Bob") Siroskey was just getting out of the shower after working over-time on a Saturday when the phone rang. It was Vincent, inviting him to an impromptu bachelor party.

Siroskey immediately said yes. Vincent was one of the friendliest employees at Efficient Engineering Co. in Troy, where they drafted machinery for engineers to build.

Questioned by prosecuting attorney Theodore Merritt, Siroskey confirmed Vincent had sneaked a bottle of vodka into the Fancy Pants Club. He estimated they made about eight drinks of vodka mixed with orange juice while watching the dancers. "I had never seen him in a better mood," Siroskey said. "He was laughing, having a good time, tipping the dancers."

And then, out of nowhere, Siroskey said he heard someone say the racist slur *Chink*.

"The music was playing and I was minding my own business, and all of a sudden I heard 'Chink' come across the stage," he said.

Siroskey admitted he had no idea who actually shouted "Chink." "I cannot say who it came from," he told Merritt. "All I know is it came from the other side of the stage."

Although he didn't know *who* said it, Siroskey insisted he definitely heard the word coming directly across from Vincent. "It was very distinct," he said. "It was like a shout." He told the jury that the racist slur upset Vincent. "Nobody usually called him a Chink."

Although Siroskey could not verify if Ebens had used a racist slur against Vincent, he confirmed the Chrysler foreman did swear at his friend. "I turned and the person on the other side of the stage was saying, 'I don't know if you are a big motherfucker or a little motherfucker' and Vince replied with 'Don't call me a motherfucker.'"

As for how the fight started, Siroskey, like Gary Koivu, confirmed that Vincent pushed Ebens first. Siroskey also remembered a chair being swung at Vincent but didn't remember who had originally picked up the chair. As the chair swung toward Vincent, Siroskey saw his friend grab the chair and throw it to the ground. By then, the club's doorman, Gary Reid, had arrived to break up the fight.

While Vincent, Gary Koivu, and Jimmy Choi were escorted out of the club, Ebens and Nitz headed to the bathroom to take care of Nitz's bleeding head. Ebens claimed Siroskey followed them into the bathroom to apologize.

But Siroskey denied this. "I just walked in and I said, 'I don't know what the problem is,'" he explained to the jury. "'We are just here to have a good time. He is getting married in nine days. It is just like a little bachelor party.'"

"You have a very cocky friend," Ebens allegedly snapped back.

"He didn't really seem satisfied with just what happened in the bar," Siroskey said.

Ebens and Nitz stormed out of the bathroom. Siroskey left soon after. When he entered the main club area, his friends were already outside. "Somebody came in and got me and said, 'Vince is being chased with a baseball bat,'" he said.

Siroskey rushed out to the parking lot, where he armed himself with a tire iron from the trunk of Koivu's car for protection. "I said to Gary, 'We are going to need something,'" he said. "'He has got a bat.'"

Just then Ebens returned to the parking lot, out of breath and unable to catch up with Vincent or Choi.

Ebens spotted the tire iron clenched in Siroskey's hand. "Come on, I will fight you with the tire iron, no problem," he shouted.

As Ebens rushed toward them, Siroskey and Koivu scrambled into the car and sped off. They drove up and down Woodward, desperately searching for Vincent. Because Koivu had not filled up the gas tank earlier, they were running low on gas. As they filled up at a gas station, the two friends realized that trying to find Vincent was like trying to find a needle in a haystack. Tired and hungry, they decided to grab some food at a nearby Burger King. They sat by the front window, thinking they might catch Vincent passing by.

"I never seen him the rest of the night," Siroskey said. Afterward he and Koivu drove to the Golden Star Restaurant in hopes that maybe Vincent had made it back there.

Instead, Golden Star owner Paul Ng delivered the bad news. "He told us that he had gotten beaten up by a baseball bat and was at Henry Ford Emergency."

"Did you go to the hospital?" Merritt asked.

"Yes."

"And was he able to talk to you?"

"No."

· · ·

But that was not the end of Siroskey's day in court. Defense attorney David Lawson immediately questioned the accuracy of Siroskey's memory, given how much alcohol he drank that night.

Siroskey admitted to being drunk that night, but just "enough."

"What do you mean by enough?" Lawson asked.

"I was not drunk. I was not stumbling. I was, you know, just like if you are at a party and it is the end of the night and you are going home."

But Lawson wasn't convinced. He grilled Siroskey about his

meeting in May 1983 with Koivu, Choi, and lawyer Liza Chan to discuss Vincent Chin's death. Lawson believed that this meeting might have influenced Siroskey to remember certain details of the night that might have not actually happened.

"Isn't it true, Mr. Siroskey, that it wasn't until Mr. Koivu and Mr. Choi started to tell you about the events that you had any memory about any encounter in the bathroom at all?" Lawson asked.

"No," Siroskey said.

Lawson held up the printed transcript of the conversation. He read a direct quote from Siroskey saying "I don't remember" when Chan asked him about what happened in the bathroom between him and Ebens and Nitz.

"So your memory of this incident sort of faded in and out?" Lawson asked. "Things were very difficult for you to remember that evening, were they not?"

"Yes," Siroskey admitted.

Lawson pressed on. "Now, you were upset as a result of the events that evening?"

"Yes, very upset."

"You had been drinking?"

"Yes."

"And your friend was seriously injured and eventually died?"

"Yes."

"And things were not clear in your head?"

But Siroskey pushed back. "I was more upset about him being hurt than trying to remember what happened."

"Of course," Lawson said. "But then you learned about the probation sentence in the State Court; is that right?"

"I read about it, yes," Siroskey said.

"And that upset you, too?"

"Sure."

Siroskey's answer gave Lawson the opening he needed. He accused Siroskey and his friends of conspiring with Chan over what had happened that night. "That is when you got together and tried to put together events that you could not recall; is that right?"

But Siroskey insisted there was no collusion. "No," he said, explaining the meeting was ". . . to help me remember what happened."

Michael Nitz's lawyer, Miriam Siefer, also cross-examined Siroskey about his testimony, especially his recollection of what happened in the bathroom with Ebens and Nitz. "So, in fact, you apologized to Mr. Nitz, didn't you?" she asked.

"I don't believe I apologized to anybody," Siroskey answered.

"Well, you told him that you were sorry for what happened?"

Siroskey once again firmly denied ever apologizing to Ebens and Nitz in the bathroom. "I never said that."

Perhaps Siroskey's hazy memory had been influenced by Jimmy Choi's speculation, Siefer suggested, even though Choi was not in the bathroom.

But Siroskey had an explanation for why Choi remembered the bathroom conversation even though he was never there in the first place. "I probably told him earlier, I guess; and I forgot then, and I re-remembered."

After Siefer's cross-examination wrapped, Merritt approached Siroskey again with a follow-up question. If Siroskey did not intend to apologize to Ebens and Nitz in the bathroom, then why did he talk to them at all?

"Just clarifying that I hope everything was over and the thing was ending, just to satisfy myself," Siroskey said.

"And what was the impression that you left with?" Merritt asked.

"I felt that he felt that he was not satisfied with just a little spat in the bar," Siroskey said. "He was kind of angry and upset himself."

"But at that time, you didn't think this was going to be such a big deal?" Merritt asked.

"No."

"And you didn't think he was going to chase Vincent Chin and kill him?"

"No."

"Thank you," Merritt said. "That is all I have."

. . .

Jimmy Choi testified that he had been talking with Gary Koivu when he overheard someone mention something about foreign cars. "I heard someone mention foreign cars coming from the direction of across the stage, which I didn't pay too much attention," he said. "I just glanced around and resumed talking to Gary again."

And then Choi claimed he heard the word *Nips,* a racist slur used against people of Japanese descent, thrown in their direction. He remembered Vincent allegedly shouting back, "We are not Japanese."

Choi also witnessed Vincent getting offended when Ebens called him a "motherfucker." Although defense attorney

Kenneth Sasse had explained to the jury during his opening statement that Ebens and other blue-collar autoworkers used the American swear word *motherfucker* casually in their everyday language, the phrase was considered especially offensive to the Chinese community.

"That [kind of remark] is one of the things that Chinese are really leery about because we respect our mothers," Choi later explained in a newspaper interview. "You have to understand, the Chinese take that word very seriously. Elders are revered. That word is the ultimate insult."

During his testimony, Choi confirmed that Ebens's swearing offended Vincent. "He got mad and said, 'Come on, let's go outside.' He came around the stage and went over to where the two gentlemen were sitting, the man with the grey hair stood, and Vincent punched him. Then they started exchanging blows."

Choi, Koivu, and doorman Gary Reid rushed over to break up the fight. Choi insisted he saw Ebens try to slam a chair at Vincent, who managed to grab it and throw it on the floor. As Reid separated Ebens and Nitz from Vincent, Choi grabbed his friend.

"Okay, cool down," Choi told Vincent. "Calm down, man. Have a good time."

"Let's go," Vincent said, breathing hard. "Let's get out of here."

Choi also confirmed that Vincent challenged Ebens to another fight when Ebens and his stepson showed up in the parking lot. "Vincent saw them and he got angry again. He said, 'Okay, let's fight again, chicken shit.' Stuff like that. And they didn't say a word."

"And what did they do?" Merritt asked.

"They just went to the car, lifted up the hatch back, and pulled out a baseball bat. Vincent said, 'I am not going to fight you with a baseball bat.' Then they kept coming, so Vincent ran away from them."

Ebens soon returned, unable to catch up with Vincent. "Where is your friend?" he demanded to the others.

Choi didn't realize that he would be next. Ebens spotted him with Koivu and Siroskey and said, "Let's get this little fucker."

"I just ran," Choi said. "I never said one word to them."

Choi managed to catch up to Vincent. "Those guys are crazy," he told him. "Let's run." They raced south on Woodward Avenue. They were surrounded by deserted buildings and dark alleys. "Nobody was there," he said.

But in the distance, they saw a brightly lit and crowded McDonald's. They decided to wait outside, hoping Koivu and Siroskey might drive by and see them. Choi broke off a piece of the wooden fence in front of the McDonald's as a makeshift defense weapon and gave an empty bottle to Vincent to use.

The two friends jumped every time they saw a dark-colored car that looked like the one Ebens and Nitz owned. To their relief, the cars would drive by. They started to relax and began laughing.

Suddenly, Vincent turned to Choi. "Scram," he said.

Choi turned around and saw Ebens and Nitz sneaking up from behind the bushes planted outside the McDonald's. He jumped to his feet. He ran across the street and then turned back to see Vincent following him.

Then Choi spotted Nitz rush up behind Vincent and grab him in a bear hug. "They were still scuffling when the older man came with the bat."

Choi saw Ebens clutch the bat with two hands as he swung it at Vincent. "He kept on swinging, like this, in a frenzy."

"It seemed like slow motion," he told the jury.

As police officers held Ebens at gunpoint, demanding he drop the bat, Choi rushed over to his friend. "He was still conscious," he said.

"Was he saying anything?" Merritt asked.

"Yes," Choi answered. "I cradled his head and I said, 'Hey Vincent, are you all right?' And he was saying, 'Fight. Fight. It is not fair.'"

"Was he speaking Chinese?" Merritt asked.

"In Chinese," Choi confirmed. He then told the jury how he shouted to the crowd, "Somebody get a bloody ambulance." When no one moved, he left Vincent to dial 911 on a pay phone inside the McDonald's. He then raced back to Vincent, who was still conscious. "Snap up, snap up, snap up," Choi told Vincent. "The ambulance will be right here." Choi held his friend's hand the whole time until the ambulance finally arrived.

As the EMTs carefully placed Vincent on a gurney, Choi turned to see Ebens talking to the police. "I didn't mean to hurt this boy," he recalled Ebens saying. "My son is hurt."

"If I had a gun, I would shoot you both right here," Choi shouted at Ebens and Nitz, shaking with fury.

Choi then grabbed Vincent's wallet and hopped into the ambulance with him. As one of the EMTs stuck their fingers into Vincent's mouth to keep him from biting his tongue, Choi begged his friend to stay awake. "Vincent, snap up, snap up."

At the hospital, the medical staff wheeled Vincent into the emergency operating room while Choi went to make the most difficult phone call of his life. "I called his fiancée and family."

. . .

It was difficult for Jimmy Choi to relive the night of his friend's death. But it was even more grueling to be cross-examined by Ebens's defense attorneys. As with Koivu and Siroskey, they grilled Choi about possibly exaggerating or even fabricating details of his story to fit the prosecution's charge that Ebens was motivated by racism.

"Now, you knew, did you not, that the investigation was whether these men were motivated in doing this act because of your friend's race?" asked Frank Eaman.

"I have a vague idea," Choi answered.

"Sir, you knew that it was significant whether any racial remarks were made or racial discussion occurred inside the Fancy Pants; did you know the significance of that?" Eaman asked.

"I knew the significance, but I did tell the truth."

A skeptical Eaman quoted Choi saying "I don't think they made any racial remarks" in the transcript of his meeting with Liza Chan in May 1983 about the fight at the Fancy Pants Club.

Choi admitted he met Chan during a stressful time in his life. He was planning to attend graduate school for management and had just finished an internship in Toronto: "And all of a sudden, this lady lawyer came to me. I was not prepared." Choi said that later he started to remember more details, including someone saying the racist slur *Nip* at the club. "As I thought about it, more things popped up to me through this case when it came up."

"Did you receive advice from anyone about what parts of this story to tell and what parts not to tell?" Eaman asked.

"I didn't receive any advice to that effect," Choi said. "I was advised to tell the truth and the whole truth."

But Eaman didn't back down. He wondered if Choi was influenced by reading media accounts about the anti-Japanese sentiments in the Detroit auto industry and a rise in discrimination against Asian Americans.

"Can you be sure what you are telling is a product of your own memory, of what other people have told you about what you have seen in the newspapers, what you have seen on TV? Can you be sure of that?"

"I can be sure what I tell you today, that is what I remember best and vividly," Choi replied.

Eaman wondered if the American Citizens for Justice had influenced Choi. "Now, you are aware, are you not, Mr. Choi, that Asian Americans around the world have marched because of this case?"

"I am aware of that," Choi said.

"Mr. Choi, because of that, and the publicity, do you feel any pressure?"

"Pressure on me?" Choi shot back. "I don't socialize with them. I have my own life to live. Why should I have pressure? I only have pressure coming here sitting down in here, that would be pressure, but nothing else. Pressure, I have to think hard to remember, to think, okay, but not from the Asian Americans."

But the defense team still wondered why Choi had first said there was no racial provocation from the defendants before later changing his mind.

Choi's answer shed light on how difficult it was for Asian Americans in the 1980s to deal with racism.

"Well, there was a time, okay, for Chinese, we try not to,

shall I say, react," Choi explained. "Usually, we can take a lot of things . . . I tried to shun all of the racial things away from me. I had a few experiences, mostly when I deal with my classmates at school, but a few times when somebody like drives by and just told me Chink, I tried to brush it aside."

Whether he realized it or not, Choi's answer revealed why the Vincent Chin killing was a watershed moment for Asian America: the price for brushing racism aside may have been too high.

## Chapter 24

# THE EMPLOYEES: "IT'S BECAUSE OF YOU"

During her testimony, twenty-year-old Sharon Fleming explained she had only been working at the Fancy Pants for two days when Vincent Chin's bachelor party showed up.

Times were tough back then in Detroit. In 1982, Michigan's unemployment rate had reached 17 percent, about twice the national average. With more than half the city on government assistance, Mayor Coleman Young declared a hunger emergency. At the time, Fleming took up dancing while raising her first child, who had just been born.

She was the second dancer to perform for Vincent and his friends and the others in the club. "They were having a good time," she noticed. But during her first song, they started arguing with other people. "Just a little bickering, it wasn't anything big."

"What was the tone of Mr. Ebens' voice?" asked prosecutor Amy Hay.

"Upset."

At the end of her three songs, Fleming went to the light switch to change the lights when she witnessed Vincent get out of his chair and head for Ebens's side of the stage. That was when the fight began, she said. "There was a chair thrown, then a punch thrown that I seen."

"Did you see who threw the chair?" Hay asked. "Did you see who threw the punch?"

"Mr. Ebens," Fleming answered.

. . .

Like Fleming, Angela "Starlene" Rudolph was a new dancer at the Fancy Pants Club. So she was happy to see Vincent Chin and his bachelor party arrive—this would be a good night in tips for her.

But when Rudolph danced for Vincent and his friends, she refused to let him tip her.

"Why did you refuse his tip?" asked defense attorney Eaman.

"Because of the way he wanted to give me the tip," she explained. "I wasn't accustomed to it. . . . He wanted to place it in my costume." According to the club rules, customers could tip the dancers only by handing over the money. Rudolph didn't want to risk her job by breaking any rules during her first week at work.

So she backed away and headed over to where Ebens and Nitz were sitting. "They were in a partying mood," she said. "They were starting to cheer me on."

While Rudolph was dancing for Ebens and Nitz, Vincent teased her for leaving his bachelor party. According to Rudolph, that was when Ebens shouted in Vincent's direction, "Boy, you don't know a good thing when you see one."

"I'm not a boy," Vincent shouted back.

"He was just using 'boy' as a figure of speech," Rudolph said.

But the more Ebens shouted at Vincent, the angrier Vincent became. Which made it awkward for Rudolph, who was doing her best to be professional onstage.

197

"I was trying to ignore the situation," she told the jury. "It was making me uncomfortable."

After she finished her set, Rudolph went back to the dressing room. She told the other dancers about the argument between Vincent and Ebens.

"We never thought anything would happen, and all of a sudden, we heard, boom, boom, boom!" Rudolph said. "Like chairs hitting walls or floors. They were fighting because I stuck my head out the door to see."

Rudolph and the other dancers were scared. There had never been a fight before in the club. They hid in the dressing room in case the violence grew worse.

"I stayed in the back the whole time," she said. "I didn't want to go out there."

. . .

Racine Colwell, twenty-four, was tired. She had been working since noon on a double shift.

Colwell danced for three songs during her set. She made at least thirty dollars in tips from Vincent and his friends. "He was just having a good time, you know, laughing and joking . . . and carrying on," she said.

Colwell pointed to a blueprint of the Fancy Pants Club layout during the trial. She confirmed that she was standing by the corner of the stage after her dance performance when she heard Ebens yelling at Vincent. She testified that he was speaking loudly because she could hear him over the music.

When asked if she had heard Ebens refer to Vincent's race, Colwell said no. "All I heard him say when I turned around is,

'It's because of you little motherfuckers that we're out of work.'" To Colwell, it was obvious what Ebens was referencing.

"I'm not a little motherfucker," she remembered Vincent shouting.

"Well, I'm not sure if you're a big one or a little one," Ebens shot back.

"And by that time he got mad," Colwell said, describing how Vincent then walked over to Ebens and pushed him.

And that was when the fight got out of control. Colwell confirmed what the other club employees had described— punches being thrown, chairs slamming against walls. She remembered seeing Michael Nitz "bleeding a lot."

Until that night, Colwell had never seen a fight in the six years she had worked at the club. "Everybody minds their own business." She said the fight lasted for only a few minutes before the club doorman escorted Vincent out of the club.

"When the doorman escorted Vince out, did Vince say anything?" Merritt asked.

"Yes, he was saying he didn't do anything and they were picking on him," Colwell said. "And the parking lot attendant told him that he should know better. He turned around and he told, I believe it was Mr. Ebens, he shouted across the room that 'I will be waiting outside, I'll be waiting outside.'"

"Did you see Vincent Chin again?" Merritt asked.

"No, I didn't." Colwell said.

Merritt turned to Judge Taylor. "That's all I have, Your Honor."

Later, during Colwell's cross-examination with Eaman, she said she did not follow the case in the media. She found out about what had happened to Vincent Chin only when a customer told her about it. "A customer brought me one that had a picture of in it, and that was it."

"That is a shame," she said about Vincent's death. "He was really nice and he never bothered nobody. I just didn't think it was fair."

Chapter 25

# THE COPS: "HE SHOULDN'T HAVE DONE IT"

Michael Gardenhire was sitting by the window of the McDonald's, eating a cheeseburger. Although he was dressed in gym shoes, blue jeans, and a plain shirt, he was also wearing his gun holster. An experienced police officer with the Highland Park Police Department for the past decade, he also worked part time as a security guard at the local McDonald's, along with Officer Morris Cotton.

As he was eating, Gardenhire noticed a commotion outside. He looked out the window to see Vincent Chin struggling to break loose from Michael Nitz, who was holding him in a bear hug as Ronald Ebens approached them with a bat. When Vincent finally broke free and ran into the middle of Woodward Avenue, he tripped and fell.

"Mr. Ebens was standing over him with the baseball bat striking him in the head," Gardenhire testified on the second day of the trial.

When defense attorney Frank Eaman asked if he had heard any racist or ethnic slurs from Ebens, Gardenhire said no. He confirmed that Ebens and Nitz had been drinking but emphasized that "they weren't in a drunken state. They knew what they were doing."

When prosecutor Amy Hay questioned Gardenhire, she handed him the actual baseball bat used to kill Vincent. She asked him to leave the witness stand and stand in the middle of the courtroom to demonstrate how he saw Ebens swing the bat.

"Just like you hit a golf ball," Gardenhire said, clutching the bat with both hands. "He had it like this. He was standing over him and just hit him in the top of his head." The police officer then swung the bat in a full arc.

"How many swings did you see?" Hay asked.

"Four," Gardenhire said.

"Thank you," Hay said. "You may resume the stand."

Gardenhire continued with his testimony. He explained how he held up his police ID badge and gun. "I instructed him to drop the bat and he started walking toward me," he said.

Gardenhire pulled the hammer back on his gun. "I instructed him a second time to drop the bat, and that's when he gave the baseball bat to me." He ordered Ebens and Nitz to sit at the curb, where he then read them their Miranda rights.

While Officer Cotton stood guard over the men, Gardenhire returned to the middle of street where Vincent still lay faceup on the pavement. He heard Vincent moan and say something in Chinese to his friend Jimmy Choi, who was holding him in his arms. "He was saying something, but I didn't understand what it was being said," he said.

But Gardenhire had no problem understanding what Ebens was saying.

"The older gentleman said, 'He shouldn't have done it, he shouldn't have done it' speaking of Mr. Chin," he said. "Then

I instructed him not to say anything else. I just told him to remain silent."

. . .

According to Larry Robinson, Ebens did not stay quiet for long.

The nineteen-year veteran officer with the Highland Park Police Department was working the late shift when he received a backup call to the McDonald's on Woodward Avenue. When he arrived, Ebens and Nitz were sitting inside the restaurant near the counter with Officer Cotton.

"I told them they were under arrest," Robinson testified. "They were going to be transported to the Highland Park police station. And to say nothing."

Ebens and Nitz nodded their heads yes. Robinson then placed both men in handcuffs. Although Nitz willingly entered the police transport car, Ebens hesitated. "Mr. Ebens did not wish to get in the car," Robinson said. So the police officer helped Ebens inside.

Robinson put the plexiglass screen up between the driver and passenger's seats. During the drive, Ebens kept talking. Robinson noticed Ebens had "glassy eyes" and an "odor of alcohol." He told the jury that Ebens swore a lot and was "very mad, very upset."

Then Robinson said he overheard Ebens tell his stepson, "Well, Mike we got that," but couldn't hear anything beyond that.

"I immediately stopped the scout car and told both of them again to say nothing, that they were under arrest," Robinson said.

. . .

Morris Cotton was in the middle of helping start a customer's stalled car with jumper cables.

The twenty-four-year-old rookie police officer was moonlighting that Saturday night as a plainclothes security guard along with fellow officer Michael Gardenhire. As he shut the car hood, someone shouted, "They are fighting! They are fighting!"

Just then, Gardenhire rushed past Cotton, his gun drawn. Cotton followed him over to the middle of the street. He saw Ebens striking Vincent Chin repeatedly with a baseball bat in "a heat of rage."

Hay also had Cotton step down from the stand and demonstrate what he saw Ebens do with the bat. "The swings were actually full swings, as if he were maybe trying to get a home run," Cotton said. "It was another swing coming right across the back of his head and you could hear the connection like you were hitting something solid."

After Ebens surrendered, Cotton knelt by Vincent's side. He noticed blood clots seeping from the back of Vincent's head. Despite his severe injuries, Vincent leaned on one elbow, trying to get up. As he staggered back, Cotton held on to him. "Stay," he told Vincent.

Just then, he heard Jimmy Choi shouting at Ebens across the street by the curb. Cotton worried that another fight might break out. He approached them while Gardenhire remained with Vincent.

"We are not going to have this," Cotton told the men. He ordered Choi to stay with Vincent until the ambulance arrived.

Meanwhile Ebens threw up his hands, his eyes glassy. "I didn't mean it," he told Cotton. "I am sorry."

He grabbed his stepson's head and turned it around so Cotton could see his injury. "Look what he did to my son," he said, mentioning the fight that had happened earlier at the club. "He busted his head open with a chair. I didn't do anything wrong. Why are you arresting me?"

"He said to me that that was a fair fight," Cotton concluded. "He stated it was fair fight."

Chapter 26

# THE EYEWITNESSES: "GOVERNMENT EXHIBIT NO. 14"

**N**o baseball bat.

The defense team for Ronald Ebens and Michael Nitz wanted to prohibit the bat—also known as Government Exhibit No. 14—from being used as evidence during the trial.

"The baseball bat has been something of a media symbol," defense attorney David Lawson argued, saying he felt it could unfairly influence the jury's decision.

But prosecutor Theodore Merritt felt the visual demonstration was necessary. "It's clear that the bat was used as the instrument of death," he said. "It's a lot easier to show someone, then to try and explain that 'Well I saw him do this. . . and that.' The visual demonstration . . . would have important relevance to the jury in determining what force was used, how many strokes were delivered, or whatever they saw."

Judge Taylor agreed with Merritt, saying visual demonstrations with the bat would be of "crucial importance" to the jury to show Ronald Ebens's mental state. But she warned that "the bat will not be waved around and banged around in the courtroom."

But during the testimonies of the eyewitnesses who saw the baseball bat wielded by Ebens at McDonald's, the judge's warning proved to be more prophetic than she had imagined.

• • •

Keith Reid, sixteen, and Donald Wiggins, fifteen, had stopped by the McDonald's after a pickup game of basketball. They sat at the window, eating their burgers, when Reid noticed "two Chinese guys" walk by. "They kept looking back," he said.

As the two men sat down outside on the curb of the McDonald's, Reid returned to eating his food. He didn't notice anything else until a car pulled up with its lights turned off in the Ivanhoe shopping center parking lot next to the McDonald's. He testified that he saw "two white Caucasian people and one Black guy," whom he recognized as Jimmy Perry from his high school. He noticed the older white man held a baseball bat in his hands.

"And what did you see happen next?" asked Merritt.

"I seen him go through the trees and in the McDonald's on the side and hit the Chinese guy in the back of the head with the baseball bat."

Donald Wiggins also confirmed he saw Ebens strike Vincent more than once with the baseball bat.

"I seen the younger guy go past the window, run past the window," Wiggins said. "Then I heard like a baseball ball hit."

Wiggins motioned for his friends to look out the window. "A man is gettin' beat with a baseball bat!" he shouted.

Like Keith Reid, Wiggins also recognized Jimmy Perry, who had emerged from the car with Ebens and Nitz. He said that he overheard Perry tell Officer Morris Cotton "that the older guy paid him $20 to find Chin."

"He didn't use 'Chin' did he?" Merritt asked.

"No."

"What did he say?"

"Chinese."

. . .

When Ronald Ebens and Michael Nitz emerged from the car outside the McDonald's, they weren't the only ones. They had picked up a passenger—Jimmy Perry.

The nineteen-year-old Perry was walking down Woodward, headed for his girlfriend's house, when a green Plymouth Horizon pulled up next to him. He saw an older white man driving the car with a younger white man in the passenger seat, blood pouring down his face. He also smelled liquor on them.

Perry immediately asked if they needed help. "Do y'all want to go to the hospital?" he asked. "It's right around the corner."

"We're looking for two Chinese guys," the older man allegedly said, according to Perry.

Perry, now twenty-one, testified that just a few minutes earlier, he had seen a "Chinese guy" standing outside a bank farther up the street.

But Perry hesitated when Ebens asked him about Vincent's whereabouts. It was rare to see white people in this part of Highland Park, much less two Chinese guys. *Something was up.*

He was about to walk away when Nitz allegedly pulled a twenty-dollar bill from his wallet and waved it at him.

"The younger guy offered me $20 to help them catch the

Chinese guy," Perry told the jury. He got into the car and sat in the back seat.

"Did you want to go to the hospital?" Perry asked Ebens, letting them know that Detroit Orthopedic Hospital was nearby on Highland and Third.

Although Ebens said yes, Perry testified, "I found out that he didn't really want to go."

As the car crawled along Woodward Avenue, Perry noticed they were driving at only about ten miles per hour when the speed limit was thirty. "They were talking about catching this Chinese guy and busting his head when they catch him," he said.

As they drove by the McDonald's, the three men spotted two Chinese men. Perry recalled Ebens saying, "There they go," and his stepson replying, "We are going to get them."

Nitz turned the car lights off as they parked next to the McDonald's in the Ivanhoe shopping center lot. As they got out of the car, Perry recognized police officer Morris Cotton.

Cotton looked over and recognized Perry as well—the two had gone to Highland Park High School together and were both on the wrestling team. Perry decided to warn Ebens and Nitz about Cotton being a police officer because he wasn't wearing his uniform.

"I told them that the police was in the parking lot," Perry said.

"Was there any response?" prosecutor Merritt asked.

"Yeah," Perry said. "They said, 'Fuck the police.'"

Perry described how both men ambushed Vincent Chin and Jimmy Choi, who didn't see them approaching. "They snuck behind them. The father went to the right, the son went to the left. Behind the truck, under the tree." Perry got out of the car and walked over to Officer Cotton.

As Perry approached Cotton, Ebens swung the bat and hit Vincent. Perry watched as Vincent raced out into the middle of Woodward Avenue, Nitz right behind him. He described how he saw Nitz grab Vincent to prevent him from escaping, and how Ebens hit him several more times in the head and body.

That's when Cotton and Officer Gardenhire, also in plain clothes, rushed out with their guns drawn. "Freeze!" they shouted.

"Did the older guy stop hitting him right away?" Merritt asked.

"No, not at first," Perry answered. "He hit him like one more time, then he stopped."

During the cross-examination, defense attorney Frank Eaman asked Perry to demonstrate how he saw Ebens swing the bat.

"Do I have to?" Perry asked, clearly uncomfortable.

"You may leave the witness stand," Eaman said.

Again, Perry hesitated. "Do I have to?"

"You don't remember how he was hit while he was on the ground?"

"Yes, I do."

"Can you show us?"

"No."

"Is there a reason why you cannot?" Eaman asked.

"I just don't," Perry said.

But Judge Taylor ordered Perry to comply with the lawyer's request. "Well, if it is a matter of your simply not wanting to do it, go ahead and respond to the question and show him, please," she said.

A very reluctant Perry left the stand. "Like this," he said as he swung the baseball bat in the air. He described how he saw Ebens hit Vincent "five or six times" in the head and shoulder.

After Ebens and Nitz were arrested, Perry testified that Cotton came over to question him. "Jimmy, what is going on, man?" Cotton asked. "What is happening?"

"I didn't do nothing," Perry immediately said, afraid his high school classmate would think that he was somehow involved in the attack. "I didn't have anything to do with them."

. . .

If only the Detroit Tigers had beat the Milwaukee Brewers on June 19, 1982, then perhaps Ronald Ebens and Michael Nitz would have been at that game instead of at the Fancy Pants Club. They had been driving toward Tiger Stadium when they heard on the radio that the Brewers were decimating the Tigers by 10 to 3. They turned around and impulsively decided to check out the club for last call before heading home.

Baseball fan Harold Fitzgerald of Roseville was actually at the game. Disappointed by the blowout, he left the stadium early, before the game ended.

As Fitzgerald drove down Woodward Avenue, he saw two people standing in the middle of the street. "This one person had his hands up around his head trying to ward off blows," he said. "And as I got closer, I saw that it was a baseball bat and he was hitting him around the head. The man that was being hit was smaller than the person with the bat. He was hitting him rather severely with that baseball bat." Fitzgerald pulled the car over and stepped out.

Fitzgerald confirmed that he saw Ebens hit Vincent four

times. "He slumped down to the ground and he was kind of twitching and he hit him a couple of good licks again on the head area. Those blows were around the skull."

Fitzgerald did not stay long enough to give his name to the police and offer any witness testimony. He explained that there was a "tremendous amount" of people outside the McDonald's who also witnessed the beating. "I just figured that my particular entry into this case was really wasn't worthwhile at that particular time."

But several months later, Fitzgerald read the newspaper article about how Judge Kaufman had given Ebens and Nitz three years' probation and a fine for the manslaughter of Vincent Chin. He recognized Vincent's photo and was troubled by the unusually lenient sentence.

Fitzgerald had just gone to church earlier that week, where his minister had coincidentally delivered a sermon on the importance of civic duty. "Our minister had been talking about our civic responsibilities, and I was pretty upset by it." He remembered seeing the name of Lily Chin's lawyer in the article. "So I called up Ms. Chan and I made an appointment for a couple days later, if she wanted to talk to me."

Fitzgerald, however, did not realize calling Liza Chan would lead to his being called to testify at the trial. And he did not realize his testimony would make newspaper headlines the next day.

"Now, would you step down, Mr. Fitzgerald," Merritt said. "Grab that baseball bat there, and just show when the man was laying on the ground, how the other man was swinging the bat."

"He did hit him very, very strongly while the man was laying down," Fitzgerald explained as he stepped out of the witness stand. "And he hit very, very, very hard, he took a very good swing of the bat at him each time."

Fitzgerald picked up the bat and swung it in the air, demonstrating exactly how hard he had seen Ebens swing the bat.

As he smashed the bat against the floor, the force he used caused the bat to split in half. Everyone in the courtroom gasped.

Judge Taylor halted proceedings, ordering the room to settle down.

Fitzgerald held up both pieces of the broken bat in his hands.

Chapter 27

# THE MOTHER:
# "MY NAME IS LILY CHIN"

"My name is Lily Chin."

These were not the words the defense team wanted to hear. Before Lily took the stand, on June 15, the third day of the trial, Ebens's attorneys had fought to exclude her as a witness.

"I suggest that the only purpose for Mrs. Chin to testify is to evoke the jurors' sympathy," David Lawson explained to Judge Taylor.

Defense attorney Frank Eaman agreed. "Mrs. Chin has become a symbol of the mother of the victim of the crime," he added. "Some jurors did identify with her. . . . Her presence will cause in the jurors' minds and recollections of some of the most inflammatory publicity."

But prosecutor Theodore Merritt protested, saying Lily Chin's presence was not a publicity stunt. Her testimony was crucial.

"She saw the victim not several hours before his death . . ." he argued. Unlike Vincent's friends, who had been drinking, Lily was sober and could therefore give a "fair evaluation" of Vincent's physical condition before he left for the Fancy Pants Club. He said the defense was trying to build a case that "everyone was so drunk that this just got out of hand. And we seriously dispute that, Your Honor. And the amount of drinking that did take place, while it may have led to someone being slightly intoxicated, it certainly was not the drunken brawl that the defense we imagine would try to portray."

Judge Taylor agreed with the prosecution. "The mother's testimony will not be excluded," she ruled. "Her testimony apparently will be relevant on several subjects. To the sobriety of her son and his drunkenness as initiated. The fact that he had not been drunk all day is a relevant fact. And that she saw him sober when he went out for the evening is relevant."

. . .

Six minutes.

That was how long Lily's testimony lasted. Although she had an interpreter with her, Lily chose to answer the questions herself.

Theodore Merritt was the only one to ask Lily questions. The defense attorneys declined to cross-examine her.

During her testimony, Lily told the jury that she came to America in 1948 and became a citizen six years later. She and her husband had adopted Vincent in 1961. He became a citizen at age ten. Her husband passed away from kidney disease one year before their son was killed.

Merritt asked if Vincent had ever gotten into fights in the past. "No, he never fight for someone, no," Lily said.

"Now, I want to ask you about June 19, 1982," Merritt said.

Lily was ready for this. "Okay," she said.

"What did your son do after he got up that day?"

Lily described her son's Saturday. How he went to the jewelry store in the morning to get his wedding band fitted. How he watched a little TV in the afternoon before heading off for his part-time waiter shift at the Golden Star Restaurant. She confirmed that he got off early from his shift and returned home at seven o'clock.

Vincent told Lily that he was going out that night. She looked out the window to see his friend Gary Koivu waiting in the car. "I asked him, 'Where you go?'" she said. "And he said that he would go to the bar, maybe to the club."

"Did you say anything to him?" Merritt asked.

"I tell him, 'Don't go to the bar anymore.'"

"Did he say anything back?"

"He said, 'Ma, don't worry. This is the last time.'"

"Did he look drunk to you? Red in the face?" Merritt asked.

"No," Lily said. She testified that Vincent was sober and did not smell of alcohol.

Merritt asked Lily one last question. "When was the next time you saw your son?"

"The next day in the morning," Lily said. "In the hospital."

Chapter 28

# THE STEPSON:
# "IT HAPPENED
# SO QUICKLY"

If only Michael Nitz and his girlfriend had not gotten into a fight.

If only the Detroit Tigers had won their game against the Milwaukee Brewers.

If only there had been no baseball bat in the trunk of Michael Nitz's car.

June 19, 1982, started out like any other Saturday. Nitz woke up at six-thirty a.m. to work at the Royal Oak branch of Art Van Furniture, where he managed their delivery system. He had been working there part time for the past three years after being laid off from Chrysler.

Nitz delivered a few pieces to customers before clocking out at four p.m. He met his stepfather, Ronald Ebens, his mother, Juanita, and his girlfriend at the Eaton Lounge, located about a half mile from their house, for an early dinner. They ate hamburgers, played shuffleboard, and shared a couple of pitchers of beer. He testified at the trial that he drank six or seven glasses of beer while they were there from six to seven p.m.

Nitz, his mother, and his girlfriend left while his stepfather stayed behind to hang out and talk with the bartender. At home, Nitz and his girlfriend got into an argument and she left.

When Ebens finally returned, he noticed his stepson looked upset. Nitz confessed that he and his girlfriend were mad at each other. "Ron, let's go," Nitz said impulsively. "Let's get out of here."

Nitz drove the two of them in his Plymouth Horizon car. They stopped at a party store to buy a six-pack of beer. Nitz downed a bottle before they drove to Ira's, a neighborhood bar. They stayed for about forty-five minutes, where Nitz drank another beer while they played a quick game of pool.

Nitz, however, was still restless and irritated by the fight with his girlfriend.

To cheer up his stepson, Ebens suggested they check out the Detroit Tigers game that was happening that night. But when they heard the Tigers were losing 10–3 to the Milwaukee Brewers, they decided to try to find another bar for last call before heading home.

As they drove down Davison in Highland Park toward their house, Ebens suggested they go to the Fancy Pants Club. "Ron mentioned to me there was a topless place he had been to before, and he said let's go there," Nitz remembered. "So we went there."

• • •

Nitz told Siefer and the jury that he and his stepfather both paid the ten-dollar entrance fee and found two seats by the stage. Nitz nodded politely to the man sitting across the stage from them. "I more or less said hello, what's going on? How are you doing?" he said.

That man was Bob Siroskey.

Siefer then asked Nitz about his stepfather's use of vulgar language in casual conversation. "Did you see Ron swear often?"

"Yes," Nitz replied, confirming that it wasn't uncommon for Ebens to jokingly refer even to his own stepson as "a little fucker." He explained that he had worked on the line with his stepfather at the Lynch Road Assembly Chrysler Plant, where swearing was customary.

"Is that the type of language used in the factory?" Siefer asked.

"All the time."

And that language was also spoken outside the factory. "Did you hear that language around your house?" Siefer asked.

"Yes," Nitz said.

Siefer wondered if Nitz had ever discussed the current economic climate of the auto industry with his stepfather. "Did you discuss foreign cars or anything?"

"No."

"Did you and Ron ever talk about how terrible it was to be laid off?"

"No, not at all," Nitz said. "He wasn't laid off. And I wasn't working for the auto industry." He explained he had worked for three years at the plant before being laid off.

"Did that bother you?" Siefer asked.

"No," Nitz said. "It gave me a chance to go back to school, time to go to school." He also confirmed that he was collecting unemployment checks.

Nitz then testified that, out of nowhere, Vincent Chin attacked his stepfather. "He came around the edge of the stage and came up running to Ron and hit Ron right in the mouth," he said. "I got up and pushed him away from Ron." Nitz then stumbled over a chair and found himself behind Vincent. He denied ever picking up a chair and swinging it at Vincent.

The next thing Nitz knew, Gary Reid, the club's doorman, had grabbed him and was pulling him toward the other side of the club. "He said I was bleeding," Nitz said.

"Did you realize you were bleeding?" Siefer asked.

"Not until I looked down and blood was dripping on my tennis shoes," Nitz recalled, adding that his left arm was starting to swell. "I couldn't straighten it up. I was hit by a chair. My back was to Ron and Chin. I really didn't see what was going on."

After the fight broke up, Nitz and his stepfather went to the bathroom to clean up. And that was when Bob Siroskey stopped by to talk to them, he claimed. "He said he was really sorry the way his friend had acted, and that he had a lot to drink and they were just out having a good time," Nitz remembered.

Still fuming, Nitz and Ebens walked out to the parking lot where Vincent immediately challenged them to another fight.

At this point, Nitz became not just angry but scared. He and his father were outnumbered by Vincent and his friends. "I was just hit over the head with a chair, and there were more of them than there were of us," he explained. "I went to my car and opened up my hatchback and took the baseball bat out."

"Did you get into fights a lot?" Siefer asked.

"No."

"When was the last time you were in a fight?"

"Back in the seventh grade."

"Have you ever used a bat in a fight before?"

"No," Nitz answered, saying that his stepfather took the bat from him and chased Vincent and later Jimmy Choi down the street.

Later, as Nitz and Ebens drove to find a nearby hospital, they spotted Jimmy Perry walking down the street. He contested Perry's earlier testimony, saying he never asked him about "two Chinese guys."

"I asked him where the hospital was," Nitz said.

"Did you offer Jimmy Perry $20 to help you catch some Chinese guys?" Siefer asked.

"No," Nitz said.

But Nitz did remember what happened when they drove by the McDonald's on Woodward Avenue and spotted Vincent and Choi sitting outside. "Ron told me to pull over," he said.

"Why didn't you keep on going to the hospital?" Siefer asked.

"I was still angry," Nitz admitted. "I was bleeding and everything else and they were just sitting there, laughing the whole time and it just got me really upset."

Nitz admitted to grabbing Vincent as he ran toward him. After Vincent fell, Nitz confirmed seeing his stepfather hit him in the head twice. But although Nitz wanted revenge on Vincent Chin, he didn't want him dead.

"Did you want to see Mr. Chin hit in the head?" Siefer asked.

"No," Nitz said.

"Did you want to see Mr. Chin killed?"

"No."

"Were you angry?" Siefer pressed.

"Yeah, I was angry at that point," Nitz admitted.

"Did you want to get back at him?"

"For what he did to me, yes."

. . .

Siefer then had Nitz look over Government Exhibit No. 20— the original statement he had written and signed for the Highland Park Police station on the night of June 19, 1982. She asked if one particular sentence, *"I don't remember what else happened,"* was "accurate." When he said yes, Siefer asked, "Why didn't you write down what happened?"

"I just wanted to get out of there," Nitz admitted. "I was hurt. My head really hurt, and I just didn't want to be at the police station anymore, and Ron had told me not to say anything to anybody. And I just really didn't want to tell anymore."

"So that is why you wrote down I don't remember."

"Right."

"But in fact, you did remember."

"Yes."

Siefer ended her questioning of Nitz by asking him if he was racist. "At any time or point did you want to get back at Mr. Chin because he was enjoying the accommodations of the Fancy Pants?"

"No," Nitz insisted.

"Did you and Ron agree to injure Vincent Chin because he was Chinese?"

"No."

"Did you ever call Vincent Chin a Chink or a Nip?"

"No."

"Anyone else ever call him a Chink or a Nip?"

"No."

"Why were you angry?" Siefer asked.

"Because he hit me over the head with a chair," Nitz said.

"That is the reason you wanted to get back at him?"

"Yes."

And with that last answer, Siefer turned to Judge Taylor and said, "I have nothing further."

· · ·

Although Michael Nitz insisted racism played no part in the killing of Vincent Chin, prosecutor Theodore Merritt was not convinced. During his cross-examination, Merritt grilled Nitz about the anti-Asian sentiments in the Detroit auto industry against Japanese import cars.

"At the time, didn't you have a fear of losing your job because of the foreign car imports?" he asked, referring to the impending layoffs at Chrysler, where Nitz used to work.

Nitz explained he was more concerned about the competition from Canadian import cars than from Japanese cars. "Because of Canadian cars they were building. They were building the same model in Canada that we were building here, and they put us out of work because their cars were selling and ours weren't."

"I see," Merritt said. "So it was just the Canadian foreign cars involved."

"Yes."

The defense had suggested Vincent Chin's friends had conspired with lawyer Liza Chan to "get their stories straight" before the trial, and now Merritt accused Nitz of the same conspiracy with his stepfather. "This event happened two years ago and since that time, you have gotten together with Ronald

Ebens and tried to jog each other's memories about that night, haven't you?" he asked.

"We have discussed it," Nitz admitted.

"And you've compared your stories."

"Not compared," Nitz objected.

Merritt clarified his question. "But you talked about the events of that night."

Nitz could not deny this. "Yes."

"You remembered something and he remembered something and you put it together," Merritt suggested.

"No," Nitz said. He insisted that he didn't remember many details about the fight in the Fancy Pants Club because he hadn't been paying attention.

Merritt questioned Nitz's testimony that as he and Ebens drove down Woodward Avenue after the fight, they were only looking for a hospital. "You say you wanted to go to the hospital but you took your time to chase two Chinese guys around Highland Park first, didn't you?"

"No," Nitz said.

Merritt still didn't buy it. If racism didn't play a part in their attack on Vincent Chin, then why didn't Nitz or Ebens chase after Gary Koivu, too?

"He didn't have anything to do with the fight," Nitz said.

"Neither did Mr. Choi," Merritt shot back.

"At that point I thought he did," Nitz explained. "There was someone else in the fight, and I assumed it was him."

"You assumed it was the other Chinese guy, is that what your testimony is?" Merritt asked.

"Yes," Nitz admitted.

Nitz also confirmed that as they were driving down Woodward Avenue, his temper had cooled.

"So you weren't really so angry anymore, is that what you're saying?" Merritt asked.

"I wasn't, no," Nitz said.

But Merritt wondered if the mere sight of two Asian American men laughing triggered any internalized racism from Nitz. "It was just the sight of seeing them in front of McDonald's that enraged you again, is that right?"

Although Nitz said the sight of Vincent and Choi did trigger his temper, he said it was simply due to his memory of Vincent hitting him over the head with a chair. "When Ron said, 'There they are,' it started all over again in my mind."

Nitz told the jury he didn't remember much about what happened after they pulled the car over and attacked Vincent.

Merritt, however, was quick to remind Nitz that he had done nothing to stop his stepfather from hurting Vincent. "While he was hitting him in the head with a baseball bat, you just stood and watched."

"It happened so quickly," Nitz said.

"Or your job was done—you had already caught him," Merritt snapped.

Nitz was confused. "I'm sorry, my job is done?"

Merritt suggested that perhaps Nitz had no sympathy for Vincent. "Now, after Vincent Chin was lying on the ground, he was bleeding, wasn't he?"

"Yes," Nitz said.

"There was a lot of blood."

"Yes, yes."

"Mr. Nitz, you knew you were in trouble at that point, didn't you?"

"No, I didn't."

But Merritt persisted. "You knew the Chinese man you had been hunting for the last half hour was now lying there in mortal condition, didn't you?"

"No," Nitz protested.

"You knew you helped put him there, didn't you?"

"No."

Merritt turned to Judge Taylor. "That is all I have, Your Honor."

The judge addressed Nitz. "You may be excused."

Nitz left the witness stand. He had told his side of the story to the court.

Chapter 29

# THE FATHER: "SOMETHING JUST SNAPPED"

Ronald Ebens didn't have to testify at his own trial. He could have stayed silent the whole time.

"Mr. Ebens has a right to remain silent and not testify," defense attorney David Lawson explained to the jury. "But he will testify and take the witness stand and tell you as best as he remembers the events of June 19, 1982. The tragic day in his life as well as in the life of Mr. Chin."

So on June 19, 1984, exactly two years from the day he met Vincent Chin, Ronald Ebens took the stand.

. . .

Ronald Ebens could drink.

It wasn't unusual for Ebens to grab a beer with co-workers after a long shift at the Lynch Road Assembly plant.

So around three-thirty p.m. on June 19, 1982, Ebens wrapped up his shift at the plant and stopped by a nearby bar for a beer with the guys he worked with. He then drove to a second bar to meet his stepson, Michael Nitz, his wife, Juanita, and Nitz's girlfriend.

On the witness stand, Ebens testified that he drank about six big glasses of beer at the start of the night. The bartender then drove Ebens home. "He had a new Corvette, okay, and I wanted a ride in it," he said. "It was just that simple."

By the time he and Nitz arrived at the Fancy Pants Club later that evening, Ebens had drunk a few more beers. They settled down in front of the stage as Angela "Starlene" Rudolph was dancing. Ebens testified that he heard people insulting her. "I remember comments coming from across the stage directed at her and telling her words what, words to the effect of what a crummy dancer she was and like that, okay," he told the jury.

Ebens shouted words of encouragement to Rudolph. "Don't worry about those guys," he told her. "Show 'em what a good dancer is."

"Those guys" were Vincent Chin and his bachelor party friends, Gary Koivu, Bob Siroskey, and Jimmy Choi.

· · ·

Defense attorney Frank Eaman asked Ebens if he swore often and said words like *fucker* in casual conversation. "Do you or have you ever used words like that before?"

"Many times," Ebens said

"Is that language unusual to you?"

"No, it isn't."

"When you use those words, was it your intention to insult anyone or provoke anyone?"

"No," Ebens said. To him, his R-rated language was how he expressed himself.

"What happened next?" Eaman asked.

"I really didn't pay much attention to him," Ebens replied. "I was watching the dancer. He proceeded around, and I guess the next time I was really aware of him was when I turned around and he was standing directly in front of me."

"Were any words exchanged?" Eaman asked.

"Not that I remember."

"What happened then?"

"He punched me," Ebens said. He testified that Vincent surprised him by punching him directly in the mouth with his fist while Ebens sat in his chair.

"Up to that point, did you call him, or anyone else for that matter, the word 'Chink'?" Eaman asked.

"No," Ebens insisted.

After that, Ebens claimed he did not remember much else. "Nothing really very clear in the next—it was just a melee broke out. I don't really—just a lot of people. I don't remember hitting anybody."

After the fight broke up, Ebens confirmed what Nitz had testified earlier—that they both had gone to the bathroom to clean up their injuries, where Bob Siroskey showed up.

Although Siroskey denied apologizing to Ebens and Nitz during his testimony, Ebens claimed the opposite. "He started right out apologizing for Vincent's behavior saying he had been drinking and was drunk," he said. "And he said he was sorry and he apologized about three different times, back to back."

When Ebens and Nitz walked out to the parking lot, Vincent,

Koivu, and Choi were still out there, waiting for their friend Siroskey.

"Come on, let's fight some more," Vincent shouted, according to Ebens.

"Were those his exact words?" Eaman asked.

"Words to that effect," Ebens said.

Ebens grabbed the baseball bat from his son and charged toward Vincent, who ran away.

Unable to catch Vincent, Ebens returned to the parking lot. That was when they spotted Jimmy Choi standing nearby. "There is that little fucker again," Nitz said, throwing an empty glass bottle at Choi.

Choi ducked and ran off. The bottle smashed against the brick wall of the building, shattering everywhere.

Ebens then confronted Koivu and Siroskey, who had just arrived in the parking lot.

"You and Siroskey exchanged words?" Eaman asked.

"Yes," Ebens said.

"Were they friendly words?"

"No." Ebens explained that his rage had taken over. "Pumped, the adrenaline pumped. I was going to push the rear glass of their car in, I was really pumped."

But Nitz stopped his stepfather from damaging Koivu's car window. "Ron, he didn't do anything," he reminded Ebens.

Ebens and Nitz then got in the car and headed down Woodward Avenue. Ebens confirmed that they then saw Jimmy Perry walking down the street.

Perry saw Ebens holding the bat in the back seat of the car. "What is your problem?" he asked.

"I said that I had been hit in the mouth and my son's head had been split, and I was looking for two Orientals," Ebens said.

Defense attorney David Lawson then took over the examination with Ebens. "Why were you looking for him?" Lawson asked Ebens about their attempts to locate Vincent.

"I was angry," Ebens said.

"What were you going to do?" Lawson asked.

Even though both Ebens and Nitz insisted they really wanted to find a hospital, Ebens admitted that revenge was still on his mind. "I was going to inflict pain," he said.

"You were going to hurt him?"

"Yes."

· · ·

Defense attorney Lawson asked Ebens how he felt when he and Nitz spotted Vincent and Choi outside the McDonald's.

"Angry."

"Why?"

"Same reason, I guess," Ebens answered. "The man had sucker punched me; and he was responsible for splitting Mike's head open. I was just angry."

Even though Perry warned Ebens that he recognized two plainclothes police officers at the McDonald's, Ebens didn't care. He charged at Vincent and Choi, still clutching the baseball bat. "You son of bitches," he yelled.

"Then what did you do?" Lawson asked.

"They jumped up and started to run, and at that time, I was on top of him and took a swing and caught Chin in the arm."

Ebens then described how Nitz had grabbed Vincent in a bear hug. Vincent fought back. And that was when Ebens flashed back to the image of a chair slamming against Nitz's head in the club earlier that night. Ebens, often described by family and friends as fierce and protective, didn't want his stepson to get hurt again.

"When I seen him scuffling, it just flashed in my mind, *'He is going to get hurt again,'*" Ebens explained. "I started toward him, and it was almost audible to me, and something just snapped. I don't remember from there on what did happen."

"Did you hit Mr. Chin?" Lawson asked.

"Not that I remember," Ebens said. And then he started to cry.

The courtroom was silent for several minutes as Ebens wept on the stand.

Lawson finally spoke. "Were you trying to kill Mr. Chin, Mr. Ebens?"

"No," Ebens managed to say between sobs.

"Do you remember what you were trying to do?"

Ebens tried to regain his composure. "No, I don't," he said.

"What is the next thing that you do remember?" Lawson asked.

"I remember looking up and seeing a revolver [pointed] at me and a man saying drop the bat."

"Did you do that?"

"Yes."

Then Lawson asked the question at the heart of the trial: "Mr. Ebens, did you do what you did to Vincent Chin on June 19, 1982, because of his race?"

"No," Ebens said, still weeping.

"Why did you do it?" Lawson asked.

"I never meant to kill him, I know that," Ebens said. "I was just angry over what happened. It was the only reason. Too much to drink and too dumb to think."

Lawson turned to Judge Taylor. "No further questions."

• • •

Prosecutor Theodore Merritt still had questions for Ronald Ebens.

Many more questions.

"You spent seventeen years at Chrysler, and a lot of those years were good years economically," Merritt said.

"Yes," Ebens replied.

"Some were not so good, right?"

"Yes."

"And in the bad times, didn't you share the general concern about Japanese imports?"

Ebens seemed confused by the question. "What is the general concern?"

Merritt spelled it out for him. "Have you ever had any problems with the effects that the Japanese import cars were having on the American automobile industry?"

"I don't follow your reasons," Ebens said.

"I'm asking you, did you have or did you ever have any concern about the effects that Japanese import cars were having on the American automobile industry?"

"Definitely, certainly."

"On June 19th at the Fancy Pants, weren't you talking about foreign cars?" Merritt asked.

"No," Ebens said.

"Didn't you say, 'It's because of you motherfuckers that we're out of work'?" Merritt asked.

"I don't remember," Ebens said.

Although Ebens claimed he could not remember exactly what he shouted at Vincent, he insisted he never said anything racist.

"You definitely know you didn't say 'Chink'?" Merritt asked.

"Yes, I do," Ebens said.

When Merritt wondered if Ebens was just too drunk to remember if he had said any racist slurs, Ebens immediately protested, saying he would never say those words.

"No, I was not so drunk," he said.

"Is that because you would never use such nasty language, Mr. Ebens?"

"I just know what words I have used in my life, that is all."

As for Jimmy Perry's testimony, Ebens denied to Merritt that they had offered him twenty dollars to help them find Vincent Chin.

"Jimmy Perry just decided to hop into your car is that it?" Merritt asked.

"Jimmy Perry offered to show us where the hospital was," Ebens answered.

"Just out of the goodness of his heart?"

"You will have to ask Jimmy Perry," Ebens said.

• • •

Throughout the cross-examination, Ebens repeated that he had been too black-out drunk to remember many—if any—details about beating Vincent Chin.

So Merritt decided to jog Ebens's memory by holding up the baseball bat.

"Let me ask you something," the prosecutor said. "Let me show you Government Exhibit 14, first of all. Is that the bat that you used to kill Vincent Chin?"

"I can't tell that," Ebens said. "I don't know."

"Could you show us how you were holding the bat when you asked Gary and Bob, 'Where is your friend?' " Merritt pressed.

Again, Ebens repeated himself. "I can't tell that, I don't know."

"Now when you were in the car, saying, 'When I catch these Chinese guys, I am going to bust their heads,' you hadn't blacked out yet?"

"I never said that," Ebens said.

"When you found Vincent Chin and said, 'There they are,' you hadn't blacked out yet?"

"I don't know."

But Merritt drilled question after question to Ebens. Had he sneaked up behind Vincent and Jimmy Choi to ambush them? Had he purposely hit Vincent in the leg to prevent him from running away? Did he remember hitting him in the chest, arm, and face?

Ebens answered "No" to Merritt's barrage of questions.

"You can't remember hitting him in the head as he lay there on the ground?" Merritt asked.

"No, I can't," Ebens said.

Merritt remained skeptical. "You can't remember telling the police that you are sorry, but look at what he did to my son, you do remember that, don't you?"

"Not really."

"You had the presence of mind to think of an explanation, didn't you?"

"I don't remember being asked for an explanation."

Merritt held the baseball bat directly in front of Ebens, offering it to him. "Mr. Ebens, maybe if you would take the bat, maybe it would bring something back."

Defense attorney David Lawson immediately objected. "I think we have had enough ramifications with the bat and I think it is meant to harass the witness," Lawson said.

Judge Taylor agreed. "Ask a question," she admonished Merritt. "It wasn't a question."

"Yes, all right," Merritt agreed. He put the bat down and faced the defendant. "Mr. Ebens, have you ever chased a man because of a drunken fight and beat him to death?"

"No, outside of this time, only Vincent Chin."

"And because he looked like Vincent Chin, isn't that right, Mr. Ebens?"

"No, it is not right."

Those were Ebens's final words on the witness stand. There was nothing more he could say.

Now it was up to the jury to decide who was right. Whose story would they believe?

Chapter 30

# THE CLOSING ARGUMENTS: "YOUR HARDEST PART IS STILL AHEAD"

Thirty-six witnesses.

Six lawyers.

Two defendants.

One judge.

One victim.

They all played a part in the trial of *United States v. Ronald Ebens and Michael Nitz.*

On June 26, 1984, the attention shifted to the twelve jurors. The Asian American population of Detroit held its breath, wondering if justice would finally be served.

"The Vincent Chin murder represents for us the destruction of a myth that Asians could work hard, rise above adversity, and get a piece of the American pie," Helen Zia said.

"This was a premeditated murder," declared Benny Wong, eighty-two, who had worked in a Ford Motor plant tool shop for forty-six years. "The two men went and got a baseball bat, and they came back to kill Vincent Chin because they mistook him for Japanese, because they were mad at Japan for flooding this country with automobiles and causing unemployment."

But Ebens and Nitz had many supporters who believed this trial should never have happened in the first place. "This is an out-and-out example of double jeopardy," said a co-worker of Ebens who declined to give his name. "These two men are being tried twice for the same crime."

"The fight could have gone either way," agreed another friend who also spoke anonymously. "There were tempers at both ends. . . . It ended up a tragedy for all three men, the dead man and his killers."

But the people ultimately responsible for the fates of Ronald Ebens and Michael Nitz were the twelve men and women on the jury. For the next three hours, they listened as the prosecution and defense delivered their final closing arguments.

## THE PROSECUTION

Prosecutor Theodore Merritt warned that it was "not easy being a juror."

"You realize that your hardest part is still ahead," he said. "You're going to have to put all of the evidence together to determine what these defendants did to Vincent Chin and why they did it."

During his closing statement, Merritt walked the jury again through the main events which led up to Vincent's death.

According to Merritt, Ebens and Nitz were jealous of Vincent Chin. They were short of cash and found the ten-dollar cover charge at the club expensive while Vincent was extravagantly showering the dancers with four hundred dollars' worth of tips. It was, he said, the ultimate example of white privilege.

"They saw an Oriental acting flamboyant, spending a lot of money," he said. "How do you think Ronald Ebens reacted to that? Was he happy for Vincent Chin's good fortune and his success?" He told the jury that it was "logical" that Ebens would say, "It's because of you little motherfuckers that we're out of work."

"Was he perhaps a little resentful?" Merritt suggested. "As he watched this Oriental enjoying himself, spending more money than he and Michael Nitz could afford to spend on those dancers . . . Ladies and gentlemen, that's the kind of attitude that started this fight."

Merritt did not deny that Vincent Chin was an active participant in this fight. But when the 149-pound twenty-seven-year-old saw Ebens pull a baseball bat out of the car and charge toward him, Vincent ran. "He ran for his life," Merritt said. "Because he knew by the look in Ronald Ebens' eye and that bat that was in his hand that this was more than a barroom fight. . . . He knew that Ebens' bigotry now was armed with a deadly weapon."

Merritt challenged the defense's claim that this fight was caused by "mere anger or desire to get even." He pointed to Ebens chasing Vincent's friend Jimmy Choi when he couldn't catch up to Vincent himself as evidence of racism. "The racial animal inside Ronald Ebens had been unleashed, and now his prey was anything Oriental." He described the chase as a "hunt" for Vincent, "to teach him a lesson."

Although Nitz did not hurt Vincent, Merritt said he was guilty of conspiracy. "Michael Nitz was in for a penny or in for a pound, and he was a conspirator who played an important role in hunting and killing Vincent Chin."

As for the recorded conversation between Liza Chan, Gary Koivu, Bob Siroskey, and Jimmy Choi, Merritt dismissed the defense's claim that this was evidence that Vincent's friends had "got together and made up the whole story to avenge the death of their friend." Instead, he said, the conversation was simply out of due diligence because the killing had happened so long ago. "They got together to try to jog their memory," he said. "These three men are men who honestly told from the stand what they did remember. And they told you when they didn't remember something." He reminded the jury that the friends' testimony was all independently corroborated.

"There was no smoking gun," he said. "The only smoke that was there was put there by the defense."

Merritt wrapped up his closing argument by declaring this was no barroom brawl gone out of control. "This was more than some barroom fight," he said. "This was violent hatred turned loose. This was years of pent-up racial hostilities and rage unleashed. This was a modern-day lynching, but there was a bat instead of a rope."

## THE DEFENSE

Although the prosecution had the burden of proving Ronald Ebens and Michael Nitz guilty, defense attorney Frank Eaman carried a different burden. He was defending the "bad guy." The villain. The man who beat Vincent Chin to death.

But Eaman was not defending what Ronald Ebens did to Vincent Chin—there was no excuse for his violent behavior.

Instead, he was defending *why* Ronald Ebens acted the way he did. Eaman believed this was an ugly case of toxic masculinity, not racism.

"Anger, intoxication, fights over women, let's examine the scene here," he said. "We have a Saturday night in Detroit . . . two men who got angry, a man whose manhood was insulted. This was an extremely volatile situation that had nothing to do with race."

Eaman criticized the American Citizens for Justice for throwing gasoline on a fire that, he said, had already been extinguished. Ebens and Nitz had already been found guilty of a "serious crime"—manslaughter. "Then something happened since then," he said. "Then people got to work, and the fact that Mr. Chin was Asian American, the fact that Mr. Ebens was an auto worker, were facts that were not lost on those fertile imaginations."

The logic behind the accusations of racism were faulty, according to Eaman. "Since when do people in Detroit who work for auto companies translate feelings about imported cars into wanting to beat an Oriental person to death and deny him his right of public accommodation?" he asked. He told the jury that each witness was "straining to inject racism into these events to help in this second prosecution."

It was Vincent Chin himself who proved Ebens was not racist, Eaman claimed. "Perhaps the strongest evidence we've heard were the words of Vincent Chin, that 'Nobody calls me a fucker,'" he explained. "What set Vincent Chin off was being called the obscenities, a motherfucker, a word that is commonly heard in factories, but that set him off because he had too much to drink and he rose and this time provoked a fight for being called a fucker. That's nothing other than a non-racial event, from the spontaneous uttering of Ebens."

As for the prosecution's attempts to depict Ronald Ebens as a "racial animal," Eaman said the opposite couldn't be more true. "The prosecution might suggest that he is not sorry for what they have done. The truth is he is.

"The truth is Ronald Ebens does not know everything he said and everything he did that night," Eaman said. "He does know it motivated him to anger and intoxication and stupidity. It is not his intent to forget the ordeal. But it was not his intent to keep him from a public place of accommodation, that was not his intent."

Did racism exist in this country? Of course, Eaman said. "We are not so blind to racial violence to say that it does not exist. It exists in the country and throughout the world."

But what happened on June 19, 1982, was not a racial incident, he maintained. And the prosecution accusing Ebens and Nitz of racism cheapened the truth. "There are also those who would claim it exists when it does not," he said. "And when they claim this, they cheapen the legitimate claims of racial discrimination and racial violence.

"None of this happened to Vincent Chin because of Mr. Chin's race," he concluded. "And none of this happened because Mr. Ebens and Mr. Nitz were acting purposefully to deny Vincent Chin his right to be in the Fancy Pants Club. And for all of these reasons, we ask that you return a verdict that would be consistent with the facts in this case of not guilty on both of the counts. Thank you."

. . .

Defense attorney Miriam Siefer, who was inspired in high school by the 1960s civil rights movement to become a public defender, told the jury that the Civil Rights Act was "one of the most important pieces of legislation ever enacted in this country."

But Siefer accused the prosecution of using the Civil Rights Act for all the wrong reasons, calling it a "perversion, where there's no credible evidence of a racist purpose." Like Eaman, she believed political pressure led to this civil rights trial.

"Ladies and gentlemen, race did not enter this picture until after Mike Nitz got probation in March of 1983 in the state courts," she said. "But this system has to have more integrity than that. You cannot just convict someone out of anger and frustration or outrage for a state court's failing. There must be credible evidence that establishes beyond a reasonable doubt that Mr. Nitz committed a federal offense."

She maintained that American Citizens for Justice had persuaded the federal court to get involved as a "last resort" to put Ebens and Nitz behind bars. Like Eaman, she believed this was a case of toxic masculinity. "There was no ugly racism turned violent on June 19, 1982, but men who were influenced by alcohol who could not control their anger and who felt the macho urge to get even."

Siefer ended her closing argument by asking the jury to recognize the difference—that although Nitz was guilty of manslaughter, he was not guilty of racism.

"I can stand before you and tell you that the evidence demonstrates that this is not a civil rights case," she said. "I ask you, and the evidence demands that you return the verdict of not guilty on each of the counts as to Mike Nitz. Thank you."

## THE LAST WORD

Because the prosecution had the burden of proof, Theodore Merritt was allowed to have the last word with his rebuttal to the defense's closing statements.

Merritt believed Ebens was not truly remorseful for what had happened, even though he broke down on the witness stand. "I ask you not to be swayed by the defendant's repeated and well-timed outburst of tears, because with those tears he's asking for mercy, he's not asking for justice."

Merritt compared Ebens's testimony to that of Vincent's mother, Lily Chin. "But the one woman who has every right to cry in this world, she sat up in here and didn't cry and gave testimony in the case about the death of her only son," he said. "And Ronald Ebens didn't cry at the scene."

Merritt continued, "Now the defense also suggests that since no one heard Vincent Chin say, 'Nobody calls me a Chink,' 'Nobody calls me a Nip,' well, that means it didn't happen." But one didn't have to use the actual specific racist term to be racist, Merritt argued. It wasn't always about the word choice—it was about the *intention* behind the words. The defense claimed these insults were meant in a macho context. But Merritt contended that because Vincent Chin was not white and racist stereotypes existed about Asian men, any insults about masculinity would always be tied to his race.

"Jimmy Choi told you as a minority he tried to learn to ignore racial insults," he said. "And the fact that Vincent Chin, a man who had lived with his mother all his life, chose to respond to the foulest obscenities about his mother instead of the racial insults to him, well, what does that prove? That's immaterial to what else he was called."

In fact, Merritt said, Vincent Chin *did* stand up to racism. "Vincent Chin decided to stop ignoring the racial insults, the obscenities about his mother, and he came over and he challenged Ronald Ebens."

Merritt wondered how Ebens would have reacted to Vincent if he had been white, too. Would he have taken the baseball bat from the trunk of his car and chased him down the street? Would he have let his temper boil over instead of cooling down? "When you go back in that jury room, you ask yourself, would Vincent Chin be alive today if he was the same color as Ronald Ebens and Michael Nitz?"

He reminded the jury about Vincent's journey to America—how he had been adopted at age six from China and become an American citizen at the age of ten. Vincent Chin's story, he said, was the same for all Americans.

"It probably sounds corny, but that is what America is about," Merritt said. "People from different races, different countries. . . . We're Americans. And as Americans, we must condemn this type of racial violence. . . . Justice to this case requires and demands a verdict of guilty. And in Vincent Chin's last words, 'It's not fair.'"

Chapter 31

# THE VERDICT: "I CAN'T BRING HIM BACK"

"Your Honor, we have reached a verdict."

After twelve hours of deliberation, the jury of seven women and five men had made a decision. At two-thirty p.m. on Thursday June 28, 1984, the clerk read the final verdict for the courtroom.

"In the case of United States of America versus Ronald Ebens and Michael Nitz, we, the jury, find the defendant Michael Nitz not guilty as to Count One and not guilty as to Count Two."

As Nitz buried his face in his hands and cried, the clerk continued to read the jury's verdict for his stepfather.

"We, the jury, find the defendant Ronald Ebens not guilty as to Count One . . ."

Ebens held his breath as the clerk read the final part of the verdict.

" . . . and guilty as to Count Two."

In other words—Ronald Ebens had been found not guilty of conspiracy but guilty of violating Vincent Chin's civil rights.

"When they read through that verdict, it was 'Not guilty,

Lily Chin and Helen Zia at a June 29, 1984, press conference held after Ronald Ebens was found guilty of violating Vincent Chin's civil rights. Although Lily grieved the tragic loss of her son Vincent, she formed a close mother-daughter bond with Zia, which lasted until Lily's passing in 2002.

'Not guilty,' 'Not guilty, 'Guilty,' Eaman said. "When they got through three 'Not guilty,' boy, we thought, *We did it! Did we do this?* And when they said the fourth 'Guilty,' it was like the anvil fell that we were always waiting for it, it was gonna fall."

Ebens sat stoically as U.S. marshals escorted the twelve jurors out of the courtroom. The jury members declined to talk to the throng of TV camera crews, photographers, and reporters waiting outside.

"To be quite honest, I expected to go to jail," Ebens reflected later. "I pleaded guilty to manslaughter on that. I did just like anybody else, I went to take my licks; I thought for sure I would go to jail. And I was prepared to go. Really. As much as you can be prepared for something like that."

After the jury left, Ebens and Nitz stood up. Ebens reached over to hug his stepson. The two men left the courtroom, not saying a word to the press outside.

The lawyers, however, had plenty to say. When asked for his reaction to the verdict, lead prosecutor Theodore Merritt told reporters, "We're satisfied."

But the defense called the entire case a "political prosecution" because 1984 was also a presidential election year. "This is an election year," Nitz's attorney Miriam Siefer said. "And this is an easy case to be liberal, an easy civil rights case for the Reagan administration which is not known to be liberal to and for civil rights."

Merritt disagreed. "That's totally false that this is in any way a political prosecution," he snapped back.

Helen Zia, who felt "justice was done," reminded the media about the long-term importance of this trial. "This case is the first federal civil rights case involving an Asian American that has ever been prosecuted," she said. "It is remarkable that the federal government recognized the problem of racial animosity toward Asian Americans at a time when civil rights laws are under fire."

Eaman still believed the case was ultimately influenced by a community's desire for vengeance. "The community has spoken and demanded his blood and the opportunity now comes to get it."

This was never about vengeance, argued James Shimoura. This was about justice. And he cautioned the public that this case was just the tip of the iceberg. "In the case of Mister Chin, I think justice has been served," he told the press. "But I think the public ought to be made aware of the fact that this is only one case, there's still discrimination against the Asians all over the country."

. . .

Eaman and the defense planned to appeal the verdict. Eaman believed the government produced "no credible evidence" of racism. "I can't blame the jury for the verdict," he said. "They were under so much pressure because of the prosecutor's appeals to their sympathy and the repeated enactment of a brutal beating by the prosecution witnesses that it was too much for them to judge the evidence impartially."

But a woman who served on the jury contested Eaman's claim, saying she and the other jurors deliberated all sides of the case.

"We tried, we wanted to be fair to both sides," she later explained. "So we tried to come up with a story, consistent with no civil rights violations, no racial remarks, and we really couldn't do it."

During deliberation, the jury did not focus on the details of the actual killing. "We were interested in motivation," the juror said, adding that the jury was not convinced by the defense's argument that "there was no racial component of this."

According to this juror, there were two witnesses who helped seal Ebens's guilty verdict—Racine Colwell and Ebens himself.

"The key witness in my view was Racine Colwell, who was one of the dancers, and the jury did agree that her testimony was

Michael Nitz found himself in the media spotlight again after being indicted along with his stepfather Ronald Ebens on civil rights charges by a federal grand jury on November 2, 1983. Although Nitz would be found not guilty in both civil rights counts, he still wept for his stepfather, who was found guilty in the first trial.

credible," she said. "The feeling I think about the other dancers and Vincent Chin's friends were that they were not as credible."

As for Ebens, the jury had trouble trusting his testimony. "His memory was very selective," the juror said. "He had a lot to drink the night of the killing. And he testified he didn't remember many details of the evening. But when asked about various racial remarks that other witnesses said they had heard, he said he was sure he didn't say these things. And that was received skeptically by the jury. We felt his memory was too selective."

. . .

For the present, Ebens was released on bond. He could go home. Soon he would be sentenced—and there was a very good chance that he could get up to life in prison.

"I just feel deeply sorry for the death of [Lily Chin]'s son," he told the press. "There's no more I can say. That's all you can say. I can't bring him back."

On September 18, Ebens and the lawyers met with Judge Taylor to discuss Ebens's sentencing.

Defense attorney Frank Eaman tried to appeal to Judge Taylor's compassion by reminding her that Ebens had no prior criminal offenses. "Mr. Ebens had a typical, normal life of a Midwesterner who grew up on a farm," he said. "Went into the service, and worked in the auto plants, and then in thirty minutes of his life he went berserk and acted out of character." He believed Ebens's anger management problem and alcohol abuse did not deserve "a harsh, cruel sentence," but rather "the compassion, understanding and assistance of a Court of Law."

Prosecutor Theodore Merritt recommended to Judge Taylor

With his then-wife, Juanita, by his side, Ronald Ebens enters federal court for sentencing on September 18, 1984, after being found guilty of one count of civil rights violations in the first trial of *United States v. Ronald Ebens and Michael Nitz*. He was sentenced to twenty-five years in prison—but the guilty verdict and sentence were overturned on appeal in 1987.

that Ebens be sentenced to thirty years in prison for showing "a wanton disregard for Mr. Chin's life—another human being." He believed that severe length of time was appropriate. "A 30-year sentence would appropriately reflect society's intolerance of this type of violent and antisocial behavior," he said.

After both lawyers finished their arguments, Judge Taylor turned to Ronald Ebens himself. "Mr. Ebens is there anything you would like to say?" she asked.

"Only, Your Honor, I have expressed my regret and remorse on several occasions, and I would just like to reiterate that one more time," he said. "I am sorry for what happened. I can't say anything more than that. At this point, I have no recourse but to depend on the American system of justice, and you, Your Honor."

"Is that all?" Judge Taylor asked.

Ebens nodded.

The judge then delivered her decision.

"It is adjudged, Mr. Ebens, that you are committed to the custody of the Attorney General for a term of 25 years."

. . .

The city of Detroit was divided on the guilty verdict and sentence. When polled by newspapers, 56 percent of the public believed the verdict was fair, while 44 percent felt it was not.

The sentence of twenty-five years in prison was a common punishment for a second-degree murder conviction. Had Judge Charles Kaufman not given Ebens and Nitz three years' probation, the maximum sentence for their original charge of manslaughter was ten to fifteen years in prison.

A heartbroken Michael Nitz told the press that his stepfather had just been trying to protect him that night. "[He] saw that I was hurt, bleeding badly," he said. "He did just what any normal father would do in that situation." Nitz said he and his family were in shock over the twenty-five-year sentence. "He's innocent to start with, but we didn't expect this."

Ebens braced himself for the future—a quarter-century in prison. "I was guilty of being the direct cause of taking a life," he told reporters. "This was definitely wrong. I've repeatedly said that I'm deeply sorry for it—I mean, I don't know what else they want a man to do. There isn't anything left that I can do."

But there was still one more thing his lawyers could do.

File an appeal.

# "IN THE SHADOWS"

For five years, Jarod had no idea Vincent Chin had been with him every day.

After graduating from college, Jarod rented a small house close to the trendy town of Ferndale, Michigan. Every day he walked down Woodward Avenue to grab a cup of coffee at his favorite coffeehouse before driving to his job at the photography studio.

And every day he passed by a marker on the corner of 9 Mile and Woodward. But he never stopped to look at it.

Instead, one day he noticed a restaurant that had recently opened across the street. It was a hipster taco joint.

Jarod began hanging out at this restaurant. He even celebrated his birthday there several times. "It was the place to go to," he said. "I spent a lot of time and money there!"

His mom, however, didn't know why he liked that restaurant so much. When he invited her to lunch there one day, she seemed unimpressed with the food.

And then one day Jarod was walking along his usual route down Woodward Avenue to pick up his morning coffee before work. When he arrived at the corner of 9 Mile and Woodward, he stopped as the traffic light turned red.

While waiting to cross the street, he glanced over at the legal milestone marker on the corner. He approached the faded blue metal stand displaying two side-by-side plaques etched in bronze, under the shadow of a nearby elm tree.

To Jarod's shock, it was the 34th Michigan Legal Milestone marker dedicated to Vincent Chin by the Ferndale City Council and created by the State Bar of Michigan and the Michigan Asian Pacific American Bar Association.

"From a Whisper to a Rallying Cry: 'It's not fair,'" Jarod read on one plaque. "These were the last anguished words whispered by Vincent Chin as he lay dying, the victim of a hate crime on June 19, 1982. His words became a rallying cry for the Asian American community outraged at the lenient sentences his assailants received, and they spawned a civil rights movement. The Vincent Chin case galvanized the Asian American community . . . and also helped form the basis for state and federal changes on important legal issues dealing with hate crimes, minimum sentencing guidelines, and victims' rights."

Jarod couldn't believe that this entire time he had been walking by a memorial dedicated to Vincent Chin and never knew it until now.

"I walked by that plaque for a year or two straight, not even reading it or even looking at it," he said. "When I read it, I was like, *this is him!*"

And then Jarod read the words on the other plaque that celebrated Ferndale as "the birthplace in 1983 for the pan-ethnic Asian American civil rights organization American Citizens for Justice."

"In response to the injustices in the 1982 beating death of Vincent Chin in Highland Park, Michigan, members of the Asian American community assembled at 22828 Woodward Avenue, the former Golden Star Chinese Restaurant located in the northeast block of Woodward and Nine Mile, where Chin was employed."

Jarod looked across the street. His favorite hipster taco joint was located at the same address—22828 Woodward Avenue.

He had been hanging out at the former Chinese restaurant where Vincent Chin had worked. He remembered how he had taken his mom there for lunch once and she didn't seem to like the food. Had she known this whole time that his favorite hangout was where she had frequented at his age and dated Vincent?

"I had no idea who he was and how much influence he had on the Asian American community," Jarod reflected. "In retrospect,

The 34th Michigan Legal Milestone marker dedicated to Vincent Chin by the Ferndale City Council, the State Bar of Michigan, and the Michigan Asian Pacific American Bar Association. It stands just across the street from the former Golden Star restaurant on Woodward Avenue where Vincent waited tables on the night of June 19, 1982, hours before he was beaten to death just a couple miles away on the same street.

Vincent Chin has always been in the shadows of wherever I have gone."

As Jarod continued to research Vincent's life, he found out the street address of where Vincent had grown up with his parents. Curious, he drove over to see what the Chin family residence looked like. To his shock, Vincent's old childhood home was located just a few blocks from the house that he rented.

Jarod began to wonder if maybe these were not coincidences at all. Was Vincent Chin trying to send him a message? "I get chills thinking about it now," he said. "I wonder if it must have been him reaching out to me."

PART FIVE

# BEYOND A REASONABLE DOUBT

The former Fancy Pants Club, in 2018. More than one hundred years after its birth
in 1915 as a "movie palace" and its transformation into a 1970s adult entertainment
dance nightclub before being permanently shut down by police in 1986, the abandoned building showed signs of life as green plants peeked through its gutted lobby.

Chapter 32

# "THIS CASE IS NOT OVER"

On January 8, 1986, the Fancy Pants Club shut its doors forever.

The Wayne County prosecutor's office officially deemed it a "public nuisance," a legal term for a criminal act having occurred on the premises. In the case of the Fancy Pants, there were allegations of prostitution. Police padlocked the doors. No one would enter the club again.

And on January 8, 1986, Ronald Ebens was still not in prison. It had been four months since Judge Anna Diggs Taylor sentenced him to a twenty-five-year jail term. Instead, he remained a prisoner in his own house, waiting while his defense attorneys David Lawson and Frank Eaman appealed his case.

In the judicial system, the losing party in a federal court trial has the right to challenge the decision by making an appeal to the U.S. Circuit Court of Appeals.

So Ebens's defense team filed an appeal to the federal Sixth Circuit Court of Appeals, claiming that a legal error influenced the outcome of the case. They criticized prosecutor Theodore Merritt's "junkyard-dog style" of prosecution during the trial, which they alleged included misleading statements. They also accused lawyer Liza Chan of coaching the witnesses Gary Koivu, Bob Siroskey, and Jimmy Choi to say they had heard racist slurs said at the Fancy Pants Club.

After their appeal was filed, a panel of three federal judges reviewed the information. Eaman and Lawson needed a majority vote to approve their appeal. Most appeals took several months.

In Ebens's case, it took much longer. On September 11, 1986—almost two years after Ebens had been sentenced to twenty-five years in jail—the court of appeals agreed unanimously to overturn that conviction. The court ruled that Judge Anna Diggs Taylor made a mistake by not allowing the taped recordings of Liza Chan's meeting with Koivu, Siroskey, and Choi to be submitted as evidence into the trial. These tapes could have been used to discredit their testimony.

James Shimoura and the American Citizens for Justice were upset by the ruling. Shimoura said the accusation that Liza Chan had coached the witnesses was "absolutely ridiculous." "What is very outrageous is that Ronald Ebens has already pleaded guilty to manslaughter charges over three years ago and he has yet to spend a day in jail," he said.

· · ·

But Ronald Ebens wasn't in the clear yet.

The appeals court did not rule out another trial. It was up to the U.S. Department of Justice to decide whether to retry Ebens.

The department made its decision quickly.

Just one week later, on September 19, 1986, the department announced that Ronald Ebens would be retried on charges of violating Vincent Chin's civil rights.

"We are quite pleased with the announcement by Justice," Shimoura said at a press conference. "It goes a long way to show

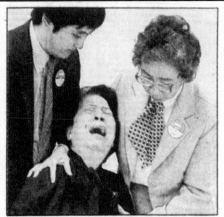

Free Press Photo by ALAN KAMUDA

**Vincent Chin's mother, Lily, is comforted by Mabel Lim and James Shimoura at a news confernce Friday.**

# New trial ordered for Chin's killer

By SUSAN GOLDBERG
Free Press Staff Writer

Ronald Ebens, who beat Chinese-American Vincent Chin to death with a baseball bat, will be retried on charges of violating Chin's civil rights, the U.S. Justice Department announced Friday.

Ebens, 47, who has remained free on $20,000 bond, was convicted of the civil rights violation in 1984 and sentenced to 25 years in prison. But his conviction was overturned last week by the U.S. 6th Circuit Court of Appeals because of what the court cited as errors in the trial, conducted by U.S. District Judge Anna Diggs Taylor.

The appeals court left it to the Justice Department to decide whether to retry Ebens, a former auto plant foreman.

Earlier Friday at a news conference in Detroit, Lily Chin, Vincent Chin's mother, tearfully asked for another trial.

"Please tell the government, 'Do not drop this case,' " said Lily Chin, who lives in San Francisco.

"I want justice for Vincent. I want justice for my son."

**CHIN, 27,** was beaten on June 19, 1982, by Ebens and his

See **CHIN**, Page 9A

September 1986: In a *Detroit Free Press* report on the announcement that Ronald Ebens would be retried due to alleged errors in the original 1984 trial, James Shimoura and Mable Lim stand by Lily Chin's side during a press conference. A devastated Lily repeatedly told the press, "I want justice for my son."

that people who have a sense of justice and moral compassion could not possibly allow this heinous, racially motivated crime to go unpunished."

Now it was defense attorney Frank Eaman's turn to be upset. "This is a political case," he said. "Political pressure was placed on Washington. When it's a political case you're going to get a political prosecution."

Ebens continued to insist that racism played no part in Vincent Chin's death. "I'm no racist," he said.

But these roller-coaster events overwhelmed Vincent's mother Lily Chin. She nearly fainted at the press conference. She wept as ACJ member Mable Lim and Shimoura gently held her in their arms.

"Please tell the government, 'Do not drop this case,'" Lily finally said. "I want justice for Vincent. I want justice for my son."

. . .

Meanwhile Frank Eaman worried that his client would not be guaranteed a fair and impartial trial in Detroit, given the case's notoriety.

"I think because of all the publicity in this case and all the lies that have been told about Ron Ebens, it's hard to ever imagine him getting a fair trial anyplace," he said.

Judge Anna Diggs Taylor, who would preside again over this new trial, agreed with Eaman. Due to the "saturation publicity" over the Vincent Chin killing, Ronald Ebens "cannot obtain a fair and impartial trial," she ruled.

As a result, on February 24, 1987, the Department of Justice ordered the second federal trial of Ronald Ebens to be moved to Cincinnati.

And on April 22, 1987, the trial of *United States v. Ronald Ebens* began.

Again.

# Chapter 33

# "WE ALL REMEMBER OUR LINES, OKAY?"

Lily Chin couldn't sleep.

The past five years felt like a nightmare she could not wake up from. This kind of pain was unusual for Lily, who was known among her friends and family for her high spirits and laughter. It broke her heart to be in Detroit, a constant reminder of her son's absence.

And now, five years after Vincent died, Lily had to relive the civil rights trial all over again. About ninety Asian Americans attended a midnight candle vigil and prayer service at the St. Monica Roman Catholic Church in Cincinnati on the night before the official start of the new trial. "We have to be reminded from time to time of the rights of people like you who come to this country," said Reverend Joseph Lutmer to the congregation.

The next day the lawyers for the prosecution and defense made their opening arguments. For the second trial, U.S. Attorney William Soisson and Assistant U.S. Attorney Floyd Clardy spoke on behalf of the government's prosecution. Lawyers Frank Eaman and David Lawson returned once again to defend Ronald Ebens.

Ronald Ebens and his wife, Juanita, attended all eight days of the trial. But Ebens chose not to testify this time.

From April 22 to 30, 1987, the witnesses who had appeared at the first trial repeated their testimony for the jury in Cincinnati. Although many of the arguments between the defense and prosecution echoed what happened during the first trial, there was one crucial difference this time.

The tapes.

. . .

The court of appeals had ruled that Judge Taylor erred in the first trial by not allowing the tape recordings of Liza Chan's May 1983 meeting with Vincent Chin's friends Gary Koivu, Bob Siroskey, and Jimmy Choi to be submitted as evidence. As a result, the tapes were allowed as evidence for the second trial.

Judge Taylor, worried about any media leaks, banned the media and the general public from listening to the tapes in the courtroom. The tapes were played in private for only the lawyers and the jury. She imposed a gag order on everyone, forbidding the attorneys, witnesses, and court personnel from discussing the tapes with the public. She also ordered that the loudspeakers be unplugged so no one outside the courtroom could overhear the tapes.

Ebens's defense attorneys claimed the tapes were proof that Chan had coached the three witnesses to embellish their stories with false claims. The jury listened to the tape playback of Chan speaking to Koivu, Siroskey, and Choi.

The quotes from Chan included:

*"We will agree this is the story, this is it. When it's a federal prose-cution, we're all going to have to be agreeing on this is what happened. Otherwise you'll all look funny on the stand."*

*"Just remember your different lines—Chink, foreign car part, big fucker, little fucker, all fuckers, don't call me a fucker. We all remember our lines, okay?"*

"There were things in the transcript that jumped out at us that sounded like witness coaching," Eaman later explained. "It's always a mistake if you want to avoid witness coaching to talk to all the witnesses at once. . . . You can hear witnesses memories evolve, like 'Yeah yeah, no, no, now I remember him saying this!,' and that's very suspect. Memory is not a videotape you replay. Memory is something that your brain creates . . . and memory is very susceptible to influence, and you can change your memory especially when you're in a group like that. You can hear the memory evolve as the interview went on, and the allegations and the memory continued to evolve during the trial."

But Vincent's friends denied that Chan had coached them. To this day, Gary Koivu remains adamant that he always told the truth. He says Chan never influenced his testimony. "I found out that they thought there was collusion among us," he reflected years later. "It wasn't going to change my testimony as far as saying something I didn't see, or remembering something I didn't hear."

Koivu said that their meeting was simply to refresh each other's memories because it had been almost a year since the incident. In hindsight, he understood why it appeared suspicious, even though their motives were innocent. "I know the optics of it," he said. "It looks like, okay, you're colluding, getting together to get one story that's gonna make it sound exactly like how it happened. But all I was doing was saying what I remembered, and Jimmy was saying what he remembered, and Bob was saying what he remembered."

Bob Siroskey admitted at the second trial that his memory "fades in and out." But he said he was sure he had heard the word *Chink* said at the Fancy Pants Club.

Defense attorney Eaman grilled Jimmy Choi, who had waited tables with Vincent at the Golden Star Restaurant, about why he waited so long to tell authorities that he too had allegedly heard racist slurs.

"Did you tell Highland Park police about foreign cars or Nips?" he asked.

"No," Choi said.

"Racial statements didn't become important until it became a civil rights case, right?" Eaman pressed.

"Yes," Choi said.

"The first time you mentioned it was to the grand jury in September 1983?" Eaman asked.

"Yes," Choi said.

But Choi still insisted on the witness stand that he had heard the word *Nip* spoken at the club.

Dancer Racine Colwell also denied that Liza Chan had ever coached her. She admitted that Chan had interviewed her before the trial but said their meeting wasn't taped. She told the jury that their interview was ethical. Chan never told her what to say, Colwell testified.

But there was one witness who was never asked to explain about the tapes.

Liza Chan.

· · ·

On the first day of the second trial in Cincinnati, Liza Chan checked into a hotel near the courthouse, preparing to testify.

But no one ever called her to the witness stand.

In fact, two days into the trial, she was told to go home. She would not be asked to testify.

"I was surprised," Chan later said. "I was fully expecting they would give me a chance to explain."

Chan wanted to tell her side of the story. That she did *not* coach Gary Koivu, Bob Siroskey, and Jimmy Choi. That she had simply recorded their interview so she wouldn't be distracted by taking notes during their conversation.

And then there was a subtle language issue that Chan believed may have given the impression that she was coaching the witnesses. Chan was born in Hong Kong and raised to speak British English. She was not familiar with American idioms and expressions. For example, when she told Koivu, Siroskey, and Choi that they needed to "get your stories straight," she did not realize that the phrase "get your stories straight" in American English had a negative connotation—that it implied lying. "I thought it meant 'tell me what you know, tell me your truth,'" she explained.

Chan's law firm boss Daniel Hoekenga and her colleague Marc Susselman also listened to the tapes. "I was a little concerned of what might be on these tapes that might be distorted," Susselman remembered. "I know Liza was agonizing." After listening to the tapes, Susselman concluded, "I was satisfied there was no problem."

"They were more used to my accent because they worked with me," Chan said. "So they understood perfectly there was nothing in there that would implicate me or show that I was coaching. And I wasn't."

As a young lawyer trying to impress her boss, Chan recorded the interview to save time. "I was under so much time pressure," she said, explaining that she innocently thought recording everyone together in one interview session would be "faster" and more convenient.

At first, Chan wasn't worried about the tapes. She believed they would prove that she was being a responsible lawyer by having a backup recording of her interviews for accuracy's sake. "I felt very comfortable that this was a record in case anyone doubted anything, my integrity, my sincerity, my honesty, my professionalism," she said. "Well wow, geez, it turned out completely the wrong way!"

In hindsight, Chan agrees that recording the interviews was not a good idea. "The optics were not good at all," she said. "It's not like I'm engaging in some criminal conspiracy, coaching or anything like that. I was a very new, very young and inexperienced civil practice lawyer. I was very disappointed I didn't get to testify and correct the record of what happened at that meeting."

· · ·

On Thursday, April 30, 1987, attorneys delivered their closing statements to the jury. The question remained the same: Why had Ronald Ebens beaten Vincent Chin to death? Was it simply a fight between two drunk and angry men that spun out of control? Or was it a case of racial violence gone fatal?

"Ronald Ebens did not consider Vincent Chin a person,"

declared Assistant U.S. Attorney William Soisson in his final words to the jury. "Ronald Ebens' racial hatred can best be demonstrated by the brutality of the beating."

"This is not a lunch counter in Atlanta," shot back defense attorney David Lawson in his closing statement. "This is not a bus in Montgomery. This is a girlie club in Highland Park. There is no evidence that this homicide is racial."

Judge Taylor reminded the twelve jurors that if they decided Ebens was guilty, they must believe it "beyond a reasonable doubt."

And with that, Ronald Ebens's fate was once again in the hands of the jury.

# Chapter 34

# "A VERY, VERY TOUGH DECISION"

For the second time in three years, Ronald Ebens and his family waited as the jury deliberated his fate.

The nine men and three women deliberated for ten and a half hours over two days.

At 3:10 p.m. on Friday, May 1, 1987, they announced their verdict.

*Not guilty.*

This time Ebens broke into tears as he heard the verdict. Juanita buried her face in her hands and sobbed. She then ran over to the defense table to hug her husband. The two then hugged defense attorneys David Lawson and Frank Eaman.

"We said all along this case was a frame-up," said a triumphant Frank Eaman. "This was never a civil rights case, and he got a fair trial."

"We're disappointed," prosecutor Floyd Clardy told the press. "We accept the verdict of the jury."

The "not guilty" verdict was unanimous. "We had a very, very tough decision to make," said jury foreman Jeffrey Heffron, a machinist from Cincinnati. He was the only juror to speak to the press. "It was no pleasure, but we came up with the only decision we could come up with. What was it the judge said,

'Beyond a reasonable doubt'—there you have it. I agonized over this for two weeks. I'm still agonizing over it now."

For Ebens, however, the agony had finally ended. "I'm still very sorry about what happened," he told the press as he and Juanita walked out of the courtroom, their arms linked together. "But you gotta realize how relieved I am after four years of waiting for this to be over. That's really all I have to say."

Frank Eaman believed the tapes of Liza Chan interviewing Gary Koivu, Bob Siroskey, and Jimmy Choi helped tip the scales in Ebens's favor. "I'm not accusing people of perjury," Eaman said. "I'm just saying their memories were helped."

Defense attorney David Lawson agreed. "It was wrong to make this a civil rights case," he said. "Ronald Ebens did not do it because of Chin's race."

The tapes concerned Helen Zia and other members of the American Citizens for Justice. Zia believed the tapes were misleading and heard out of context. "It takes a certain sophistication to discern whether it was coaching or legal questions being discussed," she said. "The tapes were enough to put a reasonable doubt in their [the jurors'] minds, and that's all it takes."

Liza Chan was heartbroken. For years she refused to talk about the trial. "I was very upset," she said much later. "I really felt very bad. That's why I have not given any interviews. I have not spoken publicly about the case. I did not appear in the documentaries. I just wanted to be done and go on with my life. I was very emotional about it, that's why I couldn't talk about it for over thirty-five years."

The "not guilty" verdict divided Detroit. Many people disagreed with the decision. Angry readers wrote letters to the *Detroit Free Press,* calling this acquittal "a green light for killers."

"As far as violating civil rights is concerned, didn't the man have a right to live?" wrote one reader. "It seems to me that killing him would count as violating his civil rights."

Another reader asked, "Ronald Ebens may be a 'free' man, but can he ever be really free?"

And not all outraged readers were Asian American. Since 1982, the controversial case had united many diverse groups. A rabbi from the suburb of West Bloomfield criticized the acquittal in a letter to the editor, saying he was filled with "great sadness and despair in the justice of our country's system. Whatever technicalities were involved, a person took the life of another merely because of his skin color and racial descent. . . . How can we speak of justice if a killer goes free except for the payment of an insignificant amount? The wounds of the victim can never be healed."

"I am not Asian American," another reader wrote, "and I feel totally outraged. When a man can kill another man in a drunken rage with a baseball bat (racially motivated or not), and can walk away, it makes a mockery of our judicial system."

James Shimoura of the ACJ expressed his shock and anger. "My heart sank thirty feet," he told the press. "I fully expected a guilty verdict. I think every Asian American shed a tear today because of this verdict."

Helen Zia saw the emotions run raw for many Asian Americans as they tried to process the unexpected acquittal. "Everybody feels it like death," she said. "We're all in total shock. What it boils down to is that we had a good shot at it, but it was up to the jury. It just goes to show just how ignorant white America is."

• • •

About seventy people attended a fifth-anniversary commemoration of Vincent Chin's death at the Forest Lawn Cemetery in Detroit in June 1987. Lily Chin's grief was compounded by Ronald Ebens's acquittal just one month earlier.

Despite Detroit's divided reaction, Ronald Ebens continued to stand up for himself. He denied ever harboring any racism against the Asian community.

"I've never been a racist," he said. "I've never had anything against anyone in this whole world. And with God as a witness, that's the truth.'"

Ebens wanted to apologize to Lily Chin, saying that he had paid for the crime "every day of my life. "I know how my mother would feel," he said. "I'd just like to tell her how sorry I am."

But Ebens would never have that chance. An inconsolable Lily refused to accept the acquittal. She turned to Helen Zia and asked, "Helen, is there anything else we can do?"

"No, there's nothing more with the civil rights case," a heartbroken Zia replied.

"One of the saddest and most difficult things I've ever done was to tell Mrs. Chin that the civil rights case was over, lost," Zia later remembered. "When she heard that there were no more legal avenues to pursue . . . I watched as the pain and disappointment washed over her."

"My life is over," Lily Chin told the press later. "Vincent's soul will never rest."

# "I REALLY DON'T WANT TO TALK ABOUT IT"

Jarod didn't mean to text his mom about Vincent Chin.

It was 2016. For the past four years, he had never once mentioned to his mom that he knew about Vincent.

But when he overheard his professional photographer mentor mention the Vincent Chin case during a group critique meeting with other photographers, Jarod revealed that his mom had been engaged to Vincent.

"I told him how I was 'related' to Vincent Chin, and my mentor was blown away," Jarod said. His mentor said it was clear Jarod was uncovering a family secret. "He urged me to do a project about it."

The more Jarod thought about it, the more excited he became. "I thought it would be powerful to have intimate family photos with the uncovering of old documents and old photographs that my family had of Vincent Chin," he said.

About a month later, Jarod went out with his friends for dinner and drinks. But he couldn't stop thinking about his mentor's suggestion. Distracted, he impulsively texted a fellow photographer to tell her about his decision to do a Vincent Chin–related photography project.

But when Jarod looked down at the screen, to his horror, he realized . . . *he had texted his mother by accident.*

His heart racing, Jarod immediately called his younger brother, who was living at home with their parents. It was late at night, and their parents were already asleep. He begged his brother to steal their mother's phone and delete his text.

But his brother didn't want to wake up their parents. He was afraid he might get in trouble. "No, you deal with it," he snapped before hanging up.

Jarod, terrified of his mom's reaction, called his brother back. They argued some more, and then his brother hung up on him again. Jarod kept calling him back. After the fifth phone call, the noise woke up their parents.

"It became this whole argument, and we woke up my mom which woke up my dad," Jarod remembered. "And then my mom saw my text."

Jarod overheard his mother in the background. "Why are you doing this?" she demanded of her son. "I really don't want to talk about it."

As Jarod stared at his phone, he realized he had no other choice.

If his mom wouldn't talk about Vincent Chin, then he would.

PART SIX

# "REMEMBER ME ALWAYS"

Chapter 35

# AMERICA BREAKS ITS PROMISE TO LILY CHIN

When Vincent was a child, he loved eating the winter melons his mother, Lily, grew in their backyard garden. Unlike American sweet melons like cantaloupe and watermelon, Chinese winter melons are soft and mild and often used in soups and stir-fried savory dishes.

But after Vincent's death, Lily rarely went outside because she remembered how much he loved her garden. She imagined him waiting for her in the backyard.

In fact, Lily saw her son everywhere.

"I don't like to go outside," she said. "Sometimes I see the young man that looks like my Vincent, and I am dizzy. I look at the table, look at supper, I cry. I just open the door, see the house, I cry. I don't like to live in here anymore."

Lily's friends and family noticed the change in her personality. Helen Zia remembered, from before, "her laughter, the way she got excited, eyes sparkling, when she was about to make a funny observation about something she had seen or heard."

And now Lily's eyes no longer sparkled. She had withdrawn from the world. She retired from her job at the brush factory. She made less than ten thousand dollars a year from Social Security and from renting out her house in Oak Park. But she refused to take any money raised by the American Citizens for Justice, insisting it should pay their legal fees from both trials.

The once fiercely activist mother now refused to talk to the media. Even though Liza Chan's colleague Marc Susselman filed a civil lawsuit for the wrongful death of her son, Lily still found herself spiraling into despair. She began to shut herself off from the community, including those closest to her, like Vikki Wong. "She come to see me, but I don't want to see her," Lily said. "She come and make me cry. She call me Mama. I tell her, you lost the Vincent, you lost the flame. I lost the Vincent, I lost my whole life."

. . .

Lily still loved Detroit. But Vincent's ghost haunted her every day, making it unbearable to stay there any longer. "I love Detroit and friends," she said. "But I cannot stay. Detroit, every night, ten, I go bed. Every night one a.m., I no sleep anymore. See Vincent."

So Lily decided to leave the city she had called home for the past thirty-seven years. She packed two suitcases and moved to a rooming house in San Francisco's Chinatown. Despite her small, six-by-ten-foot room, she at least had a view of the San Francisco–Oakland Bay Bridge. She spent her days wandering past the Chinatown shops or sitting in the park to watch the children play. But their laughter pierced Lily's heart, reminding her again of her loss.

Lily didn't know it, but she wasn't alone in her grief. After Ronald Ebens was found not guilty in the second trial, many people wrote letters in protest. On September 23, 1987, the *Detroit Free Press* printed several of those letters. The headline read, FROM OUR READERS: AMERICA BREAKS ITS PROMISE TO LILY CHIN.

"What a sad and poignant final chapter to the Vincent Chin case," one reader wrote. "My thoughts and prayers go out to Lily Chin. Although there is nothing we can do to make up for the loss of her son, at least we can all rededicate ourselves to making America the kind of place Mrs. Chin had hoped and thought it would be for her and her family."

Many people said they shared Lily's pain. "I feel the hurt," wrote another reader. "Mrs. Chin has lived here most of her life. This is her county and yet this woman feels it has let her down. I feel the emptiness in my heart for her."

Others empathized with Lily Chin's outrage and sense of betrayal. "Coming from a different country and having a different background, my family, just like most immigrants, considered America as a country of freedom where people would be treated equally and could find justice," a reader wrote. "I can understand how disappointed and upset Mrs. Chin may be about the death of her son, Vincent."

But Lily's story also served as a warning for the younger generation of Asian Americans. "As a third generation Asian American, I am very deeply saddened and angered," an Asian American reader wrote. "America is celebrating the 200th birthday of its Constitution. Unfortunately for the Chin family, there is nothing to celebrate. And for myself, I have a new understanding of discrimination."

. . .

But Lily soon realized it wasn't just Vincent's death and the acquittal of his killer that haunted her.

It was America.

In September 1987 she decided to move again. But this time, she was going back to China. "It was just too sad for her to stay in America," Zia said.

Moving back to Guangzhou proved to be a positive experience. Lily reunited with her elderly mother, who still lived in their hometown, along with her cousins and other family members.

Lily wrote many letters to Helen Zia. They were simple, filled with ordinary details about weather and shopping. Zia was relieved to see Lily returning to her old self. "Dear Helen, how are you? I feel very well. My Mama is very happy to see me. I buy new furniture. The price is cheap. The weather is good."

In another letter, Lily assured Zia that her spirits were improving. "Dear Helen, I have your letter. I am OK in Guangzhou. Canton is good. Don't worry about me, I can take care of myself."

Zia later visited Lily in China. They went on walks together, and Zia marveled at how popular Lily was in her neighborhood. "She seemed to know everybody," Zia said. "People would stop her to say hello, and they'd exchange news and jokes."

In fact, Lily had used some of the money left over from the ACJ to build a school in her town. She also wanted to start a scholarship in her son's name.

Liza Chan also visited Lily in China. At first, Chan was afraid Lily would be angry at her for having recorded her interview with Gary Koivu, Bob Siroskey, and Jimmy Choi. She felt guilty for how her tapes had led to Ebens's acquittal. But to Chan's surprise and relief, Lily still supported her.

"She never blamed me," Chan said. "We remained friends. We had wonderful times together. I felt redemption in a way because of our friendship, so that was good enough for me. That's how I felt closure from it."

Many other friends from the Vincent Chin case also visited Lily, including Stewart Kwoh of the Asian Pacific American Legal Center (APALC) in Los Angeles. Although Kwoh was grateful to see that Lily had moved on with her life, he still sensed a lingering sadness.

"What happened was not just a tragedy for her and her family, but an indictment of the U.S. justice system," he said. "She was smiling, but I could see in her eyes that she had lost everything."

. . .

But Lily would not stay away from America forever.

In 2001, Lily was diagnosed with cancer. She returned to Michigan for medical treatment.

"She didn't want people to know about her illness," Zia said. "She fought valiantly to stay as independent as she could."

Lily stayed at a health center in Farmington Hills. Her sister Amy and her family took care of her. Lily also found comfort in church. She was baptized at the Farmington Hills Chinese Bible Church over the Thanksgiving holiday.

On June 9, 2002, Lily Chin died, just two weeks before the twentieth anniversary of her son's death.

. . .

On June 15, 2002, Helen Zia delivered the eulogy for Lily Chin at her memorial service at the William Sullivan Funeral Home in Southfield, Michigan.

"If Lily Chin were to sit up right now and smile with that sparkle in her eyes, . . . she'd say, 'Waaahhh, look at so many people here today. Why you all come to see me?'" Helen said, smiling as friends and family gathered to celebrate her life.

Zia praised Lily's courage and integrity. "She was so much more than a symbol of injustice and a mother's grief," she said. "Some people call Mrs. Chin the 'Rosa Parks of Asian Americans'—and she was indeed. She stood up and refused to accept what was handed to her. The courage and willingness of this Chinese immigrant mother to speak out, despite her grief, continues to inspire people to keep up the fight for justice, against hate and violence in all its forms."

But Zia also told everyone that their fight was not over. She encouraged everyone to live up to Lily's example.

"Lily Chin reminds us that there is still much to be done, and that there is a terrible price to pay if we don't speak up," she said. "Lily Chin, a dear mother who immigrated from China and spent a lifetime working in restaurants, laundries, and factories so that her son could have a better life, showed us what is possible—and what we are all capable of. Her shining example of standing up and speaking out, even when it is most difficult, is an inspiration for all people who value fairness, equality, and justice in society."

. . .

Lily Chin was laid to rest at the Forest Lawn Cemetery in Detroit with her husband and son. The double headstone Vincent had designed for his parents now had her name etched in the red marble. The traditional Chinese lions he had drawn now stood guard over the whole family.

They were finally together again.

Chapter 36

# "YOU NEVER GET OVER IT"

On the thirtieth anniversary of Vincent Chin's death, in 2012, a reporter named Emil Guillermo was working on a story about Vincent Chin for *AsianWeek,* the largest English-language Asian American newsweekly in the country. He wrote about Asian American issues for his column, "Amok."

In his research, Guillermo found what appeared to be Ronald Ebens's home phone number. He dialed the number, even though he expected Ebens not to answer . . . or worse, to hang up on him.

Instead, to his shock, Ebens answered the phone.

This would be the first time since the 1987 verdict that Ronald Ebens had talked publicly about Vincent Chin.

Ebens told Guillermo that killing Vincent Chin was "the only wrong thing I ever done in my life."

Guillermo wrote that Ebens sounded remorseful on the phone. "He's prayed many times for forgiveness over the years," he wrote.

Although Ebens never spent a day in jail for killing Vincent Chin, he would never truly be free. On March 23, 1987, a $1.5 million settlement was reached in the civil lawsuit that had been filed for the wrongful death of Vincent Chin by Liza Chan's colleague, attorney Marc Susselman. This money represented what Vincent Chin could have earned over his lifetime had he completed his engineering degree at Lawrence Technical Institute.

The court ordered Ebens to pay two hundred dollars monthly, or 25 percent of his net income, for the rest of his life to the Chin estate. But Ebens had not worked for the past five years. And given his criminal record with a guilty charge of manslaughter, he would never work full time again. As a result, he never paid a single penny of the $1.5 million settlement.

Instead, ever since the second trial in 1987, Ebens survived on a series of low-wage jobs. He and Juanita divorced. He later remarried and moved to Nevada.

Ebens still insisted to Guillermo that racism had played no part in Vincent Chin's killing. He claimed the accusations of harboring racial bias because of the auto industry at the time were "the biggest fallacy."

"I'm sorry it happened and if there's any way to undo it, I'd do it," Ebens told Guillermo. "Nobody feels good about somebody's life being taken, okay? It changed my whole life. It's something you never get rid of. When something like that happens, if you're any kind of a person at all, you never get over it. Never."

• • •

Ronald Ebens has not talked to the press since that interview.

Every year on June 19, a small crowd of protesters gathers outside his house. They hold candles and signs saying, REMEMBER VINCENT CHIN. Local journalists and TV crews air news stories about these annual protest vigils.

Now in his early eighties, Ebens still gets phone calls from strangers who scream and harass him.

He still insists that he is not racist.

He still refuses to speak to the press about what happened.

But life clearly has been hard for him since that fateful day.

He's scraped by for years on various small jobs. He still owes the Chin estate more than $8 million in accrued interest since 1987 for the $1.5 million settlement in the unlawful death civil suit, which he can never pay. The Chin estate long ago put a lien on Ebens's house. (A lien is a legal claim over a person's property as collateral until a debt is paid off or settled.) In 2016, a judge ruled against Ebens's request to remove it.

Any ring at the door might be a reporter. Every year when protesters gather outside his house on the anniversary of Vincent's death, it tears him and his family apart. He worries about how his family has suffered because of what he did.

But no matter what, no matter how hard life has been, Ebens knows he's the lucky one. He is alive. He has a family and a close circle of friends who love and support him.

Vincent is dead. And he shouldn't be. This has always been the hardest part for him.

Although it has been almost forty years since Ronald Ebens met Vincent Chin on that fateful night, he still breaks down sometimes and weeps, knowing that Vincent will always be with him.

# Chapter 37
# "VINCENT'S SOUL WILL NEVER REST"

*VIKKI*
*There is no life without you*
*There is no joy or laughter*
*There is no brightness, no warmth*
*All the mornings after*
*So stay with me*
*And we'll face the tomorrows*
*To find if our love*
*Can overcome the sorrows*
*Remember me always*
*For my love for you is true*
*There isn't anyone else*
*I love you*
*Happy Valentine's Day*

Although he chose to pursue a practical career as an engineering draftsman to support his bride-to-be Vikki Wong and their future family, Vincent had a secret passion for writing. A bookworm since childhood, he loved to write poetry and stories.

When Vincent surprised Vikki on Valentine's Day 1979 with a love poem dedicated to her in the local newspaper, he had no idea how prophetic his words "Remember me always" would become. Vincent Chin's story would inspire later generations of Asian Americans to speak out and fight back against racism and injustice.

This inspiration began almost immediately after Ronald Ebens was acquitted in the second trial in May 1987. Helen Zia and other members of the American Citizens for Justice received phone calls and letters from people all over the country asking them to keep fighting. They included Minoru Yamasaki, the renowned architect who designed the World Trade Center, who would later speak at an ACJ event.

"If Asian people in America don't learn to stand up for themselves, these injustices will never cease," Yamasaki said.

Zia realized that although legally there was nothing else they could do for Vincent Chin, they had a new mission. "All we can do is to continue doing what we've been doing," she said. "To educate people about it and to make sure it doesn't happen again."

The ACJ was not going to "throw in the towel" because Ebens was acquitted, Zia told the press. She said the organization would continue to provide information and referrals for all Asian Americans across the country. They would also monitor similar cases of anti-Asian violence and provide advocacy for those cases.

"Some people continue to believe and to perpetuate the harmful notion that Asian Americans are the 'model minority' that does not encounter racism, discrimination, or hate crimes,"

Zia said. "This widely held stereotype has caused much damage to Asian Americans, making it difficult to get attention for the needs of Asian American communities. The stereotype that Asians in America are not targets of racial violence certainly played a significant role in Vincent Chin's case and the fact that a judge and a jury allowed his killers to go free."

The Vincent Chin case also inspired a future generation of Asian American lawyers, including Frank H. Wu, a Chinese American who was fifteen years old and living in Detroit when Vincent was killed. "It captured everything about the Asian American experience all at once, in a way that enabled me to understand my own life," Wu said. "If you talk to Asian Americans who came of age back then and became journalists or lawyers or who stood up and spoke out, so many of them will tell you it's because of the Vincent Chin case. It's that case that made me do what I do. That case changed my life." Wu would later become the first Asian American to serve as dean at Wayne State University Law School in Detroit.

Vincent Chin's name also became a rallying cry for all of Asian America. Stewart Kwoh and other Asian American and Pacific Islander leaders were inspired to establish a national organization to advocate for all Asian Americans. In 1991 the Asian Pacific American Legal Center (APALC), the Asian Law Caucus (ALC), and the Asian American Legal Education Defense Fund (AALDEF) formed the National Asian Pacific American Legal Consortium, known today as the Asian American Justice Center.

"Hate crimes still occur," said Stewart Kwoh. "And when they do, we have to make sure there is justice."

. . .

Vincent Chin's story also changed the justice system.

His case inspired veteran *Detroit Free Press* journalists John Castine and David Ashenfelter to write an exhaustive, six-part investigative series on manslaughter sentences in Michigan.

Their award-winning series, "Manslaughter: The Price of Life," was published in October 1983. Castine and Ashenfelter examined all 195 manslaughter cases in Michigan in 1982. They researched the 199 people who had killed 209 other people through shootings, stabbings, beatings, and traffic accidents.

In their reporting, the reporters discovered that manslaughter sentences were very inconsistent. It wasn't unusual for someone to receive a multiyear prison sentence for manslaughter while someone else got off with probation. Although the majority of the 199 persons sentenced in 1982 for manslaughter received prison sentences, 15 percent—29 people—were given probation without any jail time. They included Ebens and Nitz.

Yale Kamisar, a University of Michigan law professor, told the *Detroit Free Press* that it was not unusual for one person to receive probation and another to receive life in prison for manslaughter. "That's the way it is," Kamisar said. "There's no getting around it: there's enormous disparity in sentencing."

Part of the problem was that judges in Michigan did not have a standardized method for sentencing criminals found guilty of manslaughter. As a result, judges had to make their sentencing decisions based on their own education and life experience.

"Judges from diverse economic, cultural and philosophical backgrounds, with their own ideas of justice, are bound to impose their own values in the punishment they hand out for manslaughter and other crimes," Castine and Ashenfelter wrote in their series.

As for the plea bargaining of the original charge of second-degree murder to manslaughter, Castine and Ashenfelter discovered that the process had been recklessly abused. "Plea bargaining is supposed to speed up justice, allow prosecutors more time for more important cases, tailor punishment to the offender's background and record, and keep courts from collapsing under the weighty volume of cases," they wrote. But instead of unclogging the court system, the reporters learned, it had the opposite effect, because "the pleas of guilty as charged skyrocketed" and created the impression that killers were "cheating justice."

Marisa Chang, vice-president of American Citizens for Justice, credited the Vincent Chin case with lowering the number of murder charges being reduced to manslaughter. "Since the Vincent Chin case, several judges have announced that they're going to be more careful," she said. "In Wayne County, the prosecutors will no longer accept plea bargaining from murder to manslaughter."

Castine and Ashenfelter's manslaughter series also shed light on another controversy in the Vincent Chin case: the absence of people to represent the victim during sentencing.

On March 16, 1983, when Ebens and Nitz appeared before Judge Charles Kaufman to plead guilty to manslaughter, the prosecutor was not present. Vincent Chin's family and friends were also not present. In fact, Lily Chin would find out later that the sentencing had happened without her knowledge. Otherwise, she would have shown up.

The Vincent Chin case was one of the cases that led to Congress passing the Victims of Crime Act to provide funding for victim assistance in 1984. This act, along with the earlier 1982 Victim and Witness Protection Act, encouraged victim impact statements to be included in court proceedings. "At [the] time of the Chin case, there wasn't an automatic right for the victim's family to give testimony about the victim," explained Roland Hwang. "Now it's just a part of the sentencing process; it's so ingrained that no one thinks about the time when we didn't have that. Thirty-five years ago we didn't have that."

Partly thanks to Vincent Chin, future victims would no longer be silenced. They now had a voice.

• • •

Vincent Chin's federal civil rights trial was the first of its kind for an Asian American citizen. Today these crimes are known as "hate crimes." State and federal hate crime laws now exist to protect people from bias. Although the laws are different in each state, federal law protects victims who are persecuted for their race, religion, ethnicity, nationality, gender, sexual orientation, gender identity, or disability.

In 1982 there were few surveys or research that collected data on victims of hate crimes, especially Asian Americans. After visiting Detroit in 1983, Stewart Kwoh was inspired to start a hate crime tracking project with his legal organization to keep track of hate crimes committed specifically against Americans of Asian and Pacific Islander descent.

On April 23, 1990, the Hate Crime Statistics Act was signed into law by President George H. W. Bush, requiring the attorney general to collect and publish data on hate crimes. Since then the Department of Justice and the FBI have published a yearly report on hate crime statistics. Roughly half of hate crimes committed each year since 1991 were motivated by racial bias.

Since 1982, when the media began covering stories about anti–Asian American and Pacific Islander hate crimes, Vincent Chin's name has frequently been mentioned. Although Ronald Ebens and Michael Nitz were ultimately cleared of all civil rights charges, the controversy over Vincent's death would make him a symbol for Asian American civil rights. In 1989 filmmakers Christine Choy and Renee Tajima-Peña were nominated for an Academy Award for their documentary feature, *Who Killed Vincent Chin?*

Special anniversaries have also been held to commemorate Vincent's death. The most significant occurred at the ten-year, twenty-year, and thirty-year marks. On December 22, 2010, the city of Ferndale officially unveiled its legal milestone plaque commemorating the Vincent Chin case. Roland Hwang, Gary Koivu, and nurse Van Ong attended the ceremony.

But as the decades went by, Vincent's name started to fade from the public memory. New generations of Asian Americans grew up not knowing his name or his story. This prompted Curtis Chin (no relation to Vincent) to write and produce a documentary in 2009 called *Vincent Who?* His documentary is now taught in colleges across the country.

Even younger family members did not know Vincent's story, including Annie Tan. "I first found out about Vincent Chin when I was thirteen years old," Tan said. She was watching a documentary on PBS that featured a segment on Vincent Chin when "my mom pointed to the TV and said, 'That's your older cousin.' I was like, 'What? Really?'"

Tan began researching her family's background. Today she is an elementary special education teacher, writer, and activist living in New York. She has written and delivered speeches about Vincent Chin's life to keep his name alive, including an appearance in the 2020 PBS five-part documentary series *Asian Americans,* produced by Renee Tajima-Peña.

Vincent Chin's name also made a comeback when hate crimes against the Asian American and Pacific Islander community rose exponentially after the November 2016 presidential election—especially in Vincent's home state. According to the Southern Poverty Law Center, Michigan had the highest number of postelection hate crimes in the Midwest.

"History seems to be repeating itself," said James Shimoura. "Some always try to find scapegoats for social and economic ills. The target changes, but the issue remains the same."

In early 2017 Vincent Chin's name made national headlines when a rash of violent hate crimes aimed at Indian American men happened. In February 2017 two Indian men, Srinivas Kuchibhotla and Alok Madasani, were shot in a bar outside of Kansas City after the white male shooter reportedly yelled, "Get out of my country." Srinivas Kuchibhotla died in the hospital soon after he was shot. The killer, Adam Purinton, was later found guilty of federal hate crime charges and is now serving three consecutive life in prison sentences.

"Since the February death of Srinivas Kuchibhotla, the first bias fatality of the Trump era, one question has been coursing through South Asian–American circles: was this hate-crime killing in Olathe, Kansas, their 'Vincent Chin moment'?" wrote Arun Venugopal, a reporter with WNYC and a contributor to NPR. "Chin was a Chinese-American in Detroit who was beaten to death by two white men in 1982. His death is credited with sparking a pan-Asian-American activist movement."

In addition, despite recent new government restrictions on immigration to the United States, the Census Bureau reported that the Asian population was now the fastest-growing one in America.

Today there are just over 330 million people living in the United States. Of them, 22.6 million are of Asian descent, making up 6.8 percent of the total U.S. population. Researchers predict the Asian population in America will double over the next fifty years.

Hate speech against Asian Americans has also noticeably increased. Photographs have documented restaurant workers using racist slurs like *ching chong* and *Chink* to describe Asian American customers waiting to receive their takeout orders. Online viral videos have caught white people harassing Asian Americans by shouting "Go back to your country."

But today, thanks to Vincent's legacy, Asian Americans are fighting back by posting videos and photos on social media to make sure the world is a witness, and that the perpetrators are caught.

As for the increased reports of Asian hate crimes over the years, Advancing Justice | AAJC launched the first-ever national tracker of hate crimes against Asian Americans in 2017.

Ever since June 19, 1982, all these national efforts to document and keep track of the rising hate crimes against Asian Americans can be credited to Vincent Chin's legacy.

When Vincent's mother Lily Chin said, "My son's soul will never rest," she was right.

But not for the reasons she thought. Today Vincent Chin lives on as a symbol against hatred and racism.

His soul is not yet ready to rest.

Vincent Chin is buried at the Forest Lawn Cemetery in Detroit, his tombstone lying just behind his parents' grave marker.

# "WE NEED TO TALK ABOUT THIS"

"We need to talk about this."

But Vikki Wong didn't want to talk.

The day after he accidentally texted his mom about Vincent Chin, Jarod had stopped by his parents' house.

"I was kind of embarrassed," he said. "We sat down in the family room, and she asked me a bunch of questions on why I wanted to do this project, why I felt it was important. I could tell she was annoyed that I had been doing research behind her back."

It upset Jarod to see his mother in such pain. He began to wonder if maybe this had all been a bad idea. What had driven him this whole time to find out about Vincent Chin? Why would he risk hurting his mother by reminding her of the darkest tragedy in her life? Why couldn't he just move on and forget about Vincent Chin like everyone else had?

"Why do you need to bring him up?" Vikki asked again. "Why can't you let him rest in peace?"

Suddenly images flashed through Jarod's mind about all the strange coincidences that had happened to him over the past few years, from renting a house just a few blocks from Vincent's childhood home to celebrating his birthday at the site of Vincent's former Golden Star Restaurant to passing by

To this day, the legacy of Vincent Chin and his mother, Lily, lives on as a symbol for justice for the Asian American and Pacific Islander community against hatred and racism.

his memorial plaque every day on his way to work without even realizing it.

"His name, his past, it all seemed very connected to me," he said. "It was just him poking at me in the shadows, *Hey, look this way*, pushing me toward this history. It was like he was saying to me, *Don't forget about me, don't forget about this. This is a part of why you're here.*"

Jarod finally knew how to answer his mother's question.

"Because we should know about Vincent Chin."

# AFTERWORD

As I write this, more than 367,000 Americans have died from the COVID-19 coronavirus.

My Asian American friends have reported being called *Chink* and being coughed at or spat upon by strangers who blame them for the spread of this virus. Right before temporary air travel restrictions went into effect, airline passengers requested to be seated elsewhere from my family members during trips.

One day in early April 2020, I was even racially profiled at my own house. A white family of four had decided to take a rest during their neighborhood walk by standing in our driveway. At the time, social distancing of six feet was recommended and masks were not yet mandatory. We had a friendly conversation as I stood behind my front door, where they could hear my voice but not see my face. But when I opened my door to wave hello (while maintaining the mandated social distancing of six feet), the family immediately recoiled in fear because they could see that I was of Asian descent. "Get back from her," the father shouted.

. . .

Even though this viral disease affected everyone, many people, including prominent politicians, have pointed the finger at China.

For example, Senator John Cornyn (R-Texas) said in a March 18, 2020, interview with *The Hill*: "China is to blame because, the culture where people eat bats and snakes and dogs and things like that, these viruses are transmitted from the animal to the people and that's why China has been the source of a lot of these viruses like SARS, like MERS, the Swine Flu." When reporters asked Senator Cornyn if blaming China for the novel coronavirus was racist against Asian Americans, he replied, "I disagree. We're not talking about Asians, we're talking about China where these viruses emanate from and have created this pandemic."

In March 2020, during press conferences about the global pandemic, President Donald Trump insisted on referring to the coronavirus as the "Chinese virus," the "China Plague," and "China virus" even though Robert R. Redfield, the director of the Centers for Disease Control and Prevention (CDC), and other health experts, condemned these phrases as "absolutely wrong."

As a result, Americans of Asian and Pacific Islander descent became targets of racism and violence related to the pandemic. More than 30 percent of Americans reported witnessing coronavirus-related harassment and/or hate crimes against Asian Americans, according to the Center for Public Integrity. Other hate crime trackers, including the Stop AAPI Hate tracker by the Asian Pacific Policy and Planning Council, reported receiving more than 2,500 reports of racist incidents linked to the pandemic between March and August 2020.

These incidents ranged from verbal abuse, including racist slurs, to civil rights violations in the workplace to physical violence. Teenagers at a San Fernando Valley High School in California attacked a sixteen-year-old Asian American boy, sending him to the hospital with a concussion. Asian Americans in New York reported being kicked and punched by strangers on the subway.

In late March 2020 a man stabbed an Asian American man and his two children, ages two and six, along with a store employee (a white male) at a Sam's Club in Midland, Texas. He was charged with attempted capital murder and aggravated assault. The FBI is investigating this incident as a hate crime. "The suspect indicated that he stabbed the family because he thought the family was Chinese, and infecting people with coronavirus," confirmed an FBI spokesperson. According to the FBI's report, "Hate crime incidents against Asian Americans likely will surge across the United States, due to the spread of coronavirus disease . . . endangering Asian American communities. The FBI makes this assessment based on the assumption that a portion of the US public will associate COVID-19 with China and Asian American populations."

. . .

Almost forty years after his death, Vincent Chin's name is being mentioned again in the media as a warning. Especially in Michigan. The Vincent Chin case "is still remembered by many Asian Americans in metro Detroit," wrote Niraj Warikoo for the *Detroit Free Press*. "They're worried about any resurgence of anti-Asian racism."

"Trump is attempting to incite hatred, violence, and discrimination against Chinese Americans," said Michigan attorney general Dana Nessel. "We won't tolerate it in Michigan." She urged everyone to report all suspected hate crimes to the local police and to the state's hate crimes unit.

Roland Hwang once again found himself fighting back. "I'm really alarmed by Trump calling the virus a Chinese virus,"

Hwang said. "There is no geographic, political subdivisions, racial or ethnic limitation with respect to the virus." As the secretary of the Association of Chinese Americans, Hwang released the following statement: "Attaching a racial, ethnic or country name to a virus, even informally, serves only to flame the fears and biases of people against Chinese and those of Asian background to no benefit in the battle against the virus pandemic."

Michigan state senator Stephanie Chang (D-Detroit) agreed. "The virus is a virus. It does not have a race or ethnicity," she posted on her social media Twitter account.

Helen Zia also found herself fighting back again. "We can stop repeating history and prevent the scapegoating and prejudice that killed Vincent Chin," she said. "Division and violence only weakens America. During this terrible pandemic and crisis, we must also fight the anti-Asian virus and call on the best of America to stand for human dignity, together."

"The atmosphere of hate today is eerily similar to that of 1982, when Vincent was killed," agreed Academy Award–nominated filmmaker Renee Tajima-Peña of *Who Killed Vincent Chin?* "But another thing resonates with that time: people are speaking out and standing against hate."

· · ·

Because the Asian American and Pacific Islander community fought back against the surge of anti-Asian racism during the pandemic, President Trump was finally forced to address the "Chinese virus" controversy. "It is very important that we totally protect our Asian American community in the United States, and all around the world," he wrote on his official Twitter social media account.

Despite that Tweet, Trump continued to use the term *China-virus* and even joked about it with supporters at a June 21, 2020, election campaign rally in Tulsa, Oklahoma. "COVID-19, that name gets further and further away from China as opposed to calling it the Chinese virus," he said, eliciting cheers from the audience. "It's a disease without question, has more names than any disease in history. I can name, 'kung flu.' I can name, nineteen different versions of names."

The crowd's cheers at the racist term *kung flu* disturbed many prominent Asian Americans, including Chris Lu, who had served as cabinet secretary for President Barack Obama. "The fact that he got the crowd so riled up was just chilling," Lu said. "In that really primal desire to get a rise out of the crowd and get that affirmation he wants, he went to this place that has such bad consequences for Asian Americans broadly and for Asian American kids in particular. It's a joke to him but not to us."

Trump's language angered both Representative Judy Chu (D-California) and Representative Ted Lieu (D-California). Chu, along with the Congressional Asian Pacific American Caucus, released a statement in February condemning the "deeply disturbing racism targeting the Asian American community."

In July 2020, Ted Lieu assembled a bipartisan group of 150 members of Congress to demand Attorney General William Barr publicly condemn anti-Asian coronavirus-related racism and provide immediate and specific action against such acts. "We did not understand why the Department of Justice wasn't doing more in countering hate crimes," Lieu said. "The dangers faced by the Asian American community today are very real and deserve a strong and specific response by our government."

As for Trump, "it'd be great if the president condemned racism, but I just want him to stop making his own racist statements. If he could do that, that'd be very helpful," Lieu said.

Trump, however has yet to apologize for his racist rhetoric.

"It's clear that Donald Trump started to resort to xenophobic, anti-immigrant, and racist actions when he started to sag in the polls," Lieu observed. "He started to embrace the Confederacy. He started to again use statements about the pandemic that negatively affected Asian Americans."

On September 17, 2020, the U.S. House of Representatives passed a resolution denouncing anti-Asian racism related to the coronavirus pandemic. The final vote was 243–164. Representative Grace Meng (D-NY) introduced the resolution, calling for "all public officials to condemn and denounce any and all anti-Asian sentiment in any form." The resolution also criticized "anti-Asian terminology and rhetoric related to COVID-19, such as the "Chinese Virus," "Wuhan Virus," and "Kung-flu," stating that these words "perpetuated anti-Asian stigma."

In the midst of this global pandemic, Black and white racial tensions in America also reached another tipping point. The killings of several Black men and women—notably Breonna Taylor and George Floyd—by white police officers set off a chain reaction of #BlackLivesMatter protests across not just the United States but also the world. On the night of May 30, 2020, twenty-five cities, including Los Angeles, across sixteen states were not only in a COVID-19 stay-at-home quarantine but also under a mandatory eight p.m. curfew with the National Guard being called in. These protests would continue throughout the year.

During many of these protests, the Asian American and Pacific Islander community banded together with groups like #Asians4BlackLives to show solidarity, just as Reverend Jesse Jackson and the Black community did for the Asian American community during the Justice for Vincent Chin protest rallies back in the early 1980s. According to a July 28, 2020, Gallup poll, 89 percent of Asian American respondents supported these protests against racial injustice.

COVID-19 is not the only virus plaguing our world. Racism is also a virus that we must cure.

Although I do not know what the future holds, I do know this.

We will always continue to fight back against hate.

That is what Vincent Chin's legacy has taught us.

*Paula Yoo*
*Los Angeles*
*January 2021*

# TIMELINE

**1905:** David Bing Hing Chin (also referred to as C. W. Hing; Vincent's father) is born in China.

**June 18, 1920:** Lily Yee (Chin) (Vincent's mother) is born in Heping, Guangdong Province, China.

**1922:** David Chin emigrates to the United States and later enlists in the U.S. Army.

**October 30, 1939:** Ronald Ebens is born in Dixon, Illinois.

**1948:** David Chin returns to China to marry Lily Yee; they return to America and settle in Detroit.

**May 18, 1955:** Vincent Chin is born in Guangdong Province, China.

**October 31, 1958:** Michael Nitz is born in Wisconsin.

**1961:** Lily and Hing Chin adopt Vincent, and he arrives in the United States.

**1965:** Ten-year-old Vincent becomes an American citizen.

**1971:** Sixteen-year-old Vincent's family moves from Highland Park to Oak Park after Vincent's father is beaten and robbed.

**1973:** Vincent graduates from Oak Park High School.

**1978:** Vincent meets Vikki Wong.

**May 1980:** Vincent graduates from Control Data Institute with honors and receives a certificate of excellence for computer programming and operations.

**November 3, 1981:** David Chin (Vincent's father) dies of kidney disease.

**June 19, 1982:** On the evening of his bachelor party, Vincent Chin is bludgeoned to death with a baseball bat by Ronald Ebens after an earlier fight with him and Michael Nitz at a strip club.

**June 23, 1982:** Vincent Chin dies in a coma.

**June 29, 1982:** Vincent Chin's funeral is held at the Sawyer-Fuller Funeral Home in Berkley, Michigan, one day after the date for Vincent and Vikki Wong's wedding.

**February 8, 1983:** Ronald Ebens pleads guilty and Michael Nitz pleads no contest to reduced charges of manslaughter.

**March 16, 1983:** Wayne County circuit judge Charles Kaufman sentences Ebens and Nitz each to three years of probation, a $3,000 fine plus court costs, and no jail time.

**March 25, 1983:** *Detroit Free Press* columnist Nickie McWhirter posts an editorial condemning Judge Kaufman's sentencing.

**March 28, 1983:** Association of Chinese Americans writes a letter requesting that Judge Kaufman reconsider his original sentence of probation and fines for Ebens and Nitz.

**March 28, 1983:** Ronald Ebens is fired from his job as a general foreman at Chrysler Corporation's Warren Truck Plant.

**March 31, 1983:** American Citizens for Justice (ACJ) is founded.

**April 29, 1983:** Judge Kaufman hears arguments on whether to change his sentence. About a hundred protesters are present at the hearing.

**May 9, 1983:** About one thousand marchers rally in downtown Detroit to protest Ebens and Nitz's sentences.

**May 17, 1983:** Liza Chan meets with Vincent Chin's friends and crime witnesses Jimmy Choi, Gary Koivu, and Bob Sirosky and records their statements.

**June 3, 1983:** Judge Kaufman announces he will not resentence Ebens and Nitz.

**June 19, 1983:** Rallies are held across the country on the one-year anniversary of Vincent Chin's beating.

**June 29, 1983:** ACJ representatives and Lily Chin meet with the Department of Justice in Washington, D.C., to demand a federal investigation into whether Vincent Chin's civil rights were violated.

**July 1983:** The Justice Department orders the FBI to investigate whether Ebens and Nitz violated Chin's civil rights.

**August 4, 1983:** The Justice Department announces that a special federal grand jury in Detroit will hear evidence in Chin's slaying.

**September 1, 1983:** The grand jury begins its inquiry.

**October 7, 1983:** Lily Chin appears on *The Phil Donahue Show* ("Justice in America")

**November 2, 1983:** A federal grand jury indicts Ebens and Nitz on two counts: interfering with Chin's right to use and enjoy a place of public accommodation on account of his race, and conspiracy.

**June 5, 1984:** The federal trial begins at the Eastern District of Michigan court in Detroit.

**June 28, 1984:** The jury finds Ebens not guilty of conspiracy but guilty of interference with Chin's civil rights. Nitz is cleared of both charges.

**September 18, 1984:** Ebens is sentenced to twenty-five years in prison by U.S. District judge Anna Diggs Taylor. He appeals and is released on a $20,000 bond.

**March 3, 1986:** Ebens sues Chrysler for money damages and reinstatement.

**September 11, 1986:** The Sixth Circuit Court of Appeals reverses Ebens's conviction, citing improper introduction of evidence and coaching of witnesses.

**September 19, 1986:** The Justice Department announces it will retry the case against Ebens.

**February 23, 1987:** The new trial is moved to Cincinnati.

**April 22, 1987:** Ebens's new trial begins.

**May 1, 1987:** The Cincinnati jury acquits Ebens. He is cleared of all charges, meaning that neither Ebens nor Nitz would ever spend a full day in jail for the beating death of Vincent Chin.

**July 1987:** In a civil suit, Ebens is ordered to pay $1.5 million to the estate of Vincent Chin. Ebens disposes of his assets and later leaves Michigan. To date, he has not paid any of the settlement.

**September 1987:** Vincent Chin's mother, Lily Chin, later leaves the United States and moves back to Guangzhou, China.

**May 27, 1992:** Ebens loses his appeal to recover $400,000 in back pay from Chrysler. He remains unemployed.

**June 9, 2002:** Lily Chin dies, two weeks before the twentieth anniversary of her son's death.

# ACKNOWLEDGMENTS

It is an honor and privilege to tell Vincent Chin's story. Thank you to my editor, Simon Boughton and everyone at Norton Young Readers, and to my literary agent Tricia Lawrence and the Erin Murphy Literary Agency, for believing that Vincent's story should be told for future generations.

I am grateful for the many voices who spoke out to keep his name and legacy alive for this book. It was helpful and in many instances inspiring to meet those directly involved with the Vincent Chin case, including those not named here because they requested privacy. I appreciate everyone's time, expertise, and reflection on this pivotal moment in Asian American history. I know how much pain this story brought up for everyone involved who had to remember—and relive—what happened in 1982. Thank you for your honesty and candor:

Laura Black, Liza Chan, Morris Cotton, Frank Eaman, Denise Yee Grim, Roland Hwang, Gary Koivu, Stewart Kwoh, Corky Lee, Jarod Lew, Mable Lim, Van Ong, James Shimoura, Miriam Siefer, Marc Susselman, Parker Woo, and Helen Zia.

I greatly appreciate the hard work and generosity of my fellow journalists, writers, filmmakers, librarians, academics, and research archivists who provided expertise and access to important primary sources for this book. Your scholarship helped me immensely in my goal to make sure everything was presented in an accurate and authentic manner:

Juanita Anderson, Hui-Lim Ang, Leo L. Belleville, Glenn

Longacre, Sarah Kreydich, and staff (National Archives at Chicago), the Bentley Historical Library at the University of Michigan in Ann Arbor, George Brown, Jo Lloyd, and Alison Green Myers (Highlights Foundation), John Castine (*Detroit Free Press*), Curtis Chin (*Vincent Who?*), Christine Choy (*Who Killed Vincent Chin?*), Kevin Chu and staff (Museum of Chinese in America), Jim Duran (Vanderbilt Television News Archive), Nancy Etz and Grant Kessman (Creative Artists Agency), Jessica R. Friedman, Susan Grider (Vanderbilt Law Library), Elizabeth Lee, Allan Lengel, and all my friends and colleagues from *The Detroit News,* Ken Loomis and staff (U.S. Court of Appeals for the Sixth Circuit), Julia Pope (Conrad R. Lam Archives, Sladen Libraries of Henry Ford Health System), John Purdy and staff (U.S. District Court for the Eastern District of Michigan), Neda Salem and staff (Ethnic Studies Library at the University of California, Berkeley), Steve Simons (The Shuman Company), Neb Solomon, Renee Tajima-Peña (*Who Killed Vincent Chin?*), Annie Tan, Andrea Teets and staff (U.S. District Court for the Eastern District of Michigan), Frances Kai-Hwa Wang, Nia Wong (4 News Now KLXY), and Frank H. Wu.

My gratitude for my dear friends, Detroit crew, and children's literature/young adult writing colleagues, and fellow Asian American activists for your advice, critiques, and support during the writing of this book:

Edith (Edi) Campbell, William Chang, Amy Cherrix, ML Compton, Sarah Park Dahlen, Jim Diamond, Kelly DiPucchio, Dr. Marilisa Jiménez García, Jeff Kim, Dr. Laura M. Jiménez, Mike Jung, Skip King, Erin Eitter Kono, Greg Lanier, Cindy Lin, John Linardos, Ken Min, Debbie Reese, Anne Renton, Cristina

Rhodes, Ph.D., David Smith, Sandy Tanaka, Eric Wallace, Renée Watson, Bruce Wright, Jeff Yang, and Phil Yu.

Love to my family: My parents, Young and Kim Yoo, my brother David Yoo and sister-in-law Jessica Jackson-Yoo, their children Griffin and Lucy, and the extended Jackson family. Sara Yoo. Kenneth and Julie Yoo. Chris and Jolina Yoo. Susan and Sean Sang Yoon. Samuel and Monica Kwon. Lisa Kwon Choi and Vincent Choi. James and Tina Kwon. Paul and Jessica Kwon. Janice and Ted Center. Don McCorkle and Kristine Dyke. Kelly McCorkle Schafer and Tom Schafer. Jonathan Earp and Jocelyn Truong. All my nieces and nephews. And to my husband, Kyle McCorkle, and our three cats Oreo, Beethoven, and Charlotte.

For Vincent, Lily, and David Chin—Rest in peace. Rest in power.

# NOTES

### *"You Don't Know About Vincent Chin?"*

2 **"It was a very surreal moment"**: All quotations from Jarod Lew in this chapter come from author interviews on June 1, 2018, and April 17, 2019.

### *Chapter 1: "One Last Night Out with the Guys"*

7 **But now at twenty-seven**: Brian Flanigan, "Slaying Ends Couple's Dream," *Detroit Free Press*, July 1, 1982.

8 **they had scheduled their wedding**: *Fatal Encounters* (film), exec. prod. Lloyd Fales and Knute Walker (2013).

8 **"one last night out with the guys"**: Chin quoted in Helen Zia, *East West*, April 13, 1983.

8 **"Okay Mom"**: Lily Chin interview, *Who Killed Vincent Chin?* (film), dir. Christine Choy and Renee Tajima-Peña (1987), transcript, MOCA.

9 **Ronald Ebens and his stepson**: *United States v. Ronald Ebens and Michael Nitz*, No. 83-60629, Ronald Ebens witness testimony, p. 155 (U.S. District Court for the Eastern District of Michigan Southern Division, June 19, 1984), transcript, NAC.

9 **at the Chrysler plant**: Ebens interview, *Who Killed Vincent Chin?*

9 **along with almost a quarter-million autoworkers**: Lydia Chavez, "G.M. Sets Closing of 4 Parts Plants," *New York Times,* February 26, 1982.

9 **"Boy, you don't know"**: Angela Rudolph ("Starlene") interview, *Who Killed Vincent Chin?*

10 **She liked Vincent's**: *United States v. Ronald Ebens and Michael Nitz*, No. 83-60629, Racine Colwell witness testimony, p. 7 (U.S. District Court for the Eastern District of Michigan Southern Division, June 14, 1984), transcript, NAC.

10 **"It's because of you"**: Ibid. (June 13), p. 226.

10 **Ebens would later claim**: Ronald Ebens witness testimony, ibid. (June 19), p. 164.

10 **"He shoved him"**: Gary Koivu witness testimony, ibid. (June 13), p. 156.

10 **The fight escalated from there**: Racine Colwell witness testimony, ibid. (June 13), p. 229.

11 **"I was hoping once the fight"**: Gary Koivu interview, *Fatal Encounters*.

11 **Out in the parking lot**: Highland Park Police Report, June 19, 1982.

11 **He glared at Vincent**: Christine Choy interview, *Fatal Encounters*.

12 **As they drove down Woodward Avenue**: Ebens interview, *Who Killed Vincent Chin?*

12 **"All I could think of"**: Ibid.

13 **"It kind of shocked me":** Morris Cotton interview, *Who Killed Vincent Chin?*

13 **Inside the McDonald's:** Paul Weingarten, "The Unquiet Death of Vincent Chin: An Examination of the Killing Detroit Can't Forget," *Chicago Tribune*, July 31, 1983.

13 **Ebens slammed:** Ronald Ebens witness testimony, *United States v. Ebens and Nitz*, June 19, 1984, p. 183.

13 **"His eyes were glazed":** Cotton interview, *Fatal Encounters*.

13 **"Mr. Ebens was standing":** Gardenhire quoted in Weingarten, "Unquiet Death."

14 **"He was swinging":** Cotton interview, *Fatal Encounters*.

14 **The blows shattered:** Zia, *Asian American Dreams*, p. 59.

14 **Ebens swung the bat one last time:** *United States v. Ronald Ebens and Michael Nitz*, No. 83-60629, Morris Cotton witness testimony, p. 42, 44 (U.S. District Court for the Eastern District of Michigan Southern Division, June 15, 1984), transcript, NAC.

14 **"Back up!":** Morris Cotton, interview by author, June 24, 2019.

14 **"Get out of the way!":** Ibid.

14 **"And at this time":** Cotton interview, *Fatal Encounters*.

14 **"Fight":** Chin quoted in Tim Kiska, "Friend Says Chin Provoked Fight," *Detroit Free Press*, June 15, 1984.

14 **His pupils were fixed and dilated:** Ibid.

14 **"It's not fair":** Chin quoted ibid.

## Chapter 2: Murder City

15 **"I've seen a lot of violent death":** Gerald Alan Thompson interview, *Who Killed Vincent Chin?* (film), dir. Christine Choy and Renee Tajima-Peña (1987), transcript, MOCA.

15 **On the night of June 19, 1982:** Ibid.

15 **"There was brains":** Ibid.

15 **"Look what he did":** *United States v. Ronald Ebens and Michael Nitz*, No. 83-60629, Gerald Alan Thompson witness testimony, p. 55 (U.S. District Court for the Eastern District of Michigan Southern Division, June 20, 1984), transcript, NAC.

16 **"I had a critical patient":** Ibid.

16 **"I'm sorry that this happened":** Michael Gardenhire quoted in Paul Weingarten, "The Unquiet Death of Vincent Chin: An Examination of the Killing Detroit Can't Forget," *Chicago Tribune*, July 31, 1983.

16 **"he shouldn't have done it":** *United States v. Ronald Ebens and Michael Nitz*, No. 83-60629, Michael Gardenhire witness testimony, p. 88 (U.S. District Court for the Eastern District of Michigan Southern Division, June 13, 1984), transcript, NAC.

16 **As the other EMTs:** Thompson interview, *Who Killed Vincent Chin?*

16  **"I can tell you this"**: Ibid.

16  **"Come on, Vince"**: Robert Siroskey, Gary Koivu, and Jimmy Choi, interview by Liza Chan, May 17, 1983.

16  **"He's losing consciousness"**: Ibid.

16  **"They started rapping"**: Ibid.

16  **"Don't lose consciousness"**: Ibid.

17  **Van Ong thought:** Van Ong, interview by author, June 22, 2018.

17  **"I saw the dark side"**: Ibid.

17  **"We used to call ourselves"**: Laura Black, interview by author, July 7, 2018.

17  **By 10:21 p.m.:** Dr. Jeffrey Crecelius witness testimony, *United States v. Ebens and Nitz* (June 13), p. 117.

18  **Ong could barely recognize Vincent:** Ong interview by author.

18  **"I went there and asked"**: Gary Koivu interview, *Who Killed Vincent Chin?*

18  **The parking attendant:** Ibid.

18  **"That was the only place"**: Ibid.

18  ***"Where you guys been?"***: Siroskey, Koivu, and Choi interview by Chan, p. 115.

19  **"No, Vincent's in the hospital"**: Ibid.

19  **"It was pretty somber"**: Koivu interview, *Who Killed Vincent Chin?*

19  **Five percent:** Dr. Jeffrey Crecelius witness testimony, *United States v. Ebens and Nitz* (June 13), p. 118.

19  **A CAT scan revealed:** Ibid., pp. 120–21.

19  **"We tend to give a younger person"**: Ibid., p. 118.

19  **Surgery began at one a.m.:** Ibid., pp. 120–22.

20  **By six o'clock that morning:** Ibid., p. 122.

### *Chapter 3: "Mama Is Here"*

21  **So did Vincent:** Lily Chin interview, *Who Killed Vincent Chin?* (film), dir. Christine Choy and Renee Tajima-Peña (1987), transcript, MOCA.

21  **Lily yawned:** Ibid.

21  **"Vincent must have forgotten"**: Ibid.

21  **He treated Vincent like his own son:** Paul Weingarten, "The Unquiet Death of Vincent Chin: An Examination of the Killing Detroit Can't Forget," *Chicago Tribune*, July 31, 1983.

22  **"Uncle Ping"**: Chin interview, *Who Killed Vincent Chin?*

22  **He said Danny:** Ibid.

22  **"I was thinking"**: Ibid.

22  **"Don't worry, Auntie"**: Ibid.

22  **"Vincent's mother was crying"**: Gary Koivu interview, *Who Killed Vincent Chin?*

22  **"Unfortunately, this violence"**: Laura Black, interview by author, July 7, 2018.

23 **"I ask how he is":** Chin quoted in Weingarten, "Unquiet Death."

23 **Dr. Crecelius took Lily:** Ibid.

23 **The patients in ICU:** Black interview by author.

24 **And now his head:** Chin interview, *Who Killed Vincent Chin?*

24 **She and her husband:** Colin Covert, "The Ordeal of Lily Chin," *Detroit Free Press*, July 7, 1983.

24 **Lily showed the photo:** Ibid.

24 **When Vincent met:** Linda Chong, "Lily Chin Tries to Ease Pain: "Death of a Dream: Vincent Chin's Mother Gives Up on America," *Detroit Free Press,* September 9, 1987.

24 **"He was a terrific kid":** Chin interview, *Who Killed Vincent Chin?*

24 **Meanwhile, Lily kept:** Ibid.

25 **"I kept saying":** Ibid.

25 **"I remembered seeing":** Gary Koivu, interview by author, June 22, 2018.

25 **"I was with him for four days":** Vikki Wong interview, *Vincent Who?* (film), dir. Tony Lam and written/produced by Curtis Chin (2009).

25 **"I am sometimes a stubbornly":** Chin interview, *Who Killed Vincent Chin?*

25 **"His brain stopped functioning":** *United States v. Ronald Ebens and Michael Nitz,* No. 83-60629, Dr. Jeffrey Crecelius witness testimony, p. 123 (U.S. District Court for the Eastern District of Michigan Southern Division, June 13, 1984), transcript, NAC.

26 **On June 23, 1982:** Ibid.

### Chapter 4: Father's Day

27 **"We were at a bar":** *United States v. Ronald Ebens and Michael Nitz*, No. 83-60629, Morris Cotton witness testimony, pp. 48–49 (U.S. District Court for the Eastern District of Michigan Southern Division, June 15, 1984).

27 **Detective Donald Roberts, a nineteen-year veteran:** Donald Roberts witness testimony, ibid. (June 19), pp. 140–42.

27 **"There was such a commotion":** Ibid.

27 **Vincent Chin would turn out:** Paul Weingarten, "The Unquiet Death of Vincent Chin: An Examination of the Killing Detroit Can't Forget," *Chicago Tribune*, July 31, 1983.

28 **When Roberts arrived:** Roberts witness testimony, *United States v. Ebens and Nitz* (June 19), p. 142.

28 **Juanita soon arrived:** Michael Nitz witness testimony, ibid. (June 20), p. 89.

28 **Ebens had trouble sleeping:** Ronald Ebens interview, *Who Killed Vincent Chin?* (film), dir. Christine Choy and Renee Tajima-Peña (1987), transcript, MOCA.

28 **"That was the first time":** Ibid.

28 **Second-degree murder is:** "Second Degree Murder," Legal Informa-

tion Institute, Cornell Law School, https://www.law.cornell.edu/wex/ second_degree_murder. For Michigan, see "Michigan Second-Degree Murder Law—Michigan Penal Code Section 750.317," *FindLaw,* https:// statelaws.findlaw.com/michigan-law/michigan-second-degree-murder -law.html.

28   **A defense attorney showed up:** Weingarten, "Unquiet Death."

29   **"We checked the guy":** Roberts quoted ibid.

29   **"He said it sounded like a fair fight":** Morris Cotton, interview by author, June 24, 2019.

29   **"I lock up people":** Ibid.

31   **"I locked up Black people":** Ibid.

31   **"You'd go to some folks' homes":** Ibid.

31   **"They pulled their guns on us":** Ibid.

32   **During high school:** Ibid.

32   **While at Wayne State:** Ibid.

33   **"At that time, I didn't see":** Juanita Ebens interview, *Who Killed Vincent Chin?*

33   **"Vincent died today":** Juanita Ebens quoted in Michael Moore, "The Man Who Killed Vincent Chin: The Wages of Death," *Detroit Free Press,* August 30, 1987.

33   **"Two days later Ebens and Nitz:** Weingarten, "Unquiet Death."

### Chapter 5: "As Long as We Have Each Other"

34   **"Mrs. Lily F. Chin":** Quoted from image from *Who Killed Vincent Chin?* (film), dir. Christine Choy and Renee Tajima-Peña (1987), transcript, MOCA.

35   **"Vince was a happy person":** Wong quoted in Paul Weingarten, "The Unquiet Death of Vincent Chin: An Examination of the Killing Detroit Can't Forget," *Chicago Tribune,* July 31, 1983.

35   **"He was charismatic":** Denise Yee Grim, interview by author, October 3, 2018.

35   **"I was always the quiet one":** Gary Koivu interview, *Who Killed Vincent Chin?*

35   **"He always had his nose in a book":** Choi quoted in Weingarten, "Unquiet Death."

35   **"He was a comic book geek":** Grim interview by author.

36   **"I said, 'Vincent, you can't' ":** Chin quoted in Colin Covert, "The Ordeal of Lily Chin," *Detroit Free Press,* July 7, 1983.

36   **He later surprised Vikki:** Vincent Chin, "Vikki," *Detroit Free Press,* February 14, 1979.

36   **"I could tell they got along":** Gary Koivu, interview by author, June 22, 2018.

36  **"Vincent was devoted to her":** Chin quoted in Weingarten, "Unquiet Death."

36  **"She came to work":** Shafer quoted in Brian Flanigan, "Slaying Ends Couple's Dream," *Detroit Free Press*, July 1, 1982.

36  **"We thought that was nice":** Grim interview by author.

37  **"When his father died":** Choi quoted in Matt Beer, "Getting Away with Murder? The Life and Death of Vincent Chin," *Detroit News*, April 17, 1983.

37  **"Vincent wouldn't walk":** Weingarten, "Unquiet Death."

37  **"There really wasn't anybody":** Blair quoted in Beer, "Getting Away with Murder?"

37  **"Aruba!":** Chin quoted in Flanigan, "Slaying Ends Couple's Dream."

37  **"Vincent was very good":** Chin quoted in Weingarten, "Unquiet Death."

38  **"He said, 'Mama, I want' ":** Chin quoted in Linda Chong, "Lily Chin Tries to Ease Pain: Death of a Dream: Vincent Chin's Mother Gives Up on America," *Detroit News*, September 9, 1987.

38  **Dozens of gaily wrapped wedding presents:** Kin Yee interview, *Who Killed Vincent Chin?*

38  **"I felt a great sense of loss":** Gary Koivu interview, *Fatal Encounters* (film), exec. prod. Lloyd Fales and Knute Walker (Investigation Discovery, 2013).

39  **"He's standing in front":** Koivu interview, *Who Killed Vincent Chin?*

39  **They hung out together:** Koivu interview by author.

39  **"I was very quiet":** Ibid.

39  **"very friendly, always talkative":** Koivu interview, *Who Killed Vincent Chin?*

39  **"He would take a couple":** Ibid.

40  **"We didn't catch much":** Koivu interview by author.

40  **"We used to discuss old movies":** Koivu interview, *Who Killed Vincent Chin?*

40  **"I felt terrible":** Ibid.

## *Chapter 6: "The Little Yellow People"*

42  **In 1982 Detroit:** Helen Zia, *Asian American Dreams: The Emergence of an American People* (New York: Farrar, Straus & Giroux, 2000), p. 56.

42  **"It was zero about Asian Americans":** Helen Zia, interview by author, June 6, 2018.

43  **"It felt dangerous":** Zia, *Asian American Dreams,* p. 58.

43  **more than 300,000 people moved out:** "Table 23. Michigan—Race and Hispanic Origin for Selected Large Cities and Other Places: Earliest Census to 1990," U.S. Census Bureau, https://www.census.gov/content/dam/Census/library/working-papers/2005/demo/POP-twps0076.pdf. The

table shows the 1970 Detroit population as 1,511,482, and it went down to 1,203,339 in 1980, which means 308,143 people left.

44 **"I definitely stood out"**: Zia, *Asian American Dreams,* p. 56.

44 **"good Asian American child"**: Ibid., p. 55.

44 **So Zia graduated:** "Helen Zia Facts," *Biography,* https://biography .yourdictionary.com/helen-zia.

44 **"I had made a terrible mistake"**: Zia, *Asian American Dreams,* p. 55.

44 **She drove from Boston:** Ibid.

45 **"So we'd get a flat piece"**: Zia interview by author.

45 **"Once I was working"**: Ibid.

45 **"These jobs paid a lot"**: Ibid.

45 **"The auto industry was totally"**: Ibid.

46 **"new poor"**: Zia, *Asian American Dreams,* p. 57.

46 **"When I got laid off"**: Zia interview by author.

46 **"These were good jobs"**: Ibid.

47 **"[Anti-Japanese] feeling"**: Prout quoted in Paul Weingarten, "The Unquiet Death of Vincent Chin: An Examination of the Killing Detroit Can't Forget," *Chicago Tribune,* July 31, 1983.

48 **"Italian Americans or German Americans"**: Shimoura quoted in Colin Covert, "Japanese Americans in Detroit," *Detroit Free Press,* July 10, 1983.

48 **"I was born here"**: Ibid.

48 **more than 300,000 American autoworkers:** Carl Levin in *Hearings Before the Committee on Commerce, Science, and Transportation* on . . . *Domestic Content Requirements for Motor Vehicles Sold in the United States,* U.S. Senate, 97th Cong., 2nd sess., December 16 and 17, 1982 (Washington, D.C.: U.S. Government Printing Office), p. 31.

48 **"We are being shot at"**: Ibid.

49 **"the little yellow people"**: Dingell quoted in Francis X. Clines and Warren Weaver, Jr., "Briefing: Startling Comment," *New York Times,* March 16, 1982.

49 **"had never intentionally"**: Dingell quoted in Hobart Rowen, "U.S.-Japan Trade Battle Enters an Ugly Phase," *Owensboro Messenger-Inquirer* (Kentucky), April 2, 1982.

49 **"Japan is part of"**: Reagan quoted in John Phelan, "'80s Fears of a Japanese 'Economic Pearl Harbor' Look Silly Today—But They're Instructive," Foundation for Economic Education, June 14, 2019, https://tinyurl.com/y2hd2sd5.

49 **"If I were president"**: O'Neill quoted in Sam Jameson, "Seen as 'Scapegoat' for U.S. on Trade and Defense: Japanese Alarmed at American Criticism," *Los Angeles Times,* March 19, 1982.

49 **"in the backyard"**: Tom Hundley and Bob Campbell, "Japan-Bashing: Slaying of Vincent Chin Awakened Detroit Area to the Dangers of Anti-Japanese Sentiment," *Detroit Free Press,* October 27, 1985.

50 **"There was a lot of hatred"**: Zia interview by author.

50 **"I knew there was something more"**: Ibid.

### "They Keep Their History Very Quiet"

51 **"I realized this was pretty important"**: All quotations from Jarod Lew in this chapter come from author interviews on June 1, 2018, and April 17, 2019.

### Chapter 7: "You Make the Punishment Fit the Criminal"

58 **"Plea bargaining is supposed"**: David Ashenfelter and John Castine, "Manslaughter: The Price of Life—Serving Justice? Or Are the Deals Cheating Justice?" *Detroit Free Press,* October 10, 1983.

58 **the prosecutors agreed**: Paul Weingarten, "The Unquiet Death of Vincent Chin: An Examination of the Killing Detroit Can't Forget," *Chicago Tribune*, July 31, 1983.

58 **Those convicted could be**: "750.321 Manslaughter," Michigan Penal Code, Michigan Legislature, https://tinyurl.com/y6zobb37.

58 **In fact, there was no law**: Judith Cummings, "Detroit Asian Americans Protest Lenient Penalties for Murder," *New York Times,* April 26, 1983.

59 **Charles Marr, a spokesman**: Ibid.

59 **before Judge Bayles**: Weingarten, "Unquiet Death."

59 **"refresh his memory"**: Ibid.

59 **"Your Honor, Mr. Ebens"**: Saperstein quoted in Weingarten, "Unquiet Death."

59 **"split his [Nitz's] head open"**: Khoury quoted ibid.

59 **"came over, for what"**: Ebens quoted ibid.

60 **other witnesses**: Ibid.

60 **"During the melee"**: Ebens quoted ibid.

61 **"[The killing] was not so much"**: Khoury quoted, ibid.

61 **"I'm confident that this"**: Saperstein quoted ibid.

61 **"Only that I'm deeply sorry"**: Ebens quoted ibid.

61 **"They weren't the kind of people"**: Joyce Walker-Tyson, "2 Men Charged in '82 Slaying Get Probation," *Detroit Free Press,* March 18, 1983.

62 **"We're talking here"**: Kaufman quoted ibid.

62 **"I told my wife"**: Ebens quoted in Michael Moore, "The Man Who Killed Vincent Chin: The Wages of Death," *Detroit Free Press,* August 30, 1987.

### Chapter 8: An Asian American Dream Deferred

63 **"Three years' probation"**: Lily Chin interview, *Who Killed Vincent Chin?* (film), dir. Christine Choy and Renee Tajima-Peña (1987), transcript, MOCA.

63 **She had just**: Chin interview, *Who Killed Vincent Chin?*

63 **"Uncle Ping, how come":** Ibid.

63 **her father, Yee Char:** Name verified via Ancestry.com.

63 **"My father warned me":** Chin interview, *Who Killed Vincent Chin?*

63 **Growing up, her father had told Lily:** Helen Zia, *Asian American Dreams: The Emergence of an American People* (New York: Farrar, Straus & Giroux, 2000), p. 63.

65 **Chinese railroad workers would drill:** "The Use of Black Powder and Nitroglycerine on the Transcontinental Railroad," *Transcontinental Railroad*, https://railroad.lindahall.org/essays/black-powder.html.

65 *a Chinaman's chance in hell*: Jenn Fang, "Yes, the Term 'Chinaman' Is Derogatory," *Reappropriate*, July 9, 2014, http://reappropriate.co/2014/07/yes-the-term-chinaman-is-derogatory/.

65 **As a young woman during:** Colin Covert, "The Ordeal of Lily Chin," *Detroit Free Press*, July 7, 1983.

66 **David returned to China:** Lily Chin interview, *Who Killed Vincent Chin?*

66 **"Highland Park was high class":** Ibid.

66 **So from seven a.m. until midnight:** Ibid.

67 **"Some of them got jobs":** Zia quoted ibid.

67 **They rode the bus on Sundays:** Ibid.

67 **"They made ugly faces":** Chin quoted ibid.

67 **"gentleman":** Covert, "Ordeal of Lily Chin."

68 **"This is injustice to the grossest extreme":** Zia, *Asian American Dreams*, p. 64.

### Chapter 9: "This Is How Far We've Come in Two Hundred Years?"

69 **"Two men charged with":** Joyce Walker-Tyson, "2 Men Charged in '82 Slaying Get Probation," *Detroit Free Press*, March 18, 1983.

71 **How a frenzied mob:** Scott Zesch, *The Chinatown War: Chinese Los Angeles and the Massacre of 1871* (Oxford: Oxford University Press, 2012), pp. 126, 151.

71 **"It was total shock":** Helen Zia interview, *Who Killed Vincent Chin?* (film), dir. Christine Choy and Renee Tajima-Peña (1987), transcript, MOCA.

72 **"Asians were pretty much":** Roland Hwang, interview by author, May 29, 2018.

74 **"Livonia in the 1960s":** Ibid.

74 **"'What do you think'":** Roland Hwang, interview by author, June 19, 2018.

74 **"When I was in the":** James Shimoura, interview by author, June 19, 2018.

74 **"They thought he was looking":** Ibid.

75 **"I was pissed":** Ibid.

75 **"When Kaufman issued":** Hwang interview, May 29, 2018.

75 **"Still hurts just talking":** Koivu quoted in John White and Wynne Davis,

"His Life Cut Short, Vincent Chin Is Remembered for What Might Have Been," *StoryCorps*, NPR, June 23, 2017.

76 **"I just stayed by myself"**: Gary Koivu, interview by author, June 22, 2018.

76 **"I looked at the headline"**: Ibid.

76 **"I have never committed"**: Wong quoted in Cynthia Lee, "Probation in Slaying Riles Chinese," *Detroit News,* March 18, 1983.

76 **"You can kill a dog"**: Yee quoted ibid.

78 **The first Chinese immigrant to arrive**: Helen Zia, *Asian American Dreams: The Emergence of an American People* (New York: Farrar, Straus & Giroux, 2000), p. 62.

78 **Chinatown's original location on Third Avenue**: Patricia Montemurri, "Chinatown Lost: Forlorn Area is Buried in the Cass Corridor," *Detroit Free Press*, November 26, 1989.

78 **But by the 1980s, Chinatown had fallen**: Ibid.

78 **As a result, the new wave**: Ibid.

79 **"Typically Chinese"**: Sandra Bunnell, "The Dragon Dances: A Century of Chinese in Detroit with a Culture That Will Not Die," *Detroit Free Press*, January 6, 1974.

79 **"This is injustice"**: Yee quoted in Zia, *Asian American Dreams,* p. 64

79 **"We've got a problem"**: Hwang interview, May 29, 2018.

### Chapter 10: "We Must Let the World Know That We Think This Is Wrong"

80 **The Golden Star was a popular**: John Tanasychuk, "Comfort Food, Chinese Style," *Detroit Free Press,* June 21, 1996.

81 **"The entire Asian bar"**: James Shimoura, interview by author, June 19, 2018.

81 **"I thought this was a really big story"**: Helen Zia, interview by author, June 6, 2018.

82 **"These men killed my son"**: Chin quoted in Helen Zia, *Asian American Dreams: The Emergence of an American People* (New York: Farrar, Straus & Giroux, 2000), p. 65.

82 **"We must let the world know"**: Ibid, p. 64.

82 **"I stepped out of being"**: Zia interview by author.

82 **"I don't want to single"**: Ibid.

### "Are You Gonna Let Him Call You That?"

85 **"Dude, he called you"**: All quotations from Jarod Lew in this chapter come author interview on April 17, 2019.

### Chapter 11: The Warrior

89 **"The practice of law":** Liza Cheuk May Chan, *My Impossible Life* (Ann Arbor, MI: Bookbaby Publishing, 2017), p. 286.

89 **Chan had always imagined:** Ibid., pp. 112–13.

89 **This warrior fantasy:** Ibid., pp. 114–15.

90 **glomerulonephritis:** Ibid., pp. 289–90.

90 **"I was no longer":** Ibid., p. 115.

90 **While living in Detroit:** Ibid., p. 18.

90 **But Chan, who was a lesbian:** Ibid., pp. 279–80.

90 **The 1990 Immigration Act:** Sharita Gruberg, "On the 50th Anniversary of the Immigration and Nationality Act, Changes Are Needed to Protect LBTQ Immigrants," Center for American Progress, March 23, 2015, https://tinyurl.com/y4uypyor.

90 **She passed the state bar:** Chan, *My Impossible Life,* p. 282.

90 **But it was her international:** Ibid., pp. 281–82.

90 **One lawyer, Daniel J. Hoekenga:** Ibid., p. 282.

91 **Although Chan admired Hoekenga:** Ibid., pp. 282–83.

91 **"But it was too late":** Ibid., p. 286.

91 **So when Henry Yee called Chan:** Ibid., p. 296.

92 **"What are you going to do":** Ibid., p. 299.

92 **"I'll meet with Kaufman":** Ibid., pp. 298–99.

### Chapter 12: American Citizens for Justice

93 **"It was certainly unfair":** Mable Lim, interview by author, June 21, 2018.

93 **"I wrote my stories":** Helen Zia, interview by author, March 5, 2019.

94 **She was an active member:** "About ACA," Association of Chinese Americans, https://www.acadetroit.org/about-aca/about-aca.html.

94 **Growing up, Lim remembered:** Lim interview by author. Except where indicated, the remaining quotes from Lim in this chapter come from this source.

95 **As a result of growing public dissent:** Helen Zia, *Asian American Dreams: The Emergence of an American People* (New York: Farrar, Straus & Giroux, 2000), p. 65.

96 **Although the room bore the flag:** Ibid., p. 66.

96 **American Citizens for Justice:** Ibid, p. 67.

96 **"The American Citizens for Justice (ACJ)":** Helen Zia, ACJ Official Statement, May 14, 1983.

### Chapter 13: They Will Never Be the Same

97 **Twelve days after Judge Kaufman's:** "Michigan Dateline: Man Can't Push Chin-related Suit," *Detroit Free Press*, May 28, 1992.

97 **"There hasn't been any life":** Tim Kiska, "Chin's Slayer Says Conviction Now 'Is Unfair,'" *Detroit Free Press,* July 3, 1984.

97 **He was born one of six:** Author informal meeting with Ronald Ebens, July 30, 2019.

98 **"I worked on the line":** Ronald Ebens interview, *Who Killed Vincent Chin?* (film), dir. Christine Choy and Renee Tajima-Peña (1987), transcript, MOCA.

98 **After joining the ranks:** *United States v. Ronald Ebens and Michael Nitz,* No. 83-60629, Ronald Ebens witness testimony, p. 187 (U.S. District Court for the Eastern District of Michigan Southern Division, June 19, 1984), transcript, NAC.

98 **He maintained an amicable relationship:** Frank Eaman sentencing, ibid. (September 18), p. 13.

98 **"We used to have":** Sylvia Wulbrecht interview, *Who Killed Vincent Chin?*

99 **"They had all been drinking":** Ibid.

99 **"When Chin did die":** Richard Wagner interview, *Who Killed Vincent Chin?*

99 **"He's a lot less trusting":** Jim Wulbrecht interview, *Who Killed Vincent Chin?*

99 **"If you wanted to call":** Ibid.

99 **"He just dug in his pocket":** Ibid.

100 **Sylvia was frustrated:** Author informal meeting with Ronald Ebens, July 30, 2019.

100 **"Ron has to live with it":** Sylvia Wulbrecht interview, *Who Killed Vincent Chin?*

100 **"He just changed":** Debbie Walker interview, ibid. The quotes from Walker in the next paragraphs also come from this source.

101 **"Oh, are you the daughter":** Sylvia Wulbrecht, *Who Killed Vincent Chin?*

102 **"no act of self defense":** Nickie McWhirter, "A Lesson—and a License—That Kids Should Never Get," *Detroit Free Press,* March 25, 1983.

102 **"With due respect for":** Ibid.

102 **"You have raised the ugly ghost":** Ibid.

102 **"Mike loved life":** Walker interview, *Who Killed Vincent Chin?*

## *Chapter 14: "We Dropped the Ball"*

103 **a thirty-four-inch, flame-tempered:** Paul Weingarten, "The Unquiet Death of Vincent Chin: An Examination of the Killing Detroit Can't Forget," *Chicago Tribune,* July 31, 1983.

103 **"Some heavy sucker, eh?":** Roberts quoted in Matt Beer, "Getting Away with Murder? The Life and Death of Vincent Chin," *Detroit News,* April 17, 1983.

103 **"It soon became clear":** Helen Zia, *Asian American Dreams: The Emergence of an American People* (New York: Farrar, Straus & Giroux, 2000), p. 65.

105 **"We were all surprised":** Angela "Starlene" Rudolph interview, *Who*

*Killed Vincent Chin?* (film), dir. Christine Choy and Renee Tajima-Peña (1987), transcript, MOCA.

106 **"I told him about the incident":** Roberts quoted in Weingarten, "Unquiet Death."

106 **"There were mistakes":** John Castine, interview by author, February 27, 2019.

106 **"We dropped the ball":** Ibid.

106 **"the sob story":** Ibid.

107 **"If we had followed":** Ibid.

107 **For example, during the sentencing:** Weingarten, "Unquiet Death."

107 **"Your Honor, Mr. Ebens":** Saperstein quoted ibid.

107 **Witnesses, however, claimed:** Ibid.

108 **In addition, there were conflicting:** Ibid.

108 **"missing link":** Chan quoted ibid.

109 **"I walked around the premises":** Liza Cheuk May Chan, *My Impossible Life* (Ann Arbor, MI: Bookbaby Publishing, 2017), p. 313.

109 **"bought the 'wrong' car":** Ibid.

109 **Two weeks after Chan's visit:** Weingarten, "Unquiet Death."

110 **"It's because of you":** *United States v. Ronald Ebens and Michael Nitz*, No. 83-60629, Racine Colwell witness testimony, p. 226 (U.S. District Court for the Eastern District of Michigan Southern Division, June 13, 1984), transcript, NAC.

### Chapter 15: A Man of the Law

112 **"In all my years":** Kaufman quoted in Cynthia Lee, "Flak Stuns Judge in Chin Case: Kaufman Sentences in Slaying Assailed," *Detroit News,* May 11, 1983.

112 **the Michigan Supreme Court:** Robert Ankeny, "Justice Followed Usual Course in Chin Case," *Detroit News,* May 19, 1983.

112 **In 1983, Ebens and Nitz:** Paul Weingarten, "The Unquiet Death of Vincent Chin: An Examination of the Killing Detroit Can't Forget," *Chicago Tribune,* July 31, 1983.

114 **Fund for Equal Justice:** Lee, "Flak Stuns Judge."

114 **"impartial, intelligent and fair":** Ibid.

114 **"He is a man of the law":** Khoury quoted in Cynthia Lee, "Kaufman: Can't Alter Sentences—Probation for Pair in Chin Case Upheld," *Detroit News*, June 3, 1983.

114 **"When Judge Kaufman said":** Frank H. Wu, interview by author, July 24, 2018.

114 **"a $3,000 license to commit":** Yee quoted in Lee, "Flak Stuns Judge."

114 **"The hall was already set":** Kin Yee interview, *Who Killed Vincent Chin?* (film), dir. Christine Choy and Renee Tajima-Peña (c. 1988), transcript, MOCA.

115 **"It has aroused the anger":** John Castine, "Vincent Chin Case: Justice or Mockery?" *Detroit Free Press,* April 17, 1983.

115 **In addition, the ACJ requested:** Mark J. Jue, "Detroit Asians Draw Large Local Support," *East West: The Chinese-American Journal* 17, no. 29 (July 20, 1983).

115 **"We have asked Judge Kaufman":** Chan quoted in John Castine, "Lawyer Disputes Sentencing of Killers," *Detroit Free Press*, April 16, 1983.

115 **"If I had to do it over":** Kaufman quoted in Castine, "Chin Case: Justice or Mockery?"

115 **"Do you speak English?":** Kaufman quoted in Jue, "Detroit Asians Draw Local Support."

116 **"Seeing how hard my father":** Kin Yee interview, *Who Killed Vincent Chin?*

116 **"One of his remarks":** Ibid.

116 **"He told us that he was":** Yee quoted in Jue, "Detroit Asians Draw Large Local Support."

117 **A native Detroiter, Kaufman:** Jeanne May, "Charles Kaufman: Ruled in High Profile Beating Case," *Detroit Free Press*, July 1, 2004.

117 **For eighteen months, Kaufman:** "Omori Tokyo Base Camp #1," Mansell. com, https://tinyurl.com/y48porl3. Kaufman is listed as "Kaufman, Charles, 2nd Lt, O-683832,6485,USAAC."

117 **Prisoners lived in:** Laura Hillenbrand, *Unbroken: An Olympian's Journey from Airman to Castaway to Captive,* Young Adult adaptation (New York: Ember, 2014), pp. 176–77.

117 **They survived on a half bowl:** Ibid.

117 **The average American POW:** Lee, "Flak Stuns Judge."

118 **The slightest infraction:** "Tokyo Main Camp—Omori," https://tinyurl .com/y5rysy3x.

118 **More than 60 percent:** Lee, "Flak Stuns Judge."

118 **convince the Japanese guards:** Ibid.

118 **"I'm one of the few judges":** Kaufman quoted in Lee, "Flak Stuns Judge."

118 **"He has a more liberal philosophy":** Miriam Siefer interview, *Who Killed Vincent Chin?*

119 **"too severely in careless":** Judge Kaufman interview, *Who Killed Vincent Chin?*

119 **"It was a bad experience":** Kaufman quoted in Lee, "Flak Stuns Judge."

119 **"Judge Kaufman has never been":** Helen Zia, "Dispute Continues in Chin Case," letter to *Detroit News,* May 18, 1983.

119 **"We're not out for revenge":** Zia quoted in Jue, "Detroit Asians Draw Local Support."

121 **Hoekenga argued that Judge Kaufman's:** John Castine, "Judge to Review Probation of Killers of Chin," *Detroit Free Press,* April 30, 1983.

121 **"I did not misconstrue facts"**: Saperstein quoted ibid.

121 **"fair and reasonable"**: Ibid.

121 **"Talk about a crime"**: Hoekenga quoted ibid.

123 **"This is a very emotional"**: Kaufman quoted ibid.

123 **"The emotions caught up with her"**: Ibid.

123 **"I feel very positive"**: Chan quoted in Castine, "Judge to Review."

123 **"It bothers him"**: Kaufman quoted in Lee. "Flak Stuns Judge."

## Chapter 16: "Time to Talk About Race"

124 **On the night of June 19, 1982:** Morris Cotton, interview by author, June 24, 2019.

124 **At the time, even the Michigan chapter:** Helen Zia, *Asian American Dreams: The Emergence of an American People* (New York: Farrar, Straus & Giroux, 2000), p. 72.

125 **"It was big news"**: Ibid., p. 67.

125 **"'Real Americans Buy American' continues"**: Matt Beer, "Does 'Buy American' Buy Trouble? Detroit Killing Shows That Boosterism Can Breed Racism," *Detroit News,* June 2, 1983.

125 **The ACJ gained the support:** Kin H. Yee et al., "The Case for Vincent Chin: An American Tragedy in Justice," *American Citizens for Justice,* May 11, 1983.

125 **Roland Hwang and James Shimoura credit:** Roland Hwang, interview by author, May 29, 2018.

126 **"We owe a big debt"**: James Shimoura, interview by author, June 19, 2018.

126 **Other groups within the Asian and Pacific Islander:** Yee et al., "Case for Vincent Chin."

126 **"All Americans—Asians and non-Asians"**: Norman Mineta, official statement of endorsement of AJC, July 12, 1983, ESL.

126 **At the time, Asian Americans:** Robert W. Gardner, Bryant Robey, and Peter C. Smith, "Asian Americans: Growth, Change, and Diversity," Population Reference Bureau, Washington, DC, February 1989, https://files.eric.ed.gov/fulltext/ED317464.pdf.

127 **"The FBI would need"**: Zia, *Asian American Dreams*, p. 70.

127 **"A lot of people of my generation"**: Mayeda quoted in Colin Covert, "Japanese Americans in Detroit," *Detroit Free Press,* July 10, 1983.

127 **"necessary"**: Zia, *Asian American Dreams*, p. 70.

127 **"I've worked hard for"**: Quoted ibid., p. 71.

128 **"We want to win this case"**: Hwang quoted in Zia, *Asian American Dreams,* p. 71.

128 **"It was time to talk about race"**: Ibid., p. 69.

## Chapter 17: "We Want Justice"

129 **"They joked that this would be":** Helen Zia, *Asian American Dreams: The Emergence of an American People* (New York: Farrar, Straus & Giroux, 2000), p. 74.

129 **"All the protest signs you saw":** James Shimoura, interview by author, June 19, 2018.

131 **"The debate was whether":** Roland Hwang, interview by author, June 19, 2018.

131 **"Early in the decision process":** James Shimoura interview, *Vincent Who?* (film), dir. Tony Lam and written/produced by Curtis Chin (2009).

131 **On Monday, May 9, 1983:** Cynthia Lee, "Beating Death Stirs Rally: Asian American Wrath Turns to Prosecutor," *Detroit News*, May 10, 1983.

131 **Many wore red and white buttons:** Paul Weingarten, "The Unquiet Death of Vincent Chin: An Examination of the Killing Detroit Can't Forget," *Chicago Tribune*, July 31, 1983.

131 **"It's like when police officers":** Hwang interview.

131 **"Vincent was one of theirs":** Shimoura interview.

132 **"Most restaurants are hand to mouth":** Helen Zia, interview by author, June 6, 2018.

132 **"This was a huge outpouring":** Corky Lee interview, *Vincent Who?*

133 **"That's when I started questioning":** Van Ong, interview by author, June 22, 2018.

133 **The rally began:** Helen Zia, "We Want Justice for Vincent Chin! Rally Agenda," ACJ flyer, May 9, 1983, ESL.

133 **"We symbolically hit all the courts":** Shimoura interview.

134 **"They'd use their fingers":** Parker Woo, interview by author, October 16, 2018.

134 **"I'm not afraid to fight":** Ibid.

134 **"It was a tremendous rally":** Mable Lim interview, *Who Killed Vincent Chin?* (film), dir. Christine Choy and Renee Tajima-Peña (1987), transcript, MOCA.

134 **"The thing that was amazing":** Shimoura interview, *Vincent Who?*

134 **"We've never had any demonstration":** Lim interview, *Who Killed Vincent Chin?*

135 **"This was different":** Ibid.

135 **"People had never seen":** Frank H. Wu, interview by author, July 24, 2018.

135 **"Eyewitnesses have come forward":** Zia, *Asian American Dreams,* p. 75.

135 **"Ladies and gentlemen":** Lily Chin, speech at May 9, 1983, rally, handwritten transcript, ACJ archive, ESL.

136 **The protest rally ended:** Zia, *Asian American Dreams*, pp. 74–75.

136 **"A lot of us were really inspired":** Francis Wong interview, *Vincent Who?*

136 **Stewart Kwoh, a thirty-three-year-old lawyer:** Stewart Kwoh, interview by author, May 23, 2018.

137 **"I followed my path":** Ibid.

137 **"It was pretty clear":** Ibid.

138 **"The killing didn't attract much":** *CBS Evening News,* April 28, 1983, VTNA.

138 **"These attacks on Asian Americans":** "Jackson Decries Rise in Violence Against Asians," *AsianWeek,* March 23, 1984, p. 3.

138 **"It was a major turning point":** Angelo Ancheta interview, *Vincent Who?*

138 **The phrase *Asian American* was actually:** Anna Purna Kambhampaty, "In 1968, These Activists Coined the Term 'Asian America'—And Helped Shape Decades of Advocacy," *Time,* May 22, 2020.

138 **This term has evolved over the years:** "Asian Pacific American Heritage Month: May 2020," *Asian Pacific American Institute for Congressional Studies,* https://apaics.org/events/asian-pacific-american-heritage-month.

139 **"Since Vincent's death":** Kin Yee interview, *Who Killed Vincent Chin?*

### *Chapter 18: Mrs. Chin Goes to Washington*

140 **"real and sincere":** Kaufman quoted in John Castine, "Judge Refuses Any Changes in Chin Death Case Sentences," *Detroit Free Press,* June 3, 1983.

140 **"While sympathizing with the family":** Ibid.

141 **"If people feel no one should":** Kaufman quoted in Paul Weingarten, "The Unquiet Death of Vincent Chin: An Examination of the Killing Detroit Can't Forget," *Chicago Tribune,* July 31, 1983.

142 **"miscarriage of justice":** Chan quoted in John Castine, "Another Chin Case Appeal," *Detroit Free Press,* June 4, 1983.

142 **"principle guy":** Khoury quoted in Castine, "Judge Refuses Any Changes."

142 **"[They] chose to ignore":** James Shimoura, "Asian Americans Seek Justice for Vincent Chin," *Pacific Citizen,* June 3, 1983.

142 **"I think there's [enough] fault":** Bayles quoted in Weingarten, "Unquiet Death."

144 **Vikki Wong also wanted to fight:** Jarod Lew, interview by author, March 22, 2020.

144 **"This controversy just goes on":** Wong quoted in Cynthia Lee, "Kaufman: Can't Alter Sentences—Probation for Pair in Chin Case Upheld," *Detroit News,* June 3, 1983.

144 **"It still hurts me very much":** Wong quoted in Lloyd Dobbins, Peter Jeffries, and Steve Delaney. "Postmortem in Detroit," *First Look,* NBC, aired October 30, 1983, VTNA.

144 **"Many people only saw Mrs. Chin":** Helen Zia, *Vincent Chin's Story: Lily Chin: The Courage to Speak Out* (Los Angeles: Asian Americans Advancing Justice, 2008–9), https://tinyurl.com/y4rq9oly.

144 **"I never heard Mrs. Chin complain"**: Ibid.

144 **"She had a backbone of steel"**: Ibid.

144 **Lily made sure no one went hungry**: Liza Cheuk May Chan, *My Impossible Life* (Ann Arbor, MI: Bookbaby, 2017), p. 309.

145 **"And could she ever knit"**: Zia, *Vincent Chin's Story: Lily Chin.*

145 **"She knit me a hand-knit sweater:"** Roland Hwang, interview by author, May 29, 2018.

145 **"I think her favorite hobby"**: Zia, *Vincent Chin's Story: Lily Chin.*

145 **"Liza Chan spoke Toisanese"**: James Shimoura, interview by author, June 19, 2018.

145 **"Mrs. Chin was everyone's mother"**: Zia, *Vincent Chin's Story: Lily Chin.*

146 **"She simply accepted us"**: Chan, *My Impossible Life,* p. 309.

146 **"I'm Chinese"**: Chin quoted in Colin Covert, "The Ordeal of Lily Chin," *Detroit Free Press*, July 7, 1983.

146 **"She was very observant"**: Zia, *Vincent Chin's Story: Lily Chin.*

146 **On June 23, 1983**: James Dodson, "Services Held to Remember Vincent Chin Slaying Case," *Detroit Free Press,* June 20, 1983.

147 **"racial scapegoating"**: Bradley quoted ibid.

147 **Barbara Boxer:** "Judge Kaufman Replies," *AsianWeek* (May 26, 1983), 9.

147 **"All persons shall be entitled"**: Civil Rights Act, 1964, https://www.govinfo.gov/content/pkg/STATUTE-78/pdf/STATUTE-78-Pg241.pdf; "The Civil Rights Act of 1964," Teaching Tolerance, http://www.tolerance.org/sites/default/files/general/tt_marriage_equality_5.pdf.

147 **"place of exhibition"**: Ibid.

148 **On June 29, 1983**: "Justice Dept. May Take On Vincent Chin Case," *AsianWeek*, July 3, 1983, ESL.

148 **That year alone:** John Castine, "Dual Prosecution of Chin's Killers a Rarity," *Detroit Free Press,* November 29, 1983.

148 **"a brutal incident"**: Reynolds quoted in Paul Magnusson, "U.S. Likely to Probe Chin Death," *Detroit Free Press,* June 30, 1983.

148 **In fact, he confirmed that this case:** "Justice Department May Take On Vincent Chin Case," *AsianWeek,* July 3, 1983.

148 **"I don't know of a case"**: Reynolds quoted in Magnusson, "U.S. Likely to Probe Chin Death."

148 **For Reynolds, the Vincent Chin case:** Castine, "Dual Prosecution a Rarity."

148 **Bledsoe was found guilty:** "Grand Jury to Probe Chinese American's Death," Associated Press, September 8, 1983.

149 **"an equal candidate"**: Reynolds quoted in Magnusson, "U.S. Likely to Probe Chin Death."

150 **a photograph of Reynolds:** UPI photo in Paul Magnusson, "U.S. Likely to Probe Chin Death."

150 **"Mrs. Chin is a model":** "Jackson and Mrs. Chin Scheduled in C-Town," *AsianWeek,* June 1, 1984.

150 **"We are all citizens":** Lily Chin on *The Phil Donahue Show*, in *Who Killed Vincent Chin?* (film), dir. Christine Choy and Renee Tajima-Peña (1987), transcript, MOCA. The viewers' letters about her appearance are in ESL.

150 **"Vincent Chin's mother":** Zia, *Vincent Chin's Story: Lily Chin.*

151 **"We feel this is sort of":** Zia quoted in Joe Swickard and John Castine, "U.S. Indicts 2 Given Probation In Chin Death," *Detroit Free Press,* November 3, 1983.

151 **"It's all politics and you know it":** Ebens quoted ibid.

151 **"I'm grateful and hopeful":** Chin quoted ibid.

## *"In the Spotlight"*

153 **"When I was younger":** All quotations from Jarod Lew in this chapter are from author interviews, June 1, 2018, April 17, 2019, and March 23, 2020..

154 **In 2016 he was a finalist:** Jarod Lew, "Audrey" (2014), at https://portraitcompetition.si.edu/exhibition/2016-outwin-boochever-portrait-competition/audrey-2014?lang=eng.

154 **He also won a $10,000:** "Studio Art Alumnus Wins World Photography Award," Michigan State University College of Arts & Letters, September 30, 2016, http://www.cal.msu.edu/index.php?cID=855.

## *Chapter 19: The Defenders: Miriam Siefer and Frank Eaman*

159 **"I was a bookworm":** Miriam Siefer, interview by author, June 20, 2019.

159 **"I became aware":** Ibid.

159 **"I was drawn by the injustices":** Ibid.

159 **So Siefer majored in sociology:** Ibid.

159 **"I had a desire":** Ibid.

160 **"I remember being aware":** Ibid.

160 **"It was always about":** Ibid.

160 **"It was a fight at a strip bar":** Ibid.

160 **"Sometimes the media gets it wrong":** Ibid.

161 **"There's no question about it":** Miriam Siefer interview, *Who Killed Vincent Chin?* (film), dir. Christine Choy and Renee Tajima-Peña (1987), transcript, MOCA.

161 **"This case was used":** Ibid.

161 **"All of a sudden":** Ibid.

161 **"You have to see beyond":** Siefer interview by author.

161 **"It was not a civil rights case":** Siefer interview, *Who Killed Vincent Chin?*

162 **"As we marched along the street":** Frank Eaman interview, *Who Killed Vincent Chin?*

162 **"I stood up for the rights of everyone":** Frank Eaman, interview by author, January 22, 2019.

162 **"Our grandfather was an inspiration":** Ibid.

163 **"I knew most people":** Ibid.

163 **"I always knew that Asian Americans":** Ibid.

163 **"I saw the storyline develop":** Ibid.

163 **"good motives":** Frank Eaman interview, *Who Killed Vincent Chin?* transcript, MOCA.

163 **"There's nothing in Ebens's background":** Ibid.

164 **"When Ron Ebens first came in":** Ibid.

164 **"He let himself get out of control":** Eaman interview by author.

164 **"He's not guilty of doing this":** Eaman interview, *Who Killed Vincent Chin?*

164 **"I think that lawyers":** Eaman interview by author.

165 **"My representing Ron Ebens":** Eaman interview, *Who Killed Vincent Chin?*

## Chapter 20: The Trailblazer: The Honorable Anna Diggs Taylor

166 **"A steel fist in a velvet glove":** Mark Hicks, "Michigan's First Black Female Federal Judge Dies at 84," *Detroit News*, November 6, 2017.

166 **"She was very gracious":** Mayer quoted ibid.

166 **Judge Anna Diggs Taylor drew:** "Judge Anna Diggs Taylor, 1932–2017" (obituary), U.S. District Court—Eastern Michigan District, https://www .mied.uscourts.gov/PDFFIles/ADT.pdf.

168 **She had just given birth:** "Remembering Anna Diggs Taylor," *Congressional Record* 163, no. 195, November 30, 2017, https://www.congress.gov/ congressional-record/2017/11/30/senate-section/article/S7559-2?.

168 **"They were shouting":** Taylor quoted in Maynard M. Gordon, "Changing History: Local Attorneys in 1964 Mississippi Project," *Michigan Jewish History* 35 (Winter 1994): 6.

168 **"We were afraid":** Taylor obituary, U.S. District Court—Eastern Michigan.

169 **It was later alleged:** Diane McWhorter, "Since Mississippi Burned," *People*, January 9, 1989.

169 **"a watershed for equal rights":** Taylor quoted in Gordon, "Changing History," p. 6.

169 **"It was important to me":** Ibid.

169 **In 1979, President Jimmy Carter:** Tresa Baldas, "Trailblazer Detroit Federal Judge Anna Diggs Taylor Dies," *Detroit Free Press*, November 6, 2017.

169 **"I think for some of my":** "Anna Diggs Taylor," Encylopedia.com, https:// www.encyclopedia.com/education/news-wires-white-papers-and-books/ diggs-taylor-anna-1932.

170 **"Black judges have an important role":** Taylor quoted in "Remembering Diggs Taylor," *Congressional Record.*

170 **And she was true:** Ibid.

170 **"She was gracious":** Swor quoted in Baldas, "Trailblazer Detroit."

170 **It was the first case:** Elaine Woo, "Lily Chin, 82; Son's Killing Led to Rights Drive," *Los Angeles Times,* June 14, 2002.

### Chapter 21: The Jury: "You Must Keep an Open Mind"

171 **She was one of 158 people:** Don Ball, "Chin Jury Could Be Seated by Wednesday," *Detroit News,* June 10, 1984.

171 **They had to interview:** Ibid.

172 **"If they know I'm going to be on":** *United States v. Ronald Ebens and Michael Nitz,* No. 83-60629, jury voir dire, p. 34 (U.S. District Court for the Eastern District of Michigan Southern Division, June 5, 1984), transcript, NAC.

172 **"It's beginning to boil":** Ibid. (June 8), pp. 207–8.

172 **"This is an unusually publicized":** Ibid., p. 208.

172 **During the screening process:** "Jury Selection Starts in Detroit Beating Death," *New York Times,* June 5, 1984.

172 **"I have formulated some pretty strong opinions":** Jury voir dire, *United States v. Ebens and Nitz* (June 5), pp. 24–25.

172 **"The fact that she is a nude dancer":** Ibid., p. 113.

173 **"I don't like vulgar language":** Ibid. (June 6), p. 262.

173 **"Do you have any strong opinions":** Ibid. (June 5), p. 78.

173 **"Mr. Ebens and Mr. Nitz are white":** Ibid., jury voir dire (June 5), pp. 78–79.

173 **During the first day of jury selection":** "Federal Trial of Chin's Two Killers Begins," *East West,* June 13, 1984.

173 **"How many Asian friends":** Zia quoted ibid.

173 **"15 to 20 percent of the persons":** Zia quoted ibid.

174 **"The killers [and their families]":** Zia quoted ibid.

174 **"Was there anything about that":** Jury voir dire, *United States v. Ebens and Nitz* (June 5), p. 104.

174 **One woman who worked:** Ibid. (June 8), pp. 215–16.

174 **"He was in my graduating class":** Ibid. (June 7), p. 216.

175 **"I can't bury the emotion":** Ibid. (June 8), p. 218.

175 **"I just feel like no one":** Ibid. (June 6), pp. 13–14.

175 **"The boy that died":** Ibid., p. 50.

175 **"When I saw the victim's mother":** Ibid. (June 8), pp. 53–54.

175 **Ultimately, the lawyers:** Charles Hillinger, "Jury Tackles Civil Rights Question in Beating Death of Chinese American," *Los Angeles Times,* June 1984.

176  **"Your purpose as jurors"**: Jury swear in, p. 23, *United States v. Ebens and Nitz* (June 12).

176  **"You are to perform this duty"**: Ibid., pp. 18, 24.

### Chapter 22: The Opening Statements: "The Burden of Proof"

177  **"ugly racism which turned violent"**: *United States v. Ronald Ebens and Michael Nitz*, No. 83-60629, Thomas Merritt opening statement, p. 11 (U.S. District Court for the Eastern District of Michigan Southern Division, June 13, 1984), transcript, NAC.

177  **"On June 19, 1982"**: Ibid., p. 10.

178  **"The burden of proof"**: David Lawson opening statement, ibid., p. 20.

178  **"set off a chain of events"**: Ibid., p. 30.

178  **"vivid imagination"**: Kenneth Sasse opening statement, ibid., pp. 50–51.

179  **"barrage of obscenities"**: Merritt opening statement, ibid., pp. 12–13.

179  **"He's worked in the factory"**: Sasse opening statement, ibid., pp. 42-43.

179  **"When you have heard"**: Merritt opening statement, ibid., pp. 18–19.

179  **"The only thing that we ask"**: Lawson opening statement, ibid., p. 35.

### Chapter 23: The Bachelor Party: "We Are Just Here to Have a Good Time"

180  **"lifetime buddy"**: *United States v. Ronald Ebens and Michael Nitz*, No. 83-60629, Theodore Merritt opening statement, p. 11 (U.S. District Court for the Eastern District of Michigan Southern Division, June 13, 1984), transcript, NAC.

180  **"I wish I could have elaborated"**: Gary Koivu, interview by author, June 22, 2018.

180  **"He was having a good time"**: Gary Koivu witness testimony, *United States v. Ebens and Nitz*, pp. 150–51, 216.

180  **"It was obvious he had been drinking"**: Ibid., p. 216.

181  **"Don't call me a fucker"**: Ibid., pp. 154–55.

181  **"I looked across"**: Ibid.

181  **"And Ebens shoved back"**: Ibid., p. 156

181  **"I heard shouts coming"**: Ibid., p. 172.

181  **"What was the purpose"**: Ibid., p. 196–97.

182  **"Did you not express"**: Ibid., pp. 197–98.

182  **"Now, [Vincent] did not say"**: Ibid., pp. 189–90.

183  **"Mr. Koivu, you knew"**: Ibid., p. 215.

183  **On June 19, 1982**: Bob Siroskey witness testimony, ibid. (June 14), pp. 43–44.

184  **"I had never seen him"**: Ibid., pp. 46–47.

184  **"The music was playing"**: Ibid., p. 49.

184 **"I cannot say who"**: Ibid., p. 50.
184 **"It was very distinct"**: Ibid., pp. 71–72.
184 **"I turned and the person"**: Ibid., p. 49.
184 **As for how the fight started**: Ibid., p. 51.
185 **"I just walked in"**: Ibid., p. 53.
185 **"Somebody came in and got me"**: Ibid.
185 **"I said to Gary, 'We are going'"**: Ibid., p. 55.
185 **"Come on, I will fight"**: Ibid., p. 56.
186 **"I never seen him the rest"**: Ibid., p. 57.
186 **"He told us that he had gotten"**: Ibid.
186 **"What do you mean by enough"**: Ibid., p. 65.
187 **"Isn't it true, Mr. Siroskey"**: Ibid., p. 67.
187 **"So your memory of this incident"**: Ibid., p. 68.
187 **"Now, you were upset"**: Ibid., p. 77.
188 **"That is when you got"**: Ibid., p. 78.
188 **"So, in fact, you apologized"**: Ibid., p. 87.
188 **"I probably told him earlier"**: Ibid., p. 89.
189 **"Just clarifying that I hope"**: Ibid., p. 101.
189 **"I heard someone mention"**: Jimmy Choi witness testimony, ibid., pp. 127–28.
189 **"We are not Japanese"**: Ibid., p. 128.
190 **"That [kind of remark] is one"**: Choi quoted in Paul Weingarten, "The Unquiet Death of Vincent Chin: An Examination of the Killing Detroit Can't Forget," *Chicago Tribune*, July 31, 1983.
190 **"You have to understand"**: Choi quoted in Matt Beer, "Getting Away with Murder? The Life and Death of Vincent Chin," *Detroit News*, April 17, 1983.
190 **"He got mad and said"**: Jimmy Choi testimony, *United States v. Ebens and Nitz* (June 14), p. 129.
190 **Choi, Koivu, and doorman Gary Reid**: Ibid., p. 130.
190 **"Okay, cool down"**: Ibid., pp. 131–32.
190 **"Vincent saw them and he got"**: Ibid., p. 135.
191 **"Where is your friend"**: Ibid., pp. 143–44.
191 **But in the distance**: Ibid., pp. 145–46.
191 **"They were still scuffling"**: Ibid., pp. 147–48.
192 **"He kept on swinging"**: Ibid., p. 184.
192 **"It seemed like slow motion"**: Ibid., p. 150.
192 **"He was still conscious"**: Ibid., p. 151.
192 **"Snap up, snap up, snap up"**: Ibid., p. 152.
192 **"I called his fiancé and family"**: Ibid., p. 153.
193 **"Now, you knew, did you not"**: Ibid., pp. 161.
193 **"Did you receive advice"**: Ibid., p. 169.
194 **"Can you be sure"**: Ibid., p. 172.

194  **"Now, you are aware":** Ibid., pp. 191–92.

194  **"Well, there was a time":** Ibid., pp. 176–77.

### Chapter 24: The Employees: "It's Because of You"

196  **In 1982, Michigan's unemployment:** Richard C. Auxier, "Reagan's Recession," Pew Research Center, December 14, 2010, https://www.pewresearch.org/2010/12/14/reagans-recession/.

196  **With more than half:** *Who Killed Vincent Chin?* (film), dir. Christine Choy and Renee Tajima-Peña (1987), transcript, MOCA.

196  **At the time, Fleming:** *United States v. Ronald Ebens and Michael Nitz*, No. 83-60629, Sharon Fleming witness testimony, pp. 28–30 (U.S. District Court for the Eastern District of Michigan Southern Division, June 19, 1984), transcript, NAC.

196  **"They were having a good time":** Ibid., pp. 32–34.

196  **"There was a chair thrown":** Ibid., pp. 33–35.

197  **"Why did you refuse his tip":** Angela Rudolph witness testimony, ibid. (June 20), pp. 24–25.

197  **"Boy, you don't know":** Ibid., pp. 27–28.

198  **"We never thought anything":** Ibid.

198  **"I stayed in the back":** Ibid., p. 37.

198  **"He was just having":** Racine Colwell witness testimony, ibid. (June 14), pp. 7–8.

198  **"All I heard him say":** Ibid. (June 13), pp. 226–27.

199  **"I'm not a little":** Ibid.

199  **"bleeding a lot":** Ibid. (June 14), pp. 28–29.

199  **"Everybody minds their own business":** Ibid., p. 39.

199  **"When the doorman escorted":** Ibid. (June 13), pp. 230–31.

199  **"Did you see Vincent":** Ibid., p. 231.

200  **"A customer brought me":** Colwell testimony, ibid. (June 14), pp. 23–24.

200  **"That is a shame":** Ibid.

### Chapter 25: The Cops: "He Shouldn't Have Done It"

201  **Michael Gardenhire was sitting:** *United States v. Ronald Ebens and Michael Nitz*, No. 83-60629, Michael Gardenhire witness testimony, p. 114 (U.S. District Court for the Eastern District of Michigan Southern Division, June 13, 1984), transcript, NAC.

201  **"Mr. Ebens was standing":** Ibid., p. 83.

202  **"they weren't in a drunken":** Ibid., p. 90.

202  **"Just like you hit a golf ball":** Ibid., p. 86.

202  **"How many swings":** Ibid.

202  **"I instructed him to drop":** Ibid., p. 96.

202  **"I instructed him a second":** Ibid.

202 **"He was saying something"**: Ibid., p. 88.

203 **"I told them they were"**: Larry Robinson witness testimony, ibid., pp. 129–31.

203 **"glassy eyes"**: Ibid., p. 138.

203 **"very mad, very upset"**: Ibid., p. 131

203 **"Well, Mike we got that"**: Ibid.

204 **"They are fighting!"**: Morris Cotton witness testimony, ibid. (June 15), p. 45.

204 **"a heat of rage"**: Ibid., pp. 50–51.

204 **"It was another swing"**: Ibid., p. 44.

204 **"Stay"**: Ibid., pp. 47, 91.

204 **"We are not going to"**: Ibid., p. 89.

204 **"I didn't mean it"**: Ibid., p. 70.

205 **"Look what he did"**: Ibid., pp. 46, 71.

## *Chapter 26: The Eyewitnesses: "Government Exhibit No. 14"*

206 **"The baseball bat has been"**: *United States v. Ronald Ebens and Michael Nitz*, No. 83-60629, David Lawson peremptory challenge, p. 36 (U.S. District Court for the Eastern District of Michigan Southern Division, June 12, 1984), transcript, NAC.

206 **"It's clear that the bat"**: Theodore Merritt peremptory challenge, ibid., p. 45.

206 **"crucial importance"**: Judge Anna Diggs Taylor peremptory challenge, ibid., p. 55.

207 **"two Chinese guys"**: Keith Reid witness testimony, ibid. (June 15), p. 101.

207 **"two white Caucasian people"**: Ibid., p. 102.

207 **"And what did you see"**: Donald Wiggins witness testimony, ibid. (June 20), pp. 153, 159.

208 **"Do y'all want to go"**: Jimmy Perry interview, *Who Killed Vincent Chin?* (film), dir. Christine Choy and Renee Tajima-Peña (1987), transcript, MOCA.

208 **"We're looking for two"**: Ibid.

208 **"The younger guy offered"**: Jimmy Perry witness testimony, *United States v. Ebens and Nitz* (June 15), p. 13.

209 **"They were talking about catching"**: Ibid., p. 14–15.

209 **"I told them that the police"**: Ibid., pp. 17–18.

209 **"They snuck behind them"**: Ibid.

210 **"Do I have to"**: Ibid., pp. 26–27.

211 **"Jimmy, what is going on"**: Ibid., pp. 76–78.

211 **"This one person had his hands"**: Harold Fitzgerald witness testimony, *United States v. Ebens and Nitz* (June 15), p. 94.

212 **"He slumped down"**: Ibid., p. 95.

212 **"tremendous amount"**: Ibid., p. 99.

212 **"Our minister had been"**: Ibid., pp. 96–97.

212 **"Now, would you step down"**: Ibid., pp. 95–98.

213 **Fitzgerald picked up the bat:** Tim Kiska, "Witness Demonstrating Attack Breaks Bat Used to Kill Chin," *Detroit Free Press,* June 16, 1984.

## Chapter 27: The Mother: "My Name Is Lily Chin"

214 **"I suggest that the only purpose"**: *United States v. Ronald Ebens and Michael Nitz*, No. 83-60629, David Lawson peremptory challenge, p. 38 (U.S. District Court for the Eastern District of Michigan Southern Division, June 12, 1984), transcript, NAC.

214 **"Mrs. Chin has become a symbol"**: Frank Eaman peremptory challenge, ibid., p. 53.

214 **"She saw the victim"**: Theodore Merritt peremptory challenge, ibid., pp. 47–48.

215 **"The mother's testimony"**: Judge Anna Diggs Taylor peremptory challenge, ibid., p. 55.

215 **"No, he never fight"**: Lily Chin witness testimony, ibid. (June 15), p. 119.

215 **"Now, I want to ask you"**: Ibid., p. 119.

216 **"I asked him"**: Ibid., pp. 120–22.

## Chapter 28: The Stepson: "It Happened So Quickly"

217 **June 19, 1982, started out:** *United States v. Ronald Ebens and Michael Nitz*, No. 83-60629, Michael Nitz witness testimony, pp. 56–57 (U.S. District Court for the Eastern District of Michigan Southern Division, June 20, 1984), transcript, NAC.

218 **"Ron, let's go"**: Ibid., p. 59.

218 **"Ron mentioned to me"**: Ibid., pp. 62–63.

218 **"I more or less"**: Ibid., p. 66.

219 **"Did you see Ron swear"**: Ibid., pp. 67–68.

219 **"Did you discuss foreign cars"**: Ibid., pp. 68–69.

219 **"He came around the edge"**: Ibid., pp. 69–70.

220 **"He said I was bleeding"**: Ibid., p. 71.

220 **"I couldn't straighten it up"**: Ibid., p. 73.

220 **"He said he was really sorry"**: Ibid., p. 73.

220 **"I was just hit"**: Ibid., pp. 76–77.

221 **"I asked him where"**: Ibid., pp. 80–82.

221 **"Did you want to see"**: Ibid., pp. 84–85.

222 ***"I don't remember what else"***: Ibid., pp. 87–88.

222 **"I just wanted to get out"**: Ibid., pp. 88–89.

222 **"At any time or point"**: Ibid., p. 94.

223 **"At the time, didn't you"**: Ibid., p. 95.

223 **"This event happened two years ago"**: Ibid., p. 96.

224 **"You say you wanted to"**: Ibid., p. 102.

224 **"He didn't have anything"**: Ibid., p. 105.

225 **"So you weren't really"**: Ibid., p. 110.

225 **"While he was hitting him"**: Ibid., pp. 114–16.

### Chapter 29: The Father: "Something Just Snapped"

227 **"Mr. Ebens has a right"**: *United States v. Ronald Ebens and Michael Nitz*, No. 83-60629, David Lawson opening statement, p. 33 (U.S. District Court for the Eastern District of Michigan Southern Division, June 13, 1984), transcript, NAC.

227 **It wasn't unusual for Ebens:** Rich Wagner interview, *Who Killed Vincent Chin?* (film), dir. Christine Choy and Renee Tajima-Peña (1987), transcript, MOCA.

228 **"He had a new Corvette"**: Ronald Ebens witness testimony, *United States v. Ebens and Nitz* (June 19), p. 153.

228 **"I remember comments coming"**: Ibid., pp. 160–61.

228 **"Do you or have you ever"**: Ibid., pp. 162–64.

229 **"Nothing really very clear"**: Ibid., p. 166.

229 **"He started right out apologizing"**: Ibid., p. 169.

230 **"Come on, lets fight"**: Ibid., p. 171.

230 **"There is that little"**: Ibid., pp. 174–75.

230 **"You and Siroskey exchanged"**: Ibid., p. 177.

230 **"What is your problem?"**: Ibid., pp. 178–79.

231 **"Why were you looking"**: Ibid., pp. 180–81.

231 **"Angry." "Why?" "Same reason"**: Ibid., p. 182.

231 **"You son of bitches"**: Ibid., p. 183.

232 **"When I seen him scuffling"**: Ibid., pp. 184–85.

232 **"Mr. Ebens, did you do"**: Ibid., pp. 189–90.

233 **"You spent seventeen years"**: Ibid., pp. 192–93.

234 **"Didn't you say"**: Ibid., p. 196.

234 **"No, I was not so drunk"**: Ibid., p. 199.

234 **"Jimmy Perry just decided"**: Ibid., pp. 204–5.

235 **"Let me ask you"**: Ibid., p. 206.

235 **"You can't remember hitting him"**: Ebens testimony, ibid., pp. 207–9.

### Chapter 30: The Closing Arguments: "Your Hardest Part Is Still Ahead"

237 **"The Vincent Chin murder"**: Zia quoted in Charles Hillinger, "Jury Tackles Civil Rights Question in Beating Death of Chinese American," *Los Angeles Times*, June 24, 1984.

237 **"This was a premeditated murder"**: Wong quoted ibid.

238 **"This is an out-and-out example"**: Anonymous quoted ibid.

238 **"You realize that your hardest"**: *United States v. Ronald Ebens and Michael Nitz*, No. 83-60629, Theodore Merritt closing arguments, p. 5 (U.S. District Court for the Eastern District of Michigan Southern Division, June 26, 1984), transcript, NAC.

239 **four hundred dollars' worth**: Jimmy Choi witness testimony, ibid. (June 14), p. 187.

239 **"They saw an Oriental acting"**: Ibid., Theodore Merritt closing arguments (June 26), pp. 21–22.

239 **"He ran for his life"**: Ibid., pp. 10–11.

239 **"mere anger or desire"**: Ibid., pp. 22–23.

239 **"Michael Nitz was in"**: Ibid., p. 26.

240 **"got together and made up"**: Ibid., p. 27.

240 **"They got together to try"**: Ibid., p. 29.

240 **"This was more than some barroom fight"**: Ibid., p. 31.

241 **"Anger, intoxication, fights"**: Frank Eaman, closing arguments, ibid., p. 53.

241 **"Then something happened since"**: Ibid., p. 41.

241 **"Since when do people in Detroit"**: Ibid., p. 51.

241 **"straining to inject racism"**: Ibid., p. 45.

241 **"Perhaps the strongest evidence"**: Ibid., pp. 59–60.

242 **"The prosecution might suggest"**: Ibid., p. 60.

242 **"The truth is Ronald Ebens"**: Ibid., p. 65.

242 **"We are not so blind"**: Ibid., p. 52.

242 **"There are also those who"**: Ibid.

242 **"None of this happened"**: Ibid., p. 69.

243 **"one of the most important"**: Miriam Siefer closing arguments, ibid., p. 101.

243 **"Ladies and gentlemen, race"**: Ibid., pp. 99–100.

243 **"There was no ugly racism"**: Ibid., p. 100.

243 **"I can stand before you"**: Ibid., pp. 100–1.

244 **"I ask you not to be swayed"**: Theodore Merritt closing arguments, ibid., p. 114.

244 **"Now the defense also suggests"**: Ibid., p. 108.

244 **"Jimmy Choi told you as a minority"**: Ibid.

245 **"Vincent Chin decided to stop"**: Ibid., p. 107.

245 **"When you go back in that jury room, you ask yourself"**: Ibid., p. 121.

245 **"It probably sounds corny"**: Ibid., p. 120.

## Chapter 31: The Verdict: "I Can't Bring Him Back"

246 **"Your Honor, we have reached a verdict":** *United States v. Ronald Ebens and Michael Nitz*, No. 83-60629, verdict, pp. 2–3 (U.S. District Court for the Eastern District of Michigan Southern Division, June 28, 1984), transcript, NAC.

246 **"In the case of United States":** Ibid.

246 **"When they read through that":** Frank Eaman interview, *Who Killed Vincent Chin?* (film), dir. Christine Choy and Renee Tajima-Peña (1987), transcript, MOCA.

247 **Ebens sat stoically as U.S. marshals:** Don Ball, "One Guilty, One Freed in Chin Case," *Detroit News*, June 29, 1984.

247 **"To be quite honest":** Ronald Ebens interview, *Who Killed Vincent Chin?*

248 **After the jury left:** Tim Kiska, "One of Two Guilty in Chin Rights Case: Man Who Swung Bat Is Convicted," *Detroit Free Press*, June 29, 1984.

248 **"We're satisfied":** Merritt quoted in Ball, "One Guilty, One Freed."

248 **"This is an election year":** Siefer quoted in "Jury Convicts Killer of Vincent Chin in Civil Rights Case," NBC News, June 28, 1984, VTNA.

248 **"That's totally false":** Merritt quoted ibid.

248 **"justice was done":** Zia quoted in Rob Zeiger, "Acquittal 'Not Fair': Lily Chin," *Detroit News*, June 29, 1984.

248 **"The community has spoken":** Eaman quoted in "Jury Convicts Killer of Vincent Chin in Civil Rights Case," NBC News, June 28 1984, VTNA.

249 **"In the case of Mister Chin":** Shimoura quoted ibid.

249 **"I can't blame the jury":** Eaman quoted in Ball, "One Guilty, One Freed."

249 **"We tried, we wanted to be fair":** Unnamed juror interviews, *Who Killed Vincent Chin?*.

251 **"I just feel deeply sorry":** Ebens quoted in Jack Kresnak, "Ebens Says Vincent Chin's Mother Was 'Used,'" *Detroit Free Press*, July 2, 1984.

251 **"Mr. Ebens had a typical":** Frank Eaman sentencing, *United States v. Ebens and Nitz* (September 18), pp. 11, 16.

252 **"a wanton disregard":** Theodore Merritt sentencing, ibid., pp. 6, 9.

252 **"Mr. Ebens is there anything":** Ronald Ebens sentencing, ibid., p. 16.

253 **"Is that all?":** Judge Anna Diggs Taylor sentencing, ibid., p. 17.

253 **The sentence of twenty-five years:** Joe Swickard, "In Chin Slaying Case; Ebens Gets 25-Year Sentence," *Detroit Free Press*, September 19, 1984.

253 **"[He] saw that I was hurt":** Nitz quoted in Kresnak, "Ebens Says Mother Was 'Used.'"

253 **"He's innocent to start with":** Nitz quoted in Swickard, "In Chin Slaying Case."

253 **"I was guilty of being":** Ebens quoted in Tim Kiska, "Chin's Slayer Says Conviction Now Is 'Unfair,'" *Detroit Free Press*, July 3, 1984

### *"In the Shadows"*

255   **"It was the place to go":** All quotes from Jarod Lew in this chapter come from interview by author, April 17, 2019.

### Chapter 32: *"This Case Is Not Over"*

261   **"public nuisance":** "Highland Park: Lounge, Club Closed," *Detroit Free Press*, January 8, 1986.

261   **"junkyard-dog style":** Tim Kiska, "Chin's Slayer Says Conviction Now Is 'Unfair,' *Detroit Free Press*, July 3, 1984.

262   **discredit their testimony:** Bill McGraw, " 'I'm No Racist,' Chin's Killer Says," *Detroit Free Press*, September 17, 1986.

262   **"absolutely ridiculous":** Shimoura quoted in McGraw, " 'I'm No Racist.' "

262   **"What is very outrageous":** Shimoura quoted in Bill McGraw, "Verdict Voided in Chin Killing," *Detroit Free Press*, September 12, 1986.

262   **"We are quite pleased":** Shimoura quoted in Susan Goldberg, "New Trial Ordered for Chin's Killer," *Detroit Free Press*, September 20, 1986.

264   **"This is a political case":** Eaman quoted ibid.

264   **"I'm no racist":** Ebens quoted in McGraw, " 'I'm No Racist.' "

264   **"Please tell the government":** Chin quoted in Goldberg, "New Trial Ordered."

264   **"I think because of all":** Eaman quoted in Frederick Standish, "Retrial Ordered in 1982 Vincent Chin Killing," Associated Press, September 20, 1986.

264   **"cannot obtain a fair":** Taylor quoted in Bill McGraw, "Trial of Vincent Chin's Assailant Moved to Ohio Due to Publicity," *Detroit Free Press*, February 24, 1987.

### Chapter 33: *"We All Remember Our Lines, Okay?"*

266   **"We have to be reminded":** Lutner quoted in "Asian Americans Unify for Retrial," Associated Press, April 21, 1987.

267   **Judge Taylor, worried about:** Denise L. Stinson, "Spectators Unable to Hear Tapes: Lawyers Say Recordings Are Crucial in Civil Rights Trial," *Cincinnati Enquirer*, April 23, 1987.

267   **She also ordered that the:** Sharon Moloney, "Defense Claims Witnesses in Chin Case Were Coached," *Cincinnati Post*, April 23, 1987.

268   ***"We will agree this is":*** Chan quoted in Tim Kiska, "Chin's Slayer Says Conviction Now Is 'Unfair,' " *Detroit Free Press*, July 3, 1984. See also the original transcript at MOCA, p. 62.

268   **"There were things in the":** Frank Eaman, interview by author, January 22, 2019.

268   **"I found out that they":** Gary Koivu, interview by author, June 22, 2018.

269   **"fades in and out":** Siroskey quoted in Moloney, "Defense Claims Witnesses."

269 **"Did you tell Highland Park":** Eaman and Choi quoted in Jacquelyn Boyle, "Witness to Chin Fight Was Silent at First About Racial Slurs," *Detroit Free Press*, April 23, 1987.

269 **But Choi still insisted:** "Witness Testifies Accused Was at Beating-Death Scene," Associated Press, April 23, 1987.

269 **Chan never told her:** Jacquelynn Boyle, "Witnesses in Chin Slaying Trial Say Lawyer Didn't Coach Them," *Detroit Free Press*, April 24, 1987.

270 **"I was surprised":** Liza Chan, interview by author, June 22, 2019.

270 **"I thought it meant":** Ibid.

270 **"I was a little concerned":** Marc Susselman, interview by author, June 22, 2019.

270 **"They were more used to":** Chan interview

271 **"I was under so much":** Ibid.

271 **"I felt very comfortable":** Ibid.

271 **"The optics were not good":** Ibid.

271 **"Ronald Ebens did not consider":** Soisson quoted in Jacquelynn Boyle, "Deliberations to Resume Today in Retrial of Vincent Chin," *Detroit Free Press,* May 1, 1987.

272 **"This is not a lunch counter":** Lawson quoted in Gannett News Service, "Racial Motive Charged in 1982 Beating Death," *Cincinnati Enquirer,* May 1, 1987.

### *Chapter 34: "A Very, Very Tough Decision"*

273 **This time Ebens broke:** Associated Press, "Slayer Is Acquitted of Civil Rights Violation," *New York Times,* May 2, 1987.

273 **Juanita buried her face:** Denise L. Stinson, "Jury Acquits Ebens in Chin Case: Verdict Angers Asian Americans," *Detroit News*, May 1, 1987.

273 **"We said all along":** Eaman quoted in AP, "Slayer Is Acquitted."

273 **"We had a very, very tough decision":** Heffron quoted Jacquelynn Boyle, "Jury Clears Ebens in Chin Case: Defendant 'Still Very Sorry'; Asian Americans Outraged at Verdict," *Detroit Free Press*, May 2, 1987.

274 **"I'm still very sorry":** Ronald Ebens interview, *Who Killed Vincent Chin?* (film), dir. Christine Choy and Renee Tajima-Peña (1987), transcript, MOCA.

274 **"I'm not accusing people of perjury":** Eaman and Lawson quoted in Jacquelynn Boyle, "Tapes Were Difference in Chin Case: Retrial Judge Allowed Recordings," *Detroit Free Press*, May 3, 1987.

274 **"It was wrong":** Ibid.

274 **"It takes a certain sophistication":** Zia quoted in "Civil Rights Retrial Determines—Ebens Not Guilty; Vincent Chin's Killers Free Forever," *New York Nichibei*, May 7, 1987, ESL.

274 **"I was very upset":** Liza Chan, interview by author, June 22, 2019.

274 **"a green light for killers"**: "No, Ebens, You Are Not the Good Guy" (letter to editor), *Detroit Free Press*, September 11, 1987.

275 **"As far as violating civil rights"**: "Vincent Chin: Isn't Life a Civil Right?" (letter to editor), *Detroit Free Press,* May 18, 1987.

275 **"Ronald Ebens may be"**: Ibid.

275 **"great sadness and despair"**: Ibid.

275 **"I am not Asian American"**: Ibid.

275 **"My heart sank"**: Shimoura quoted in AP, "Slayer Is Acquitted."

275 **"Everybody feels it like death"**: Zia quoted in "Civil Rights Retrial Determines."

276 **"I've never been a racist"**: Ebens quoted in Bill McGraw, " 'I'm No Racist,' Chin's Killer Says," *Detroit Free Press*, September 17, 1986.

277 **"every day of my life"**: Ibid.

277 **"Helen, is there anything else"**: Helen Zia, *Vincent Chin's Story: Lily Chin: The Courage to Speak Out* (Los Angeles: Asian Americans Advancing Justice, 2008–9), https://tinyurl.com/y4rq9oly.

277 **"My life is over"**: Chin quoted in Helen Zia, *Asian American Dreams: The Emergence of an American People* (New York: Farrar, Straus & Giroux, 2000), p. 80.

### *"I Really Don't Want to Talk About It"*

279 **"I told him how I was"**: Jarod Lew, interview by author, April 17, 2019.

279 **"I thought it would be powerful"**: Ibid.

### *Chapter 35: America Breaks Its Promise to Lily Chin*

283 **"I don't like to go outside"**: Chin quoted in Paul Weingarten, "The Unquiet Death of Vincent Chin: An Examination of the Killing Detroit Can't Forget," *Chicago Tribune*, July 31, 1983.

283 **"her laughter, the way she"**: Helen Zia, *Vincent Chin's Story: Lily Chin: The Courage to Speak Out* (Los Angeles: Asian Americans Advancing Justice, 2008–9), https://tinyurl.com/y4rq9oly.

283 **She retired from her job**: Ti-Hua Chang, "Lily: Her Son Is Dead, But Lily Chin Cannot Forget: 'Vincent! Mama Is Coming,' " *Michigan Magazine,* October 12, 1986.

284 **"She come to see me"**: Chin quoted in Weingarten, "Unquiet Death."

284 **"I love Detroit and friends"**: Chin quoted in Chang, "Lily: Son Is Dead."

284 **She packed two suitcases**: Ibid.

285 **"What a sad and poignant"**: "America Breaks Its Promise to Lily Chin," *Detroit Free Press*, September 23, 1987.

285 **"I feel the hurt"**: Ibid.

285 **"Coming from a different country"**: Ibid.

285 **"As a third generation"**: Ibid.

286 **"It was just too sad"**: Helen Zia, *Vincent Chin's Story: Lily Chin: The Courage to Speak Out* (Los Angeles: Asian Americans Advancing Justice, 2008–9), https://tinyurl.com/y4rq9oly.

286 **"Dear Helen, how are you"**: Ibid.

286 **"Dear Helen, I have your letter"**: Ibid.

286 **"She seemed to know everybody"**: Ibid.

287 **"She never blamed me"**: Liza Chan, interview by author, June 22, 2019.

287 **"What happened was not just"**: "30 Years Later: Stewart Kwoh Recalls Vincent Chin Case," Asian Americans Advancing Justice, 2012, https://tinyurl.com/yxkcyedk.

287 **"She didn't want people"**: Zia, *Vincent Chin's Story: Lily Chin.*

287 **Lily stayed at a health center**: Ibid.

288 **"If Lily Chin were to sit"**: Ibid.

288 **"She was so much more"**: Ibid.

288 **"Lily Chin reminds us"**: Ibid.

### Chapter 36: "You Never Get Over It"

290 **"the only wrong thing"**: Ebens quoted in Emil Guillermo, "Ronald Ebens, the Man Who Killed Vincent Chin, Apologizes 30 Years Later," *AsianWeek*, June 22, 2012, http://aaldef.org/blog/ronald-ebens-the-man-who-killed-vincent-chin-apologizes-30-years-later.html.

290 **"He's prayed many times"**: Ibid.

290 **Although Ebens never spent a day**: Michael Moore, "The Man Who Killed Vincent Chin: The Wages of Death," *Detroit Free Press,* August 30, 1987.

291 **The court ordered Ebens**: Ibid.

291 **"the biggest fallacy"**: Ebens quoted in Guillermo, "Ronald Ebens."

291 **"I'm sorry it happened"**: Ibid.

292 **He still owes the Chin estate**: Emil Guillermo, "Judge Rules Against Man Responsible for Vincent Chin's Death Lien on Nevada Home Stays," *NBC News*, January 12, 2016, VTNA.

292 **Vincent will always be with him**: Author informal meeting with Ronald Ebens, July 30, 2019.

### Chapter 37: "Vincent's Soul Will Never Rest"

293 **"VIKKI"**: Vincent Chin, "Vikki," *Detroit Free Press*, February 14, 1979.

294 **"If Asian people in America"**: Yamasaki quoted in Helen Zia, *Asian American Dreams: The Emergence of an American People* (New York: Farrar, Straus & Giroux, 2000), p. 77.

294 **"All we can do is to continue"**: Zia quoted in "Civil Rights Retrial Determines—Ebens Not Guilty; Vincent Chin's Killers Free Forever," *New York Nichibei,* May 7, 1987, ESL.

294 **"throw in the towel"**: Ibid.

294 **"Some people continue to believe"**: Helen Zia, *Vincent Chin's Story: Lily Chin: The Courage to Speak Out* (Los Angeles: Asian Americans Advancing Justice, 2008–9), https://tinyurl.com/y4rq9oly.

295 **"It captured everything"**: Frank H. Wu, interview by author, June 4, 2018.

295 **"Hate crimes still occur"**: "30 Years Later: Stewart Kwoh Recalls Vincent Chin Case," Asian Americans Advancing Justice, 2012, https://tinyurl .com/yxkcyedk.

296 **Castine and Ashenfelter examined:** David Ashenfelter and John Castine, "Manslaughter: The Price of Life—It's One Crime, Many Punishments," *Detroit Free Press,* October 9, 1983.

296 **It wasn't unusual for someone:** Ibid.

296 **Although the majority:** Ibid.

296 **"That's the way it is":** Kamisar quoted ibid.

297 **"Judges from diverse economic":** Ibid.

297 **"Plea bargaining is supposed to":** David Ashenfelter and John Castine, "Manslaughter: The Price of Life—Serving Justice? Or Are the Deals Cheating Justice?," *Detroit Free Press,* October 10, 1983

297 **"Since the Vincent Chin case":** Chang quoted in Mark J. Jue, "Detroit Asians Draw Large Local Support," *East West: The Chinese American Journal* 17, no. 29 (July 20, 1983).

298 **The Vincent Chin case was:** "Specific Justice Systems and Victims' Rights," Office for Victims of Crime, https://www.ncjrs.gov/ovc_archives/ nvaa99/chap3-2.htm.

298 **"At [the] time of the Vincent Chin case":** "Q&A with Roland Hwang," Asian Americans Advancing Justice, June 19, 2017, https://advancingjustice -la.org/blog/qa-roland-hwang.

298 **After visiting Detroit in 1983:** Stewart Kwoh, interview by author, May 23, 2018.

299 **On April 23, 1990, the Hate Crime:** "H.R. 1048—Hate Crime Statistics Act," https://www.congress.gov/bill/101st-congress/house-bill/1048.

299 **Roughly half of hate crimes:** "Hate Crime Statistics," Federal Bureau of Investigation, https://www.fbi.gov/services/cjis/ucr/hate-crime.

300 **"I first found out":** Annie Tan, interview by author, September 23, 2018.

300 *Asian Americans*: "PBS and WETA Announce Groundbreaking Documentary Series *Asian Americans*," PBS, https://www.pbs.org/about/blogs/ news/pbs-and-weta-announce-groundbreaking-documentary-series -asian-americans.

300 **"History seems to be":** Shimoura quoted in Niraj Warikoo, "Vincent Chin Murder 35 Years Later: History Repeating Itself?" *Detroit Free Press,* June 23, 2017.

300 **"Get out of my country"**: "Kansas Shooting: Adam Purinton Given Three Life Sentences for Hate Crime," BBC, August 7, 2018.

301 **"Since the February death"**: Arun Venugopal, "Indian Americans Reckon with Reality of Hate Crimes," Code Switch, NPR, May 15, 2017.

301 **Today there are just over 330 million**: "United States Population," https://tradingeconomics.com/united-states/population.

301 **Researchers predict**: "Asian American and Pacific Islander Heritage Month: May 2020, U.S. Census Bureau, April 30, 2020, https://www .census.gov/newsroom/facts-for-features/2020/aian.html.

301 **Photographs have documented**: Jorge Rivas, "Calling Asians Racist Slurs on Fast Food Receipts Is Now a National Trend," *ColorLines,* January 9, 2012.

301 **"Go back to your country"**: Ashley Collman, "Asian-American Man Films a Female College Professor Storming Off After Telling Him and His Wife to 'Go Back to Your Home Country,'" *Daily Mail,* March 6, 2018.

301 **As for the increased reports**: "Asian Americans Advancing Justice Strengthens Hate Tracking Initiative on 35th Anniversary of Vincent Chin Attack," Asian Americans Advancing Justice, June 19, 2017, https:// tinyurl.com/yxaxvlf3.

302 **"My son's soul will never rest"**: Chin quoted in Zia, *Asian American Dreams,* p. 80.

## *"We Need To Talk About This"*

303 **"I was kind of embarrassed"**: Jarod Lew, interview by author, June 1, 2018.

## *Afterword*

307 **more than 367,000 Americans:** "COVID-19 Dashboard by the Center for Systems Science and Engineering (CSSE) at Johns Hopkins University," ArcGIS, Johns Hopkins University, https://tinyurl.com/uwns6z5.

307 **"China is to blame"**: Katie Shepherd, "John Cornyn Criticized Chinese for Eating Snakes," *Washington Post*, March 19, 2020; and John Cornyn interview, *Hill* video, via Twitter, https://twitter.com/thehill/ status/1240364608390606850.

308 **"I disagree. We're not"**: Julian Shen-Berro, "Sen. Cornyn: China to Blame for Coronavirus, Because 'People Eat Bats,'" NBC News, March 18, 2020. (DOI: https://www.nbcnews.com/news/asian-america/sen-cornyn- china-blame-coronavirus-because-people-eat-bats-n1163431).

308 **In March 2020:** Kimmy Yam, "Progress Is Why Viruses Aren't Named After Locations Anymore, Experts Say," NBC News, March 22, 2020.

308 **"absolutely wrong"**: Colby Itkowitz, "CDC Director Rejects Label

'Chinese Virus' After Trump, McCarthy Tweets," *Washington Post,* March 10, 2020.

308 **More than 30 percent:** Alex Ellerbeck and Center for Public Integrity, "Over 30 Percent of Americans Have Witnessed COVID-19 Bias Against Asians, Poll Says," NBC News and Center for Public Integrity, April 28, 2020.

308 **Other hate crime trackers:** "Stop AAPI Hate Reporting Center," A3PCON: Asian Pacific Policy and Planning Council, https://www.asia npacificpolicyandplanningcouncil.org/stop-aapi-hate/; and Nicholas Turton, "Anti-Asian Incidents Across U.S. Near 1,900 over 8-Week Period," Chinese for Affirmative Action, June 9, 2020, https://caasf.org/ press-release/anti-asian-incidents-across-u-s-near-1900-over-8-week -period/.

308 **These incidents ranged:** Sabrina Tavernise and Richard A. Oppel, Jr., "Spit On, Yelled At, Attacked: Chinese Americas Fear for Their Safety," *New York Times,* March 23, 2020.

309 **"The suspect indicated":** David Matthews, "Stabbing Attack on Asian Family Ruled a Coronavirus-Related Hate Crime: FBI," *New York Daily News,* April 1, 2020.

309 **"is still remembered":** Niraj Warikoo, "Chinese Americans in Michigan Anxious About Racism over Coronavirus," *Detroit Free Press,* March 19, 2020.

309 **"Trump is attempting":** Nessel quoted ibid.

309 **"I'm really alarmed":** Hwang quoted ibid.

310 **"The virus is a virus":** Chang quoted ibid.

310 **"We can stop repeating":** Helen Zia, interview by author, March 23, 2020.

310 **"The atmosphere of hate":** Rene Tajima-Peña, interview by author, March 23, 2020.

310 **"It is very important":** Trump quoted in Kimmy Yam, "Trump Calls On U.S. to 'Protect Our Asian American Community' Hours After Referring to 'Chinese Virus,'" NBC News, March 23, 2020.

311 **"COVID-19, that name gets further":** Guardian Staff, "Donald Trump calls Covid-19 'kung flu' at Tulsa Rally," *Guardian,* June 20, 2020.

311 **"The fact that he got the crowd":** David Nakamura, "With 'Kung Flu,' Trump Sparks Backlash over Racist Language—And a Rallying Cry for Supporters," *Washington Post,* June 24, 2020.

311 **"deeply disturbing racism targeting":** Kimmy Yam, "Asian American Lawmakers Urge Congress Members to Help Stop Coronavirus-fueled Xenophobia," CNN, February 28, 2020.

311 **"We did not understand":** Lieu quoted in Kimmy Yam, "150 Members

of Congress Demand Justice Department Action Against Anti-Asian COVID-19 Racism," NBC News, July 22, 2020.

312 **"It's clear that":** Ibid.

312 **"On September 17, 2020, The U.S. House of Representatives passed":** Veronica Stracqualursi, "House Passes Resolution Condemning Anti-Asian Sentiment," CNN, September 17, 2020.

312 **twenty-five cities:** "25 Cities Across 16 States Have Now Imposed Curfews," CNN, May 30, 2020.

313 **a July 28, 2020, Gallup poll:** Savannah Behrmann, "Poll: Nearly Two-Thirds Of Americans Support Protest Against Racial Injustice," *USA Today,* July 28, 2020.

# SOURCES

## List of Archives

BHL     Bentley Historical Library, University of Michigan
ESL     Ethnic Studies Library, University of California at Berkeley
MOCA   Museum of Chinese in America, New York
NAC    National Archives at Chicago
VTNA   Vanderbilt Television News Archive

## For Further Reading

### BOOKS

Ambrose, Stephen E. *Nothing Like it in the World: The Men Who Built the Transcontinental Railroad, 1863–1869*. New York: Simon & Schuster, 2000.

Chan, Liza Cheuk May. *My Impossible Life*. Ann Arbor, MI: Bookbaby Publishing, 2017.

Chang, Gordon H. *Fateful Ties: A History of America's Preoccupation with China*. Cambridge, MA: Harvard University Press, 2015.

———. *Ghosts of Gold Mountain: The Epic Story of the Chinese Who Built the Transcontinental Railroad*. Boston: Houghton Mifflin Harcourt, 2019.

Chang, Gordon H., and Shelley Fisher Fishkin, with Hilton Obenzinger and Roland Hsu. *The Chinese and the Iron Road: Building the Transcontinental Railroad*. Stanford, CA: Stanford University Press, 2019.

Chang, Iris. *The Chinese in America: A Narrative History*. New York: Penguin Books, 2003.

Darden, Joe. T, and Richard W. Thomas. *Detroit: Race Riots, Racial Conflicts, and Efforts to Bridge the Racial Divide*. East Lansing: Michigan State University Press, 2013.

Lee, Erika. *The Making of Asian America. A History*. New York: Simon & Schuster, 2015.

Liu, Eric. *The Accidental Asian: Notes of a Native Speaker*. New York, NY: Vintage Books, 1998.

———. *A Chinaman's Chance: One Family's Journey and the Chinese American Dream*. New York, NY: PublicAffairs, 2014.

Perl, Lila. *Great Journeys: To the Golden Mountain—The Story of the Chinese Who Built the Transcontinental Railroad*. Tarrytown, NJ: Benchmark Books, 2003.

Shen, Jean Yu-Wen, and Thomas C. Chen. *Asian American Studies Now*. New Brunswick, NJ: Rutgers University Press, 2010.

Schlund-Vials, Cathy J., K. Scott Wong, and Jason Oliver Chang. *Asian America: A Primary Source Reader.* New Haven, CT: Yale University Press, 2017.

Steiner, Stan. *Fusang: The Chinese Who Built America.* New York: Harper & Row, 1979.

Takaki, Ronald. *Strangers from a Different Shore: A History of Asian Americans.* New York, NY: Little, Brown, 1989.

———. *A Different Mirror: A History of Multicultural America.* New York, NY: Little, Brown, 1993.

Wu, Frank H. *Yellow: Race in America Beyond Black and White.* New York, NY: Basic Books, 2002.

Zesch, Scott. *The Chinatown War: Chinese Los Angeles and the Massacre of 1871.* Oxford: Oxford University Press, 2012.

Zia, Helen. *Asian American Dreams: The Emergence of an American People.* New York: Farrar, Straus & Giroux, 2000.

## VIDEO

Chin, Curtis and Tony Lam. *Vincent Who?* Los Angeles, CA: Asian Pacific Americans for Progress, Q&A Film, and Tony Lam Films, 2009.

Choy, Christine and Renee Tajima-Peña. *Who Killed Vincent Chin?* New York, NY: Filmmakers Library, 1990.

Tajima-Peña, Renee. *Asian Americans.* Washington, DC: WETA Washington, DC, Center for Asian American Media (CAAM) for PBS, Independent Television Service (ITVS), Flash Cuts and Tajima-Peña Productions, 2020.

## ONLINE

A3PCON: Asian Pacific Policy & Planning Council, http://www.asian-pacificpolicyandplanningcouncil.org

Asian Americans Advancing Justice, https://advancingjustice-la.org

*Chinese Railroad Workers in North America Project at Stanford University,* https://web.stanford.edu/group/chineserailroad/cgi-bin/website.

Stop AAPI Hate, https://stopaapihate.org

Venugopal, Arun. "Indian Americans Reckon With Reality of Hate Crimes." *Code Switch,* NPR, May 15, 2017, https://tinyurl.com/y6m5hdkt.

# PICTURE CREDITS

# INDEX

Page numbers in *italics* indicate photos/news clippings.

# INDEX